Essays
and
Arguments

Essays and Arguments

A Handbook for Writing Student Essays

Revised Edition

Ian Johnston

broadview press

Library and Archives Canada Cataloguing in Publication

Johnston, Ian C., 1938–, author
    Essays and arguments : a handbook for writing student essays / Ian Johnston. — Revised edition.

Includes index.
ISBN 978-1-55481-257-8 (paperback)

    1. English language—Rhetoric. 2. Persuasion (Rhetoric). 3. Report writing. I. Title.

PE1431.J64 2015   808'.042   C2015-901687-8

Broadview Press is an independent, international publishing house, incorporated in 1985.

We welcome comments and suggestions regarding any aspect of our publications—please feel free to contact us at the addresses below or at broadview@broadviewpress.com.

North America
PO Box 1243
Peterborough, Ontario
K9J 7H5, Canada
555 Riverwalk Parkway
Tonawanda, NY 14150
USA
Tel: (705) 743-8990
Fax: (705) 743-8353
email: customerservice@
broadviewpress.com

UK, Europe, Central Asia,
Middle East, Africa, India, and
Southeast Asia
Eurospan Group
3 Henrietta St.
London WC2E 8LU
United Kingdom
Tel: 44 (0) 1767 604972
Fax: 44 (0) 1767 601640
email: eurospan@
turpin-distribution.com

Australia and New Zealand
Footprint Books
1/6a Prosperity Parade
Warriewood, NSW 2102
Australia
Tel: +61 2 9997 3973
Fax: +61 2 9997 3185
email: info@footprint.com.au

www.broadviewpress.com

Edited by Laura Buzzard
Cover design by Michel Vrana
Interior typesetting by Jennifer Blais
Typeset in Arno Pro

Broadview Press acknowledges the financial support of the Government of Canada through the Canada Book Fund for our publishing activities.

PRINTED IN CANADA

Contents

Author's Note

This book is an extensively rewritten version of a handbook with the same title prepared many years ago and posted on the internet in May 2000. In revising the original text I have received a great deal of very useful editorial assistance from Broadview Press, especially from Laura Buzzard. I would be remiss if I did not take this occasion to thank Laura profusely for her always friendly, intelligent, and pertinent suggestions.

Introduction

1.1 | The Purpose of This Text

The ability to read and write arguments is an important skill central to an undergraduate education. In one way or another, almost every assignment students have to deal with in college or university is, from the outset, concerned with this issue. While the subject matter varies from one course to another, in virtually all disciplines one major purpose is to develop each student's ability to read, understand, evaluate, construct, and communicate arguments.

At first, many students find these tasks intimidating, and most find them very difficult to accomplish well. The material in this book seeks to address this problem by offering a basic introduction to some of the more important elements in the analysis and construction of arguments. The discussion begins with some very basic ideas and moves on quickly to a few points essential for effective written argumentation. The main emphasis here is on practical advice that will prove immediately useful to undergraduate students. For that reason, I stress certain recommended procedures for organizing and writing an academic essay, and I provide many detailed examples.

In choosing such an emphasis, I do not intend to convey the impression that there is only one way to carry out an essay assignment or that anyone who fails to follow closely what these pages outline is doomed to academic failure. Such a claim would be presumptuous and silly. My concern here is to assist a student who requires quick, brief, and effective help in writing a successful undergraduate essay.

1.2 | A Word to the Student Reader: Why Essay Writing Matters

Carrying out an essay-writing assignment can be a time-consuming and stressful experience, especially for inexperienced students, who may not be entirely sure about the purpose of the exercise. To begin with, let me offer a few very general initial remarks regarding why essays are important assignments and how best to approach them.

One of the major purposes of an undergraduate education is to encourage the student to sharpen her perceptions; in order to understand and enjoy and function in the world around us more fully, maturely, imaginatively, and usefully, we first have to develop our abilities to *see* and *hear* things with a sensitive appreciation for their detailed particularity. A second major purpose, closely allied to this task, is helping the student learn to communicate her perceptions in a precise, intelligent, and persuasive manner, because that is how we share much of our knowledge with others.

Young students are often remarkably perceptive, but their perceptions are frequently rather scattered and unfocused, and they tend to lack a vocabulary sufficiently flexible and precise to describe their perceptions accurately. In addition, as I have observed above, they often are unsure how to communicate their insights in a logically coherent piece of writing, so that other people can derive the full benefit of what they have to say.

An essay assignment is an academic exercise designed to address these matters. Of course, the assignment is concerned with basic writing skills and various conventions for incorporating research findings into an essay, and so on, but its truly important goal is to encourage the student to look at something closely, see what is there, recognize its significance, and then communicate that insight well. An essay assignment on a work of literature, for example, is, more than anything else, meant to help the student practice, improve, and articulate her awareness of the ways in which particular words, phrases, images, descriptions, figures of speech, and, most importantly, recurring patterns in the language communicate things essential to an intelligent appreciation of the work and, beyond that, of literature in general.

Since improving one's perceptions and one's ability to communicate those perceptions takes time, no instructor expects a startlingly insightful argument from a student who is just beginning his academic studies (that is not to say, however, that an instructor is not delighted to get such an essay). Hence, you should not worry excessively about whether or not your interpretation of a story or your treatment of a social, historical, scientific, or political issue sounds naive. You should make the essay something that reflects your engagement with the topic, even if you are not sure you have anything very interesting or original to say. You should, at all costs, avoid hiding behind a mountain of borrowed opinions or spending anxious nights frozen and motionless in front of a computer supplicating help from some distant, anonymous cyberpresence. Trust your own insights, and focus on making sure that what you do have to say is honest, clear, and logically organized.

Parenthetically, it might be worth remarking that honing one's perceptions and improving one's ability to describe those perceptions go hand in hand. I remember fondly a professor who was in the habit of haranguing us with slogans to this effect: "If you cannot describe your perceptions accurately, then you don't have accurate perceptions," "If you can't communicate it, you haven't seen it, and you don't know it," and so on. I have no wish to discuss these undoubtedly disputatious assertions, but I can attest to the fact that, as my descriptive vocabulary and my ability to use it grew, I was certainly able to see, appreciate, and understand more clearly than before.

Communicating one's perceptions in essay form generally begins with relatively unsophisticated attempts. Such exercises help to build up a writer's confidence. Then, as he practices the art of writing an essay and starts to become familiar with other people's attempts to do the same, through attending lectures, conversing with others, and reading other people's work, he learns more about what to look for and how to communicate his insights. Once he has gained sufficient confidence in his ability to write an essay, he is then in a position to experiment with all sorts of different argumentative strategies. At that point, he can consign this book to the dustbin or hand it to someone else and educate himself further by attending to how other good writers present their arguments.

One final point. At every stage of writing an essay you can derive enormous help from discussions with other people about what you are doing, especially with those who are working on the same or a similar assignment. Such conversations provide an informal opportunity for you to examine and respond to each other's efforts and to learn from each other. There is simply no better or more agreeable way to educate your perceptions and improve your ability to communicate them. Of course, it sometimes takes courage to engage in this process, for students often feel somewhat vulnerable when they expose their written work to criticism from their peers. But the rewards can be extremely valuable. It might help to remember that the single most important educational resource you are purchasing when you pay your tuition fees is access to other students. Do not hesitate to draw on that vital resource.

Some Basic First Principles

2.1 | Initial Comments on Arguments

Since this book deals with arguments, let's begin with a basic question: What is an argument? Put most simply, an argument is an attempt to persuade someone of something. It is prompted usually by disagreement, confusion, ignorance, or curiosity about an issue that the arguer wishes to resolve or illuminate. In the most general sense, arguments, friendly and otherwise, go on all the time. They are a staple ingredient of many conversations, as well as the heart of any inquiry into the truth or probability of something (for example, a judicial process, scientific research project, policy analysis, business plan, laboratory report, book review, and so on). Arguments can also, of course, be internal, as, for example, when we are faced with a difficult or confusing decision (Should I marry this man or woman? Is it right for me to oppose capital punishment? Which candidate should I vote for? Should I mortgage my house? Why did I dislike that film so much? What is the right thing for me to do in these circumstances? And so forth).

The final goal of an argument is usually to provide reasons that are sufficiently persuasive to convince someone of a conclusion (regarding a recommended course of action, the causes of an event, the probable truth of an analysis, the validity of an interpretation, the rightness of a decision, and so on). Arguments can also often have an important negative purpose: to convince someone that something is not the case or is probably untrue.

2.2 | Trivial Arguments

Some arguments are relatively trivial and easy to resolve. For example, if I claim that I am taller than you and if you disagree, then we may dispute the fact. However, this argument immediately suggests a quick resolution: we stand back to back and let one or more third parties measure the difference. Similarly, if I assert that New York City is the capital of New York State and you claim that I am wrong because Albany is the capital, then we can resolve that argument quickly by referring to an acceptable authority on the subject.

Arguments like the ones above are easy to deal with so long as two conditions hold: first, that there is a quick, authoritative way of resolving the difference (e.g., by standing back to back or by consulting a book) and, second, that both disputants agree to acknowledge that authority. In the above cases, if I do not trust the testimony of the third parties assessing our height difference or if I do not trust the book we consult, then the argument is not resolved, and it will continue to be unresolved until the arguers are persuaded to agree by some mutually acceptable authority.

In some cases where an argument can be resolved only by an appeal to an authority, the disputing parties may fail to agree on a suitable authority or may acknowledge different, irreconcilable authorities. Such arguments, no matter how energetic, will be eternally inconclusive and, for the most part, uninteresting (for example, disputes between people who assert that the only authority for the history of the earth is the Book of Genesis and those who assert that the only authority for that history is the modern scientific account). In such cases, the best resolution one can hope for is that the disputants amicably agree to disagree. If there is no such agreement, then the dispute may well turn into something nasty (e.g., a violent quarrel between competing factions).

Arguments similar to the first two mentioned above (about height and about the capital of New York State) are, as mentioned, usually relatively trivial. Their resolution is easy and quick because there is an immediate authority to establish the facts (i.e., what is true) and there is normally general agreement about that authority. Thus, once that authority has ruled on the issue, the argument is over.

This point seems obvious enough (and it is), but, as we shall see, it is crucially important not to base an essay (or any other assignment that requires a significant argument) on a trivial claim. Since any such claim can be resolved by a quick appeal to standard authorities, there is nothing meaningful to dispute. Some student essays in which an argument is called for set the essay up as asserting something very obvious (a matter of fact). When that occurs the essay ceases to be an argument of any consequence, and the essay is a poor one, because the writer is defending the obvious, something no rational person would dispute. An essay with a central claim like one of the following, for instance, is asserting something obvious:

1. Emma, the heroine of Jane Austen's novel, lives in a village in nineteenth-century England.

2. The French Revolution, which started in 1789, had many consequences.

3. There is much discussion in America today about illegal immigration.

4. John Stuart Mill's chief concern in *On Liberty* is to promote individual freedom in modern society.

5. In *A Vindication of the Rights of Woman* Mary Wollstonecraft talks a great deal about education.

6. *Snow Crash* belongs to a modern novelistic genre called cyberpunk.

7. Smoking cigarettes can be very damaging to one's health.

These are statements of established fact. We could dispute them (I suppose), but a prolonged argument would be fruitless, since we simply have to check the text of *Emma* or *Vindication* or the pages of a newspaper or a reliable source to resolve any disagreement.

2.3 | More Complex Arguments

Arguments become more complex when we are not immediately certain how to resolve them. For example, if I claim that I am a faster runner than you and if you disagree, then we have a dispute. It might seem that this difference of opinion could be easily settled by having a race. But before we can do that, we will first have to agree on what form the race should take. Are we talking about a sprint, a middle distance, a long distance, or some combination of races? In other words, we will have to reach agreement on what that phrase *faster runner* means and what might provide an acceptable measurement of that quality. Until we can do that, we will be unable to resolve the issue.

And obviously if I make the claim that I am a better athlete or more intelligent than you, the definition of the key term (*better athlete* or *more intelligent*) and the methods we use to determine the differences between us are going to be considerably more difficult to define in a manner agreeable to both of us. In fact, before we can even begin to resolve the initial dispute about which of us is a better athlete or more intelligent, we will probably have to have at least two potentially complicated preliminary arguments: What does the phrase *better athlete* or *more intelligent* mean, and, once we have established that, what is the appropriate way to measure that quality?

Arguments like the one just mentioned are quite common. In social science, for example, discussions of issues such as *poverty*, or *the middle class*, or *religious belief*, and so on, are often characterized by vigorous disagreements about what those terms mean and about the appropriate methods for identifying those included by the term. Similarly, in present-day public discussions, there are many differing views on what we mean by *climate change* and what might provide an accurate measurement of the phenomenon.

The complexity of some arguments is obvious enough if we consider disputes about the guilt or innocence of an accused person. Here we cannot simply stand the disputants back to back, nor can we devise a series of physical challenges or consult a special book to resolve the question. To obtain a conclusion, we have to set up an agreed-upon process in which the different possibilities are presented, explored, challenged—in short, argued— and then finally adjudicated by a disinterested third party (a judge and/or jury), all within the context of some acknowledged rules. The entire process requires from all participants a shared agreement about the appropriateness of the means undertaken to resolve the dispute.

2.4 | The Importance of Reason

In our Western society, for causes too complex to discuss here, we long ago determined that the appropriate way in which public arguments must be conducted is through proper reasoning. In later sections we will be considering more closely what this phrase means, but for the moment it is important to note that in making this decision we, in effect, rejected various other traditional ways in which arguments have been dealt with—appeals to religious tribunals or to rituals based on hereditary power and privilege or to sacred texts, astrology, augury, oracles, spiritual revelations, numerology, and so on.

Thus, to construct effective public arguments one must, first and foremost, have an understanding of the rules of reasoning. One of the major aims of an undergraduate education in almost all areas is to develop such an understanding. Of course, our society still permits people in their private lives to resolve their arguments and make private decisions (which often amount to the same thing) in any manner they wish, short of inflicting physical harm on others. So it is quite permissible in one's private affairs to toss coins, defer to spirit mediums, roll the dice, consult the *I Ching*, play games of rock-paper-scissors, and so on. In the world of work, politics, education, business, research, and public debate, however, the primary requirement of an effective argument is that it must be rational—that is, it must follow the rules of reason. Moreover, in this public sphere, as we all recognize, there is often a great deal of irrationality at work (e.g., in many political speeches and television advertisements), and thus an important part of being an educated citizen is possessing the skill to recognize this irrationality, especially when it is posing as a reasonable argument, since manipulating citizens through misleading (but often emotionally appealing) arguments is a major feature of modern life.

What are these rules of reason? Well, that is what this book is concerned with, at least on a very basic, common-sense level. The pages that follow offer some specific guidelines about the nature of a reasonable argument, about various methods for producing one in essay form, and about some of the ways written arguments can go astray. There is no attempt here to offer a comprehensive treatment of what can be a very complex subject. At the same time, the different sections do cover much of what an undergraduate needs to know in order to construct effective arguments.

2.5 | An Overview of the Major Tools

To make reasonable arguments in your essays, you need to be able to use three basic tools: definition, deduction, and induction. We will be discussing these in more detail later, but for the time being it is important to understand clearly the general meaning of each of them.

2.5.1 | Definition

The first essential tool is *definition*. No argument can proceed very far unless the basis of the argument and the meaning of all terms central to the debate are clear. If the parties to the dispute have different notions of what they are arguing about, then they may end up arguing about different things (what is called *arguing at cross purposes*). If I claim to be a faster runner than you on the grounds that I regularly compete in marathons, and you claim to be a faster runner than me on the grounds that you practice sprinting drills daily, we are likely arguing at cross purposes until we settle on what we mean by *faster runner*.

Clear definition is usually straightforward enough, but, as we shall see, it can present difficulties, especially if the writer fails to clarify with sufficient precision what the argument is about (and is not about) or if a key term has competing definitions or is ambiguous, confusing, or self-serving, as in the following argument:

Nothing is better than a good teacher.

A bad teacher is better than nothing.

Therefore a bad teacher is better than a good teacher.

In some instances, a definition can lie at the heart of particularly fierce disputes. Here, for example, are two persuasive arguments that reach opposite conclusions about a very contentious public issue:

Argument 1
Killing an innocent person is always wrong.

A fetus is an innocent person.

Therefore, killing a fetus is always wrong.

Argument 2
A woman has the right to full control
over her own body at all times.

The fetus is a part of a woman's body.

Therefore a woman has the right to exercise
full control over a fetus at all times.

Most people have no trouble accepting the opening general statements of both of these arguments. The difference of opinion arises from the claims made in the two second statements concerning the definition of the fetus. If one accepts the opening statement and the definition given in Argument 1, then one must accept the conclusion of the first argument; if one accepts the opening statement and the definition given in Argument 2, then one must accept the conclusion of the second argument. If one is uncertain about both definitions of the fetus, then one will remain uncertain about both arguments.

How is one to adjudicate between these two definitions of a fetus? That is the heart of the abortion argument. Attempts to resolve it involve a number of different strategies including appeals to religious authorities, to scientific studies of conception and embryonic development, or to law and human rights. Because there is no agreement about who has final authority in defining the fetus precisely, these arguments, while very persuasive to some people, fail to resolve the issue.

Definition is discussed more fully in Section 5.

2.5.2 | *Deduction*

The second essential tool is *deductive reasoning* or *deduction*. An argument is deductive when it shows that, if some statements (called *premises*) are all true, then the argument's conclusion *must* be true. Here are some examples:

1. All human beings are mortal. Anita Smith is a human being. Therefore, Anita Smith is mortal.

2. If it's raining, the game will be cancelled. If the game is cancelled, I'll be free tonight. Thus, if it's raining, I'll be free tonight.

3. School-age children resident in this state have a legal right to a free public education. Mandy Jenkins is a school-age child resident in this state. Therefore, Mandy Jenkins has a legal right to a free public education in this state.

4. Mr. Smith believes that communism is the most efficient economic system. So, at least one person believes that communism is more efficient than capitalism.

5. The interior angles of a triangle always add up to 180 degrees. The angles of this figure add up to 360 degrees. Thus, this figure cannot possibly be a triangle.

In deductive arguments, the truth of the premises must be something about which there is no dispute. Their truth must be obvious to all or else demonstrated prior to the argument. If they are not shown or known to be true, then the argument will not be persuasive.

This means there are two ways in which a deductive argument can go wrong: (1) if its premises have not been established and accepted, then the argument will fail to be convincing, and (2) if its premises fail to guarantee that its conclusion is true, then it is not *valid* and is unsound, even if its premises are true. Consider the following:

> Mr. Smith believes that communism is better than capitalism. So, at least one person believes that communism is more efficient than capitalism.

This argument looks much like Example 4 above. However, this argument is not a valid deductive argument. Even if we all agree that the premise is true, it does not follow that Mr. Smith (or anyone else) believes that communism is more efficient than capitalism. Just because Mr. Smith believes that communism is *better* than capitalism does not necessarily mean that he believes it is *more efficient*. He may believe that it is more efficient, or he may believe that it is better for other reasons. The conclusion in this case may be *very likely* to be true, but a valid deductive argument must demonstrate its conclusion with certainty, and this argument fails to do so.

Notice the terminology here. The term *valid* means that the premises guarantee the truth of the conclusion (i.e., the conclusion follows logically from the premises; thus, the argument has been constructed properly, and, if the premises are true, then the conclusion must be true). If, however, the premises do not guarantee the truth of the conclusion (as in the above example), then the argument is not valid.

It is possible to construct a valid deductive argument that is unsound. Consider the following example:

All people from middle-eastern countries
sympathize with Islamic terrorists.

Sasha is from a middle-eastern country.

Therefore, Sasha sympathizes with Islamic terrorists.

This deductive argument is valid (i.e., it has been constructed properly: the conclusion arises logically from the two premises). However, the argument is unsound, because the first premise is false.

A very common form of deductive argument begins by asserting a *principle* or *law* or *definition* or *scientific proposition* whose truth is generally acknowledged, then moves to a more particular claim about something or someone specific, and ends with a conclusion derived from the first two statements (as in Examples 1 and 5 above).

In some deductive arguments, one of the premises may be hypothetical (that is, it may state that one thing must follow from another). Here is an example:

If there's a drought in Brazil this year, then
there will be a global coffee shortage.

Brazil is about to experience a major drought this year.

Therefore, there will be a global coffee shortage.

An argument of this sort is especially common in science when an experimenter wishes to test a particular theory or hypothesis. She will frame a conditional statement and make a prediction (*If this claim is true ... then this must follow*). On the basis of this hypothesis, she will then conduct an experiment and observe the result. In almost all cases, that result will indicate one of two conclusions: if the predicted result does not occur, she will reject the hypothesis; if the predicted result does occur, she will not reject the hypothesis but continue to accept it as a working possibility.

For example, in the eighteenth century Edward Jenner, an English doctor, noticed that dairymaids who became infected with cowpox, a relatively mild disease, never seemed to catch smallpox, at that time a common and frequently lethal disease. His observations prompted him to formulate a hypothesis, conduct an experiment, and reach a conclusion, as follows:

> If cowpox effectively prevents smallpox, then
> a person who has been infected with cowpox
> will be immune to a smallpox infection.
>
> In an experiment in which a young boy (James Phipps)
> was deliberately infected with cowpox and forty-eight
> days later deliberately infected with smallpox, the
> young boy demonstrated an immunity to smallpox.
>
> Therefore in this case we have
> corroboration for the hypothesis.

The result did not *prove* the hypothesis, for the result could have been a coincidence or other factors might have been at work. But it did indicate to Jenner that he should not reject the hypothesis, for, on the basis of this experiment, he could conclude that the hypothesis had not been proven false. To demonstrate the truth of the hypothesis more convincingly he had to conduct many more tests.

A different result (i.e., a smallpox infection in the experimental subject, James Phipps) would have demonstrated that the hypothesis should be rejected, as in the following example:

> If animals pass onto their offspring characteristics acquired
> during the lifetime of the parent, then the offspring of dogs

whose tails have been surgically shortened when they were
puppies will manifest some evidence of this treatment in the
structure of their tails.

Experiments with several generations of dogs that have
had their tails shortened when they were still puppies reveal
that the newborn dogs always have a tail structure identical
to that of their parents before surgery.

Therefore, we cannot claim that the characteristic of a
surgically shortened tail is passed on as a heritable trait.

The opening claim in the above argument is offering a hypothesis (*"If this claim is true ..."*), and making a prediction (*"then this will follow"*). The second statement (the observation) is contrary to the prediction, and the conclusion is that the hypothesis must be false. Arguments like these led scientists to doubt and eventually to reject the widely held notion that characteristics acquired during the lifetime of an animal could be inherited.

This deductive procedure is useful in non-scientific arguments as well:

1. If my client committed the crime, he must have been in
    the building. But we know he was not in the building.
    Therefore, he could not have committed the crime.

2. If there were weapons of mass destruction in Iraq, they
    would surely have been found. But no weapons of
    mass destruction have been found, so they must never
    have existed.

3. If capital punishment is an effective deterrent to
    murder, then states with capital punishment will have
    significantly lower murder rates than states that do not
    have capital punishment. But there is no significant

difference between murder rates in states with capital punishment and in those without it. Therefore, the claim that capital punishment deters murder is false.

Making correct deductions (i.e., reaching a definite conclusion derived from premises) is not always easy, for there are a number of pitfalls (we will be looking at a few of them later).

2.5.3 | *Induction*

The third tool of reasoning is *induction* or *inductive reasoning*, a process in which we proceed from premises to a conclusion that, on the basis of the premises, we agree is probably true. For instance, if I start observing the colour of crows, I notice that they all seem to be black. At some point, having made many, many particular observations, always with the same result, I will conclude that all crows are black.

Unlike deductive reasoning, inductive reasoning does not produce certainty (i.e., it does not guarantee the truth of the conclusion). For instance, in the above argument about crows, I am not entitled to the conclusion that *all* crows are *certainly* black, since I have not observed all crows. However, the sheer number of observations entitles me to make that claim with a very high degree of probability, especially when I discover that no one else has ever seen a crow anywhere that was not black.

Here are a few short examples of inductive arguments:

1. The last three days I've had trouble starting my car. It's likely that I need a new battery.

2. Preliminary tests on the fish taken from this lake reveal potentially dangerous levels of mercury. And residents of the area have reported rashes after exposure to the lake's waters. Therefore, we could have a serious pollution problem on our hands.

3. Throughout the play, Nora constantly succeeds in turning any conversation into a discussion about herself, and she has trouble listening to what others have to say about anything else. From this, we get a strong sense that she is extremely self-centred.

4. For the past ten years, this river has flooded its banks every spring. The odds are good that it will do so again this spring.

5. A review of the various attempts to invade Afghanistan over the past fifteen hundred years shows that the area has never been completely conquered. This suggests that a new attempt is likely to run into serious trouble.

6. Poll numbers measuring the mayor's popularity have declined by over 25 per cent in the last six months and are now at their lowest point during his incumbency. His re-election looks as if it is going to be more difficult than we were assuming.

Notice how in these arguments the conclusions are derived from facts and are expressed as possibilities rather than as certainties. Any argument that is made to show that a conclusion is probably true (as opposed to certainly true) is an inductive argument.

2.5.4 | *Deduction and Induction in Combination*

In practice, deduction and induction are frequently combined. An argument might be deductive on the whole, for example, while each of its premises is established inductively. Consider the above-mentioned argument about inheritance.

> If animals pass onto their offspring characteristics acquired during the lifetime of the parent, then the offspring of dogs whose tails have been surgically

shortened when they were puppies should manifest some evidence of this treatment in the structure of their tails.

Experiments with several generations of dogs that have had their tails shortened when they were still puppies reveal that the newborn dogs have a tail structure identical to that of their parents before surgery.

Therefore, we cannot claim that the characteristic of a surgically shortened tail is passed on as a heritable trait.

The overall argument here is deductive. However, the second claim is established through inductive reasoning (based on observations and experiment). It could be challenged if, for example, a subsequent experiment had a different outcome (such a finding would challenge the truth of the second premise and thus cast doubt on the entire argument).

2.6 | Recognizing the Form of Simple Arguments

Here are some short arguments in which the writer presents a conclusion (which is in italics) and provides some reasons for that conclusion. Indicate beside each argument whether it is an example of deductive (D) or inductive (I) reasoning. If you are not sure, use a question mark.

Note that this exercise is not asking whether or not the argument is a good one or whether or not you agree with it. It is asking you to indicate the form of reasoning used (deductive or inductive). The criterion to bear in mind is the degree of certainty in the conclusion (inductive arguments lead to probabilistic conclusions; deductive arguments lead to statements of certainty).

1. Things equal to the same thing are equal to each other. Therefore if A equals B and if B equals C, *then A must equal C.*

2. The principle of free speech is one of the most important elements of our liberal democracy. Therefore *this student newspaper must be free to print opinions offensive to many people.*

3. Last year six per cent of the machines manufactured in that plant had defective motors. *We may well have a serious problem that we need to investigate further.*

4. All human beings suffering from a painful, fatal illness have the right to assisted suicide. *Therefore this terminally ill, suffering patient has the right to an assisted suicide.*

5. In this essay the writer frequently uses words like "perhaps," "maybe," and "alternatively." *This feature of the style suggests that the writer lacks confidence in her analysis.*

6. Model X gets better mileage, costs less to purchase and to maintain, and has a better all-round rating in *Consumer Reports* than does Model Y. *Therefore, it probably makes more sense for me to purchase Model X rather than Model Y.*

7. We all agree that the murder must have been committed by one of the three in the house—the husband, the wife, or the cook—and we've determined that neither the cook nor the wife could have done it. *Therefore, the husband must have done it.*

2.7 | Exercises in Deduction and Induction

Here, as a bonus for those readers who like to think about amusing logical puzzles, are five brain-teasers. The important thing here is not necessarily to get the right answer on your own (since many people do not find such puzzles intriguing), but rather, once you know the answer, to follow the logic of the thinking that produced it.

Problem A

You are a police officer on a highway patrol. You come across an accident in which two cars have collided in an off-highway rest area. Each driver claims that he has been at the rest area for over two hours eating lunch and sleeping and that the other driver drove in from the highway and ran into his car a few minutes ago. You cannot tell from the position of the vehicles or from the asphalt which one is telling the truth. There are no witnesses. Can you think of how you might sort out the claims on the spot? What form(s) of reasoning have you used?

Problem B

Two friends of yours are having a bitter argument over the question of whether or not two people could have exactly the same number of hairs on their heads. They want you to determine the answer to the question. Can you think of some way to settle the question with certainty, without resorting to counting hairs?

Problem C

A man is walking to the town of Ipswich. He comes to a fork in the road, with the two branches leading in two different directions. He knows that one of them goes to Ipswich, but he doesn't know which one. He also knows that in the house right beside the fork in the road there are two brothers, identical twins, both of whom know the road to Ipswich. He knows that one brother always lies and that the other always tells the truth, but he cannot tell them apart. What single question can he ask to whoever answers his knock on the door that will indicate to him the correct road to Ipswich?

Problem D

Three people are placed directly in line facing a wall. The one at the back can see the two in front of him, the one in the middle can see the person immediately in front, and the one at the front can see only the wall. Each of them is wearing a hat taken from a supply of three black hats and two white hats (the three people know this), but they do not know the colour of the hat on their own heads. They are told to remain in line silently until one of them can guess the colour of the hat on his or her head. That person gets a large cash prize. After five minutes of standing in line, the one facing the wall (at the front of the line) correctly identifies the colour of the hat on her head. What colour must it be? How did she arrive at the correct conclusion? Note that she did not guess.

Problem E

[The following problem was recently part of an interview with students wishing to enroll as undergraduates in the Computer Science degree program at the University of Oxford.]

You are the senior member of a group of 7 pirates (in descending order of seniority: you, Pirates B, C, D, E, F, and G), who have to decide how to divide up 100 gold coins, according to strict pirate rules, as follows: (a) the senior pirate (i.e., you) proposes a way of dividing the money; (b) the whole group (including you) votes on the proposal. If half or more of the votes are in favour, the proposal is adopted; if fewer than half are in favour, the senior pirate is thrown overboard, and the process starts again, with the next senior pirate making the proposal; (c) the pirates are all perfectly rational and entirely ruthless, each one concerned only about getting as much of the money as possible. What division would you, as senior pirate, suggest?

2.8 | Further Observations on Deduction and Induction

2.8.1 | The Strength or Persuasiveness of an Argument

As we have briefly discussed already, the persuasiveness of a deductive argument depends upon two things: first, there must be agreement about the truth of the premises, and, second, the conclusion must be guaranteed by those premises (i.e., the argument must be valid). Here is a simple familiar example:

All human beings must eventually die.

Mr. Jones is a human being.

Therefore, Mr. Jones will eventually die.

We all accept the truth of the first statement, based on our education and experience. We accept the truth of the second statement through our knowledge of Mr. Jones. And the conclusion (the third statement) seems to follow logically from the first two (i.e., the principle in the first premise has been applied to the specific case of Mr. Jones correctly).

Now, what is important to notice about such a deductive argument, as mentioned earlier, is that the truth of the conclusion is compelling. If we are rational, then we have to agree. To agree that the premises are true and the argument is valid, and then to decline to accept the truth of the conclusion would be to violate a basic principle of reason. I am free in a modern liberal society to reject that conclusion, but I cannot do so and claim that I am acting rationally. Hence, someone who can frame an argument in a deductive structure has the most powerful means of rational persuasion available.

That feature of a deductive argument also means, as we shall see, that if a deductive argument is constructed properly (i.e., is valid) and we find the conclusion problematic, then the fault must be with one of the premises: they cannot all be true and yet produce an erroneous conclusion.

The persuasiveness of an inductive argument will usually depend upon the nature of the evidence presented (its quality or quantity or both), so that the conclusion may range from possible to almost certainly true (though never completely certain). Consider these two examples:

1. That player rolled the dice twice in a row and got a double six both times. I think the dice may be loaded.

2. That player rolled the dice twelve times in a row and got a double six each time. I think the dice are almost certainly loaded.

Obviously, the increased number of observations in the second example makes the conclusion much more certain than in the first argument (because the statistical probability of twelve consecutive double sixes is so small).

Since it can be difficult to know what types and quantity of evidence are needed to reach a given conclusion, undergraduate courses spend a good deal of time teaching students what counts as evidence in a particular discipline and how one sets about collecting and evaluating that information (e.g., through laboratory or field procedures, strategies for reading literature, evaluating historical facts, conducting polls, carrying out effective research, interpreting statistical results, and so on). For a further discussion of this matter see 2.8.7.

2.8.2 | *Agreed-Upon Principles and Facts*

As I have stated, many arguments incorporate an appeal to some already established general principle or agreed-upon fact. Where do we find such principles and facts? They can come from a number of places. The important thing is that we all acknowledge them as true.

1. Some truths are self-evident and require no proof. Mathematics, for example, starts with some general principles which are self-evidently true (axioms), that is, everyone agrees that they must be true (e.g., the whole of a figure is made up of the sum of its parts and is greater than any single one of its parts; things equal to the same thing are equal to each other; if I subtract the same amount from two things which are equal, the remainders will be equal; and so on). We cannot prove these, but we agree that they are true, and we would tend to believe that anyone who denied their truth was irrational. Similarly, mathematical claims properly derived from these initial assumptions are accepted as true (e.g., in a right-angled triangle the square of the hypotenuse is equal to the sum of the squares of the other two sides).

2. Some truths are established by definitions. For example, if we agree that one defining characteristic of an *insect* is that it must have six legs, then we can establish as a general principle "All insects must have six legs." Similarly if we agree that the word *deter* means *to discourage someone from doing something*, then we can establish that the following statement is self-evidently true "If capital punishment deters people from committing murder, then, all other things being equal, where capital punishment is in effect, there will be fewer murders committed than where there is no capital punishment."

3. We share certain basic moral principles (through our culture or our training or as human beings); for example, torturing innocent victims for pleasure is wrong; society has a duty to help the mentally ill; and so on. Again, these are not capable of iron-clad proof, but we (or most of us) agree with most of them without further discussion. Members of a particular

social, religious, or professional group will often share a very clear set of principles that enables them to resolve arguments among themselves (although often in the multicultural world beyond the meeting house the public may not accept the same principles). That, indeed, is one of the attractions of a small group: resolving arguments is much easier among people who share a common set of principles or a code of ethics.

4. Certain documents enshrine principles which we, as citizens of Canada or America or the world, are expected to share. These are the documents which form declarations of various human rights (e.g., constitutional rights, international rights, human rights).

5. Most of us agree with the general principles that in a liberal democracy the elected government has the right to make the laws and that the citizens, under normal circumstances, have an obligation to obey the laws. Thus, the statement of a legal requirement (i.e., a law as defined by present legislation) can be treated as an agreed-upon principle.

6. An opening general principle may be a hypothesis which we wish to check by constructing an argument upon it and then testing the conclusion. This procedure is central to the process of thinking we call *scientific reasoning*. We may not know that this general principle is true, but we agree to it provisionally in order to produce a conclusion that we can examine.

7. Many of the initial statements in an argument will be well-known truths or probabilities whose reliability has been established through experiment and observation (i.e., inductively). The proofs have been so reliable that we now take the assertion as universally agreed upon and can construct an argument upon it (e.g., smoking cigarettes is

bad for one's health). Many scientific arguments rest on a deductive structure which starts with a statement of this sort, a shared truth which has been established beyond all reasonable doubt.

2.8.3 | *Applying General Principles to Particular Claims*

One common structure for an argument takes the form of three steps: (1) an agreed-upon general principle, (2) a particular claim that is generally agreed to be true, and (3) a conclusion drawn by applying the general principle to the specific case. If Statements 1 and 2 are agreed-upon and combined correctly, Statement 3 (the conclusion) will be compelling.

In such arguments, often a key point of dispute is whether the particular claim (Step 2) of the argument is, in fact, covered by the agreed-upon general principle (Step 1) or whether it lies outside the scope of that general principle. Consider the following argument:

> This college has established a clear policy that it will not tolerate any harassment on the basis of gender.

> The photography exhibition in the lobby of the college theatre is offensive to many students in the LGBTQ community.

> Therefore the photography exhibition in the lobby of the college theatre should be closed down.

Even if we agree that the first and second premises are true, we can still question whether the general principle is relevant in this particular case: Does the anti-harassment policy apply to artistic exhibitions that offend some people? Until we have a clear answer to that question, the conclusion of the above argument will remain problematic.

In other words, in deductive arguments based on an appeal to an agreed-upon principle, law, policy, or rule, we have to be careful to make sure that what is specified in that general statement can be reasonably applied to the particular issue at hand. If there is any doubt about that, then the argument will be unpersuasive. Here are a few more examples of modern arguments where this problem arises:

> Since smoking is illegal in this airport lounge, it is also illegal to use an e-cigarette device. [Does a law against smoking apply to a vaping device that produces no smoke?]

> This company's dress code is clearly an infringement of my right to freedom of expression. [Does the right to freedom of expression extend to the clothing and accessories one wears at work?]

> No action should be taken against this high school teacher for distributing anti-Semitic pamphlets on school property. She is exercising her right to freedom of speech. [Does the notion of free speech apply in this case?]

Often such arguments can be decided only by an appropriate authority, such as a school board, a municipal council, a state or provincial legislature, or (in the most contested cases) a Supreme Court. Such authorities have to decide whether a general principle—one enshrined in a constitution, a charter of rights, and/or in past precedents—can be applied to a specific law or institutional practice and, if so, then how such a judgement might affect that specific law or practice (e.g., how Second Amendment rights affect municipal gun laws, how Charter minority language rights must shape educational policies in a particular school district, and so on).

The point to remember here is that in dealing with arguments of this sort, you need to be careful to ensure that the general principle invoked is indeed appropriate in the particular case under discussion. In framing your own arguments, you will usually have to make that point clear to the reader (for examples see 7.1.1 below).

Some of the most intriguing scientific debates—those involving the classification of a hitherto unknown specimen—involve similar arguments. How should the existing classification system, which establishes the rules for assigning such specimens to a particular order, class, and species, deal with them? This question can prompt long and hotly contested arguments, with a great deal riding on the outcome. One of the best known in the history of science is the long dispute in the early nineteenth century between radical French biologists and their more conservative English counterparts over the duck-billed platypus, a remarkably different animal with an ambiguous reproductive system: Was this creature a new class of vertebrate intermediate between mammals and birds and thus powerful new evidence for evolution, or was it simply a new species of mammal without any significant evolutionary implications? When the argument was finally resolved in favour of those classifying the animal as a species of mammal, the British government proclaimed the result a triumphant victory of conservative imperial Britain over godless post-revolutionary France.

2.8.4 | Falsification Theories of Science

Many philosophers of science claim that the essence of science is the use of deductive reasoning to construct predictions on the basis of a hypothesis. If the predictions turn out to be accurate, then the hypothesis is corroborated (and is thus, inductively, more likely to be true). If the predictions are inaccurate, then the hypothesis must be inadequate or false.

Here is an example from the history of science of how this might work in scientific practice:

All planets in our solar system move in
circular orbits around the sun.

Mars is a planet in our solar system.

.Therefore, Mars moves in a circular orbit around the sun.

The logic of this argument is compelling if we accept the hypothesis that the planets move in circular orbits around the sun and agree that Mars is a planet. For many years, this was accepted without question. However, once people started rigorously and repeatedly testing the prediction made by this argument, by observing Mars with improved instruments, they quickly learned that the prediction is false. Mars's orbit is not circular. Therefore there is something wrong with this argument: either Mars is not a planet (and thus the second premise of the argument is incorrect), or the hypothesis (that all planets in our solar system move in circular orbits around the sun) must be wrong.

Astronomers had to go back and come up with another argument, and Johannes Kepler posited the hypothesis that planets in our solar system move in ellipses, with the sun at one focal point. This hypothesis led to a new argument which produced a different conclusion: Mars must move in an elliptical orbit with the sun at one focal point of the ellipse. This conclusion then became subject to rigorous testing.

According to this view of science (which has its critics) science never asserts that a hypothesis is true; rather, it is constantly testing claims by drawing deductive conclusions (i.e., predictions) from those claims and subjecting these predictions to testing. What remains is not necessarily something true, but something which has not yet been proved false. This, such falsificationists say, accounts for the fact that science is progressive, that is, its knowledge gets increasingly more secure (i.e., less false), because it is always discarding or improving theories whose predictions fail experimental testing. Alternatively put, one might say that as a theory survives repeated testing, the confidence of scientists in the probable truth of that theory increases.

Thus, for example, the concept of biological evolution may not be true in all senses of that word (although it might be): the case is simply that no one has ever been able to prove it false. Scientists will, of course, speak of the theory as *scientifically true*, because what they mean by that phrase is that it has successfully passed every scientific test that could have proved it false (and there have been innumerable such tests, since, among other things, every discovery of a fossil amounts to yet another potential challenge to the theory). This point, incidentally, should remind us that science is not the pursuit or discovery of the Truth (with a capital T), but the pursuit and discovery of *scientific truth*. Many people, of course, assert that these are the same thing; others, however, reject that claim.

Scientific truth, according to this view of science, is a concept that can be applied only to claims that can be tested and potentially falsified. Hence, there are a great many disputatious assertions that lie beyond the realm of science (e.g., "God exists," "God does not exist," "We ought to lead morally good lives," "Human beings are intrinsically valuable," "That work of literature is a masterpiece," "To be a worthy citizen one should vote in local elections," and so on). The scientific method of arguing is incapable of addressing, let alone resolving, arguments about statements like these, because such assertions do not generate predictions that can be scientifically tested.

Scientific theories (hypotheses) often run far ahead of the experimental tests that provide evidence for them (in many cases the thinkers who produce the theory are not the ones who conduct the experiments to test it). Nonetheless, the logical consistency and elegant equations in the theory, together with its apparent explanatory power, will often persuade people that the theory is a new scientific explanation for something. However, until the theory has been thoroughly tested, it remains a metaphysical speculation.

One should note, in passing, that when the test of a conclusion in a scientific experiment produces a negative result, the first reaction of scientists is usually not to reject the hypothesis. Instead they will check the test carefully, just in case some error in the measurements or calculations, a fault in the instruments, or (in some cases) fraud has skewed the results. Alternatively, they will often adjust the hypothesis to take care of the anomaly.

It is worth stressing here the importance of this method of arguing in science (and science students especially should take note). Science is not simply the collection of evidence in order to construct a theory. It is better characterized as the construction of a theoretical general principle (a hypothesis) on the basis of which certain conclusions are derived in the form of predictions. The predictions are then independently tested by experiment and observation. In this process, the number of experiments may be quite small, but they will often be crucial tests of a theory (one significant negative result, for example, can cast doubt on the entire hypothesis).

2.8.5 | The Problem of Hidden or Misleading Assumptions

A good argument should always set out clearly the premises upon which its conclusion rests. Sometimes a careless or deceptive writer will fail to do that and will offer an argument in which a major assumption is concealed. Consider the following argument:

> American commercial fishing boats have the exclusive right to harvest those fish, because the fish are coming to American rivers to spawn.

This argument rests upon an appeal to a shared principle on which the validity of the conclusion depends. However, that assumed principle is not stated. The principle is something like this: "The commercial fishing boats of the country where fish come to spawn have an exclusive right to harvest those fish." The assumption, which may or may not be true or agreed-upon, needs to be clearly included in the argument.

Here are a few more examples of similar arguments:

1. We need to reduce the random violence in our streets. We should be insisting on tougher sentences for crimes of assault.

2. People who smoke inflict damage on themselves. Therefore, insurance companies should not pay the medical expenses for treating conditions related to their smoking.

3. All our instructors should have post-graduate university degrees. We need to have good teachers.

4. Dr. Wilson provided information about a patient's medical records to Acme Insurance without the patient's consent. He is clearly an unethical physician.

Notice that each of these arguments has only one premise, and the validity of the conclusion depends upon a second premise, an assumption that is not included. Can you formulate a statement of that assumption for each of the arguments above? The unstated assumption, of course, may be true, but the writer is not being particularly candid by not including it. In some cases, the assumption may be false, and the writer is concealing it in order to make his bad argument appear more plausible.

In your own writing, try to avoid offering arguments like these (and remain alert to them when reading other people's arguments). Make sure you inform the reader in sufficient detail of all the principles or facts essential to your argument.

Another problem similar to the one just mentioned occurs when an argument attacks an opponent rather than focusing on that opponent's argument (this fallacy is called an *ad hominem* argument).

1. I don't consider his opinions worth listening to. He's a convicted criminal and has been through bankruptcy proceedings twice.

2. How can her advice on marriage be reliable? She's a flaming lesbian and a radical feminist and, on top of that, comes from San Francisco.

Such a tactic is obviously a crude (but often emotionally effective) way to appeal to the prejudices of the reader. It is relying upon the reader to supply the missing assumption (e.g., "No convicted criminal who has been through bankruptcy twice can have opinions worth listening to," "No lesbian or feminist or resident of San Francisco can offer reliable advice on marriage, let alone someone who is all three at once").

Another logical fallacy similar to the problem of hidden assumptions is a *slippery slope* argument, which usually takes the following form: "If X happens, then Y is bound to take place."

1. If we give the terminally ill a right to assisted suicide, we will soon have death clinics in every supermarket.

2. Teaching religion in the schools is inviting trouble. If we allow that, we will soon have armed religious sects battling it out in the streets.

3. We should not legalize marijuana because that will inevitably lead to an increase in heroin use.

Such conclusions about what might or will happen (usually something bad) are fallacious because there is no persuasive argument offered as to why that future situation must come about as a result of the initial event (i.e., there's a hidden assumption that it will, but no proof is offered). Similar arguments about the future benefits of some action are also suspect if they do not establish a persuasive link between the action and the future benefit.

1.   If we raise the minimum wage, that will be good for the local economy.

2.   We should bring back Latin in the school curriculum. Students will understand their own language better.

These arguments, as stated, are weak, because they do not offer any reason why we can expect the alleged benefit to result from the recommended action.

2.8.6 | *Negative Proofs: Eliminating the Alternatives*

A very powerful and common structure for an argument involves providing a list of alternatives and then showing that all but one of the alternatives are impossible, improbable, or impractical. This then leads naturally to the conclusion that the one remaining option must be advisable or true or highly probable. In other words, we establish the truth of the conclusion, not so much by focusing on it directly, but by eliminating all other possibilities. Notice the following examples:

Argument 1
Only two people's fingerprints were found on the murder weapon, those of Ms. Smith and of Mr. Wesson. Thus, one of · the two must have fired the fatal bullet.

At the time of the murder, Ms. Smith was on an extended holiday in Europe; she did not return until three days after the killing.

Therefore, Ms. Smith could not have fired the fatal shot, and Mr. Wesson must have.

Argument 2
We have three options for dealing with this crisis: we can ignore it and hope it will solve itself, we can deal with it immediately ourselves, or we can work co-operatively with the federal government to resolve it.

The issue is too serious to ignore, and we simply do not have the resources necessary to deal with it immediately ourselves.

Therefore, we must work co-operatively with the federal government to resolve it.

Argument 3
Hamlet delays killing Claudius either because he is a coward, or because he never has a suitable opportunity, or because he does not believe the ghost, or because he is suffering from some inner problem.

We know that Hamlet is not a coward, and he repeatedly states that he believes the ghost; moreover, he has frequent and easy access to Claudius, so there is no lack of opportunity.

Thus, he must be suffering from some inner problem.

This form of argument is extremely important and common in business, political and social policy, risk analysis, literary interpretation, judicial proceedings, and science, anywhere one has to adjudicate between competing options and does so by showing that all of them except one are impossible or very inadvisable, or that all of them are less persuasive than a particular one. It is also a common method many people use to make their own personal decisions.

There is, however, one common misuse of this argument you should remain alert to, a logical error called *false dilemma*.

This occurs when the list of alternatives provided at the start of the argument is not complete but is, deliberately or not, misleading, because it does not include all the options.

Here are some simple examples of this logical error:

Argument 1
We have only two choices in dealing with a worker who is drinking alcohol on the job: we can ignore the problem, or we can fire the worker for cause.

We cannot afford to ignore the problem, because the drinking creates dangers for the other workers and hurts productivity.

Therefore we have to fire any worker who is drinking alcohol on the job.

Argument 2
Everyone agrees that there are only two accounts of the creation of animal and plant species, the one in Genesis and the one provided by Darwin.

Clearly, there are inconsistencies, inaccuracies, and errors in Darwin's account.

Therefore, the only acceptable account for the creation of animal and plant species is the one in Genesis.

Argument 3
Either we give back all our land to the First Nations communities, as they are demanding, or we require them to become equal citizens without any special status, just like everyone else.

We cannot afford to give back all the land.

Therefore, we have to require First Nations people to become equal citizens without any special status, just like everyone else.

Each of these arguments begins with a list of options or alternatives, and each list is misleadingly incomplete. If you accept the list, however, as a genuine and complete statement of all the options, then you may be easily misled by the rest of the argument. In any argument, therefore, where you are considering or including a range of options, make sure the list is complete. If you are excluding something, make sure you explain why that is not an option.

2.8.7 | *Overstating the Conclusion*

A good argument should have a compelling conclusion—that is, it should have a conclusion that is reasonable to believe on the basis of the argument's premises. However, that conclusion is compelling *only* if the language used to express it matches the language in the premises. One common problem is a tendency to overstate the conclusion by using language that does not match the language in the premises.

Many native land claims are justified by Canadian law.

This petition is a native land claim.

Therefore, this petition is justified by Canadian law.

The conclusion here is very firm (*is justified*), but the first premise does not entitle you to such a firm conclusion, since it does not say *all* (hence the argument is not valid). The argument would be valid if the first premise referred to *all native land claims* instead of *many*—but it would not be very persuasive, since the first premise would be untrue: it is unlikely that *all* native land claims ever made have been justified by Canadian law. A more persuasive approach would be to change the conclusion to replace *is* with *may be*.

Here is another example:

> Julia scored more goals than anyone else on her hockey team last year.
>
> Julia's coach often puts her on the ice in crucial late-game situations.
>
> Therefore, Julia is the best player on her team.

The conclusion here is, once again, very firm (*is the best player on her team*), but the first and second statements do not entitle you to such a strong conclusion. A better one would be something like "Therefore, Julia is a good hockey player" or "Therefore, Julia is one of the better hockey players on her team."

A common source of trouble here are words in the conclusion that are superlatives (like *the best player*) or that express certainty (like *is justified*). Do not use these words when your opening assumptions do not entitle you to make that claim. If the language does match that in the premises, then the conclusion is more likely to be compelling.

In inductive arguments based on evidence, one of the most challenging issues is a question like the following: "How much evidence do I need before I draw a conclusion? What sort of conclusion am I entitled to draw on the basis of the evidence I do have? How confident can I be that this conclusion is probable?" Much of your study at university will be dealing with these questions, particularly if you are a student of social science, where the analysis of statistical evidence is a crucial part of the curriculum.

There is not time here to go into the details of what can be a very complex subject, but at a very basic level we can suggest the following points to watch for in inductive arguments:

1. The strength of the conclusion is going to depend upon the quality and the quantity of the observations (evidence) you introduce. No generalization based on a single piece of unreliable evidence is very persuasive.

2. The evidence included in the premises must be good evidence. Again, you will be learning what that phrase means in different subjects, but, in general, the evidence should meet the following criteria: it should be accurate, up-to-date, based on a reliable source, and easy to verify or replicate. It should not be subjective, fabricated, or based on a clearly biased or suspicious source. In literary arguments, the evidence normally will come directly from the text under discussion or from secondary sources (i.e., books or articles written about that text). It will not come from something subjective (e.g., what you think the childhood experiences of the heroine might or might not have been like or from the recesses of your own memories).

3. Part of the previous point requires you to identify clearly any special authorities to whom you appeal for evidence. In an academic paper you should never just refer vaguely to experts (in phrases like "Scientific studies have shown ...," "Many critics maintain that ...," "It has been verified that ..." and so on). If you want to use phrases like that, then you are going to have to provide specific references. Claims based on unnamed authorities immediately make that part of the argument suspect.

4. Most importantly, as we saw earlier, the language in the conclusion of an argument must match the degree of certainty in the evidence. An inductive argument, especially one about literature, will normally entitle you only to talk about what is probably the case rather than to use a vocabulary indicating certainty (so words like *proves*, *demonstrates*, and so on,

which indicate a firm certainty, are generally less advisable than words like *suggests, raises the possibility, perhaps indicates,* and so on), unless the probability is so high as to be almost certain. Statistical conclusions based on population surveys (i.e., polls) normally include a statement about how confident one can be that the conclusion is correct.

A tendency to overstate the conclusion, that is, to make the conclusion much more definite than the evidence suggests or to offer insufficient or poor evidence is a quick way to reduce the persuasiveness of an inductive argument. These habits make the argument sound as if it is jumping to firm conclusions far too quickly, perhaps because the author has already made up his mind and is pushing for the conclusion he wants.

One should, of course, also avoid any tendency to understate the conclusions to an inductive argument. This practice is, I would estimate, less common than the habit of overstating the conclusion, but it still can be prejudicial to your argument (by making you sound as if you have little confidence in the case you are presenting). If you have a suitable amount of excellent evidence, do not be timid about making a confident conclusion.

2.8.8 | Exercise in Simple Inductive Arguments

Below are some simple inductive arguments, with some evidence presented and a conclusion. Comment on each argument, in light of the comments above. If you think the conclusion might be improved, then provide an improved version.

1. The ghost in *Hamlet* spends more time complaining about his ex-wife's remarriage than the fact that his brother murdered him. Clearly this demonstrates he is obsessed with his inadequate sexuality.

2. The ghost in *Hamlet* comes into Gertrude's bedroom to confront Hamlet, but his ex-wife cannot see him. This suggests something interesting: that Hamlet Senior, renowned as a warrior king, may not feel quite so commanding and competent in the bedroom.

3. The driver's blood alcohol level was three times the legal limit. Three separate witnesses indicate that he was driving on the wrong side of the road without lights on, and the preliminary analysis shows that he was driving well above the speed limit. And the brakes on his car were defective. He might be to blame in the accident.

4. We have conducted an experiment ten times under standard conditions in which we added a small piece of zinc to hydrochloric acid. Every time hydrogen gas was produced. Thus, the interaction of zinc and hydrochloric acid under similar conditions will always produce hydrogen gas.

5. In this poem, nature is always described as "green," "verdant," "ripe," "blooming," and "fertile." The writer is here suggesting that nature is a rich source of life.

6. Odysseus obviously has a very cruel streak. We see this when he grinds out the eye of Polyphemos, the Cyclops, with a sharpened and burning pole and at the end when he slaughters the suitors and punishes the servants, some of them very brutally.

7. The Liberal candidates promised that they would repeal the sales tax. Once in office, they refused to carry out that legislation. They are all liars.

8. Some released sex offenders have committed new offences. We should never release any sex offenders, since they will always reoffend.

9. My astrologer and the Ouija board have told me repeatedly that it will rain on Friday. I think we should call off the picnic.

2.9 | Some Potential Problems in Arguments

In addition to the ones we have already discussed, there are many other common ways in which arguments can go astray. The following paragraphs describe some of these (the list is not intended to be exhaustive).

1. Do not end up *begging the question*, that is, assuming the truth of what you have set out to prove. For example, consider the following arguments:

    a. The government must reduce spending because the government is spending too much money.

    b. People should not break the law because breaking the law is bad.

    c. Odysseus spends little time at home because he is always away.

    d. I failed the course because my marks were too low.

    Notice how these are essentially saying: "X is the case because X is the case." The writer has offered as evidence what he is setting out to prove.

2. Be careful not to bring in a *non sequitur*, that is, some evidence which is apparently irrelevant to the point you are trying to argue.

    a. Hamlet is clearly insane because Polonius doesn't want his daughter associating with him.

    b. I failed the course because my teacher was overweight.

c.   I won't vote for Candidate Jones because
     her cousin is a vegetarian.

In each of these examples, there does not seem to be a connection between the claim made and the reason given. If
there is a connection between the teacher's weight and your
failure or the dietary beliefs of Candidate Jones's cousin and
your voting decision, you will have to set that out in detail.
As it stands, the teacher's weight and the cousin's eating
preferences here seem like a *non sequitur*, something irrelevant to your conclusions (the connection is not apparent to
the reader).

3.   Remember that *coincidence is not cause*. That is, just because
     B happens after A, that does not necessarily mean that A
     causes B. For example:

a.   I cannot recommend that medication. I know
     two people who got nasty colds after taking it.

b.   We have to get rid of the Dean. We didn't have
     this financial problem until she arrived.

c.   The witches are clearly the source of evil in
     Macbeth, because he starts thinking about
     being king right after he meets them.

The medication may cause bad side effects, and the Dean
may be responsible for the financial mess, but you cannot
establish that persuasively simply by asserting that one event
happened after another. You need much more detailed evidence in order to substantiate the claim. And the conclusion
about the witches could lead to a serious problem with an
interpretation of the play. This error, as you will find out if

you study correlation in a statistics course, can be a major source of mistakes in certain areas of social science and science. It is also a popular tactic in deliberately misleading political speeches (e.g., "We never had that problem before she became mayor!").

4. Do not appeal to the authority of someone or some organization simply because he or she is well known, even if that person is an expert, unless you can point to a specific study or facts associated with the name: e.g., "Bill Clinton says we are right to be extending free trade. So we should be." Bill Clinton might be right, but simply mentioning his name doesn't provide any meat to the argument. Of course, if the people you mention are recognized experts, then their authority may carry some persuasive weight without your mentioning a specific study (e.g., "Two epidemiologists I consulted told me that the Ebola epidemic in Africa poses no major threat to North America"). In an academic paper, however, such a remark would require a citation.

5. In the absence of compelling reasons to do otherwise, you should normally avoid unnecessarily complicated explanations when there are simpler ones available. For example, in a choice between two interpretations or hypotheses, you should select the one that requires the fewest assumptions. This principle is called *Occam's Razor*. It plays a vital role in sorting out argumentative possibilities and provides a useful check against ingenious but often bizarre explanations—e.g., the notion that Hamlet is really a woman who has been raised as a man.

   Occam's Razor does not apply, however, if the more complicated interpretation accounts for more of the evidence than the simpler one. Hence, when you are evaluating two different possible explanations for something, you need to consider two questions: "Which is the simpler and more obvious hypothesis?" and "Which provides a satisfactory explanation for more of the event, or the phenomenon, or the text?"

6. Do not attempt to further your argument by shifting the *burden of proof*. In most arguments the responsibility for making a case in favour of a particular assertion lies with the person making the claim, not with those who refuse to accept it. Notice, for example, how the following arguments attempt to shift the burden of proof:

   a. Until you can prove that angels do not exist, I will continue to believe in them.

   b. It is entirely plausible that Hamlet is a girl who has been raised as a boy. There is no evidence in the play to disprove this interpretation.

   Just because it is impossible to prove something is not true does not therefore make it true.

There are many other ways in which arguments, deductive and inductive, can go astray, most of which are easy enough to recognize. Anyone who would like to look at a fairly comprehensive and convenient list should consult the Internet Encyclopedia of Philosophy (http://www.iep.utm.edu/fallacy/).

2.10 | Exercise in Evaluating Short Arguments

Comment on the persuasiveness of each of the following arguments. Note that some are deductive and others inductive. If you can perceive a specific problem, then identify it. If you think the argument is quite persuasive, then indicate that.

1. The survey questionnaire on student plagiarism was completed by 85 per cent of the faculty. Three-quarters

of the respondents said they definitely felt that plagiarism in first-year papers was on the increase. I think we may have a problem here that we should investigate further.

2. In the opening of the *Odyssey* the gods repeatedly state that anyone who violates someone else's home must be punished. This strongly suggests that there is some divine moral order in the world of this book.

3. The economy started to go downhill right after the present government was elected. Clearly, they do not know how to run a national economy.

4. Of course, his argument is hopelessly wrong. After all, he's a Roman Catholic priest. What do you expect?

5. That film is pornographic; two or three scenes feature full male and female nudity.

6. This is a really good poem because it has a sonnet structure, with a basic blank verse rhythm, and a strong repetitive rhyme scheme.

7. Look, for the entire season this player led the team in scoring, in rebounding, in assists, and in blocked shots, and he played in every game during the season. He is clearly a strong candidate for the most valuable player on the team.

8. Students should all have to study first-year English at college because they all need at least two semesters of English. And my mother is in favour of the regulation, too.

3.0

Organizing a Written Argument

Conversational arguments tend to have a freewheeling nature, with interruptions, abrupt changes, unsubstantiated opinions, repetitions, illogical jumps, and so forth. A written argumentative essay, by contrast, requires a formal structure, because the most essential quality of such a piece of writing is *clarity*: the reader must understand the central claim of the argument and the contribution that each part of the essay makes to that argument. If the reader gets confused about particular details, then the persuasiveness of the case the writer is attempting to make will suffer, sometimes irreparably.

3.1 | Understanding the Assignment

The first important part of preparing a written argument is to understand clearly the precise nature of the assignment. What exactly have you been asked to do? Make sure you understand that clearly. If you do not, you may produce a splendid essay, but still not succeed with the assignment.

For example, if you are asked to *describe* something or to provide a *summary*, a *précis*, or an *abstract* of a piece of writing, then no argument is required. You are simply being asked to provide a concise restatement of what someone else has said. Undergraduate courses rarely involve such assignments, except in certain forms of scientific and technical writing. A request to *discuss, evaluate, assess, interpret,* or *consider,* by contrast, is asking the writer to provide an argument of the sort this book explores. It is important to note the exact language the assignment uses; for example, a requirement to *compare* two works or two aspects of the same work is different from a requirement to *contrast* the two elements. Comparing two things involves exploring their similarities and differences, while contrasting two things involves focusing on their differences.

Writing a *review* of a book, film, play, or artistic exhibition is different from writing a *critical interpretation, evaluation,* or *assessment* of the same work. Both are arguments, but a review is usually more informal and personal. It strives to reach a wider general audience (including both those familiar with the work and those unfamiliar with it). A critical interpretation is a more formal argument about the book, film, play, or exhibition, written for those who are already familiar with it.

Some assignments require the essay writer to incorporate a certain amount of research material, and sometimes that material is specified (i.e., particular named secondary sources). Other assignments leave the essay writer free to incorporate research material or to proceed on his own, and still others require the writer to avoid research materials entirely.

Some assignments give the student a great deal of latitude in adapting the argument to what she wants to talk about; others make very particular demands. Notice, for example, how specific the wording is in the following examples:

1. Discuss three scientific objections to Darwin's theory of natural selection raised by Darwin's contemporaries. Why were these significant? Note that this assignment does not require you to consider how these objections were answered by later scientific discoveries.

2. What is the significance of Achilles' first long answer to Odysseus in Book 9 of the *Iliad*? What do we learn there about what has been happening to Achilles away from the battle? Confine your essay to a close look at this one speech.

3. In Book 10 of the *Republic*, Plato insists that in the state he is describing art will be strictly censored. Why does he make this recommendation? Can you defend what he proposes?

4. We hear a good deal nowadays about granting the terminally ill a "right to die" or a "right to an assisted suicide." Why would anyone oppose conferring such a right? Offer two or three reasons why such opposition might be worth considering.

The language in these assignments is very specific. It identifies a particular subject and directs how the writer is to shape his response to it (even, in the case of the first and the last, including a numerical stipulation).

Compare those topics just listed above with others that offer the writer wider possibilities:

1. What is the significance of the witches in *Macbeth*?

2. Write an essay evaluating an aspect of Wollstonecraft's argument in *A Vindication of the Rights of Woman*.

3. Discuss the significance in *Genealogy of Morals* of Nietzsche's remark "Only that which has no history can be defined."

4. Make a case for or against the proposal to build the Northern Gateway pipeline.

5. Why is *Citizen Kane* considered a landmark in the history of film-making?

6. Evaluate the role of Tecumseh in the War of 1812.

These topics are much more open. They specify a general subject, but provide no particular directions for or limitations on the writer (other than, in all likelihood, a recommended length for the essay), and thus there are a number of different ways one might shape an argument in response. In such cases, the writer is going to have to do a certain amount of additional preliminary work to sort out just how she might deal with the topic.

In the pages which follow here, I make a number of recommendations about how to set about organizing an essay. These recommendations may at times be assuming that the student has more freedom of choice than a particular essay topic permits. Where that happens, the student should always remember that the stipulations in the topic take precedence: her essay should always remain within any limits set by the topic and address directly any specific requirements it sets out. If you are unclear about what a particular assignment might or might not require, you should clarify the matter with your instructor as soon as possible. Generally speaking, it is unwise to trust your fellow students to resolve any doubts you have, since they may have misunderstood the relevant details. This caveat is especially important if the format of the writing assignment is something you are not familiar with.

3.2 | The Importance of Structure: Paragraphs

In order to present a clear argument, the essay needs a coherent *structure*, that is, it must guide the reader in a logical manner through the stages of the argument in such a way that she always knows where she is at every stage and has a sense of where she is going when the essay moves from one major point to the next. The logical structure of an argumentative essay is determined by the sequence of paragraphs the writer organizes and by what those paragraphs contain. Thus, before we can usefully discuss various ways to organize an argument in essay form, we need to consider a few things about paragraphs.

A paragraph is a *unified* and *coherent* sequence of sentences that belong together because they all are working to carry out the same function (they have a common purpose). The *unity* of a paragraph comes from its concentration on that single function, and the *coherence* of the paragraph comes from the way the sequence of sentences in it carry out that function in a logical manner.

Now, for reasons that will be apparent later on, in order to carry out their function properly most paragraphs in written arguments should be substantial. In other words, they should be long and detailed enough to do the job. What that means, in practice, is that they should, in most cases, be somewhere between 150 and 250 words each (at least).

An assignment to write an essay usually comes with a recommended length expressed as a number of words or of double-spaced printed pages (the latter unit of measurement is equivalent to about 250 words per page). However, in order to organize the essay properly, the writer needs to know, not the total number of words, but rather how many paragraphs she has to work with. Consequently, where a word or page limit is specified, you should immediately translate this recommended page or word limit into a paragraph number (by dividing the total number of words by 200). That will give you an approximate sense of how many building blocks (i.e., paragraphs) the essay will have.

An essay of, say, 1000 words (four double-spaced pages) will thus become an essay of about 5 paragraphs; a research paper of 3000 words, an essay of approximately 15 paragraphs, and so on.

You need to do this because the number of paragraphs at your disposal will play a major role in determining the structure of the essay. An assignment to write, say, a 750-word essay on hydraulic fracking will have a very different structure from an assignment to write a 2500-word essay on the same topic.

Organizing the structure of the essay begins once you have determined what you wish to argue about and have estimated the number of paragraphs you have at your disposal. These paragraphs will have to offer (in a logical sequence) at least three things:

AN INTRODUCTION (defining what the argument is about)

A MAIN BODY (a sequence of paragraphs making the argument)

A CONCLUSION (a final summary of the argument).

The Introduction and Conclusion (normally the first and last paragraphs of the essay) will each take at least one paragraph. Hence, the Main Body of the argument will have available a minimum of two fewer paragraphs than the total number established by the guidelines to the assignment. Thus, in an assignment calling for a 1000-word essay, you have approximately 3 or 4 paragraphs with which to make the argument.

3.3 | A Note on the Tone of the Argument

Before we move on to consider ways to start organizing the essay in detail and to launch the process of writing an introduction, we should briefly consider the important question of the *tone* of the essay. This issue is obviously not a matter of structure, but it is appropriate here to spend a few moments considering it, because the tone of your writing can have a decisive effect on the persuasiveness of the argument.

An academic essay is an exercise in writing a formal prose argument. Consequently, it is not a place to be too freely colloquial. On the other hand, in contrast to the stultifying nature of a great deal of academic prose, an undergraduate essay should be relatively easy to follow for an educated general reader. So, to put the matter simply, the writer should chart a path somewhere between slang and jargon, between the street and the scholarly conference. She should write the essay as if she were writing a letter to an intelligent aunt or uncle who is keenly interested in what she has to say but is in no mood to put up with bar-room or internet lingo, chat-room abbreviations, and profanity or to endure tedious attempts to overinflate the importance of the argument with whatever specialized technical language is currently fashionable in the discipline. In other words, that relative would like to read some natural, friendly, correct, polite, and energetic prose.

Here are a few principles to guide you (the list is not meant to be exhaustive).

1. Write naturally, bearing in mind that your readers may not appreciate slang or insults or swearing. Do not try to twist your natural style into something different because you think that will make your argument more impressive, friendly, amusing, or persuasive. Avoid being flippant or too casually dismissive. Keep the language clear and straightforward. Do not use unnecessarily technical terminology or too many passive verbs (if you don't know what a passive verb is, then find out, and learn to keep that form of the verb to a minimum).

2. Put some energy and conviction—some passion—into your prose, especially when you are expressing an opinion. In the first draft of an essay, it is sometimes a good idea to overstate your opinion in order to add some energy to the argument.

If you overdo it, you can always scale back later, when you review the initial draft. Avoid words which make you sound too cautious, too much like a timid wimp (e.g., *interesting*, *positive*, *negative*, and so on). Notice the difference between the sentences in each of the following pairs:

a.   The ending leaves one with a negative
      feeling about the film.

      The ending of the film is an incomprehensible
      mess—a hodgepodge of violence, special effects, and
      unconvincing, badly written verbal exchanges offered up
      as meaningful dialogue.

b.   The character of the heroine is interesting. She has many
      positive qualities but by the end is not very likeable.

      The character of the heroine is mysteriously fascinating
      throughout. She is obviously a brilliant, courageous
      woman, but by the end has become strangely repellent.

c.   The government's failure to act in this matter
      has been problematic and not very positive.

      The government's failure to act in this matter has been a
      public disgrace and has turned a manageable problem
      into an urgent and unnecessary crisis.

3. Do not, however, let your commitment to an energetic style
    take you overboard, especially when you are denouncing
    someone else. You can certainly be firm, even energetically
    dismissive ("But that view is ridiculous," "The company's
    study is fatally flawed, slipshod, and not worth taking seri-
    ously," "The hero at this point seems to be acting like a com-
    plete fool"). But do not be abusive or insulting ("People who

believe that are cretinous idiots," "Corporations are fascist pigs," "Our state legislature is made up of nothing but spend-thrift, bleeding-heart liberals and illiterate, Bible-thumping rednecks," and so on). Such a style calls into question your own commitment to reasonable argument and, in an extreme case (like a reference to someone as a *Nazi* or *femi-nazi*), can demolish your argument on the spot. Harsh words, like *Nazi, fascist, tyrannical*, and so on, are appropriate only when they accurately describe a person or situation (i.e., when the literal meaning applies, as in, for example, "During the war, he expressed racist views in keeping with the ide-ology of the Nazis"), not when they are simply employed as cheap, over-the-top insults.

4. As a general rule, don't overuse the pronouns "I" and "me." Occasional use of these personal pronouns is quite accept-able, but try to avoid unnecessarily repetitive use of the expressions *I think* or *in my opinion, in my view, to me,* and so on. Some students seem to believe that sprinkling these phrases like salt all through the essay will deflect criticism, because, after all, the writer is entitled to a personal opinion, which the reader must respect. However, these phrases are not really necessary, because the reader understands that the entire essay is an argument in defence of a personal view-point. Regardless, an opinion is only as good as the argument supporting it; just because an argumentative position is one person's opinion doesn't mean that it is a reasonable opinion worth listening to. Moreover, the habit of constantly remind-ing the reader of yourself can also make the tone of the argu-ment very defensive, as if you are trying to protect yourself from criticism and do not have the confidence to state your positions firmly.

5. Do not let statements of how you feel about an issue carry too much of the argument. The essay is a rational argument

designed to persuade the reader that the view of the writer about a specific subject is worth attending to. The heart of that argument is a series of reasons based upon the analysis of evidence or of shared principles or of both. As such, an academic essay should not confine itself to or base itself primarily upon an expression of the writer's personal feelings or beliefs, however passionate and eloquent these may be. Obviously, a strong emotional response to a particular experience or issue may well stimulate a student's interest in writing about what he finds so stimulating, and if the writer has deeply held convictions about a subject, such feelings can play an important part in the persuasiveness of his or her case. But the core of the essay should be an argument based on impersonal reasoning.

You can think about an assignment to write an argumentative essay as an invitation to join in a public discussion about a disputatious issue. The task at hand is not necessarily to tell others how you feel about the issue, but rather to offer a worthwhile contribution to the ongoing debate by appealing to their reason, to their respect for principles, evidence, and clear logic. Passionate personal pleas or denunciations obviously are an important part of human responses to particular events, but they are usually out of place in reasonable arguments. In many cases, they tend to reveal far more about the person making the appeal than they do about the issues involved.

4.0

Setting Up the Argument

In considering the importance of defining an argument at the start of an essay, this section and the next discuss two different but related concepts: first, establishing clearly what the argument is about (the concern of this section) and, second, explaining any key terms and providing background information essential to a clear understanding of the argument (the concern of the next section). The main point here is that an argument cannot usefully proceed until we all know exactly what the issue is, share a common understanding of any potentially ambiguous terms, and possess information essential to grasping what is to follow.

In some arguments, the second requirement (explaining key terms and providing information) may not be necessary because the central terms are all clear enough and readers already have all the information they need (although, as we shall see, that is not something one should assume too readily). In all argumentative essays, however, the first requirement is absolutely essential.

4.1 | Defining the Argument

The first requirement of any written argument is that it must establish clearly what the precise issue is. That is, the opening phase of the argument has to identify the *subject* matter of the argument and the *precise claim on that subject* which the arguer is seeking to persuade the reader to accept. In almost all cases, you will need to do this before you start the main body of the argument (i.e., at the very beginning, in a section commonly called the *Introduction*).

The introduction to an argument is so crucial that if it is done poorly then there is virtually no recovery. No matter how you deal with the rest of your case, if the reader is unclear about what you are trying to do, then the relevance of that case becomes muddled. This fault is particularly common in under-graduate essays and research papers, because students frequently rush the opening of the essay in their haste to get the argument launched.

There are a number of different ways to establish an argument effectively, and we will be going through some examples shortly. However the writer sets out the introduction, it must achieve three things, as follows:

1. The introduction must alert the reader to the general subject area being considered (e.g., a film, a political issue, a social concern, a historical event, a work of literature, a scientific concept, and so on), in answer to the question: "In general terms, what area of experience is this essay dealing with?"

2. The introduction must narrow down that general subject so as to define a very specific *focus* for the argument, in answer

to the reader's question: "Just what very particular part of this general subject area is this argument concentrating on?"

3. The introduction must set out an argumentative opinion about the focus mentioned above in Step 2. This argumentative opinion, which is the central claim you are making in the argument and which you want the reader to accept, is called the *thesis* of the argument.

As we shall see later, some arguments will require more introductory material than this, but all essay and research paper arguments require these three parts in the introduction.

4.1.1 | *Two Simple Examples*

In a relatively short essay, you can usually deal with the three requirements of an Introduction in a single substantial paragraph (almost invariably the opening paragraph). Here are two typical examples.

> *Introduction A*
> Few issues in medical ethics are more complicated than what has come to be called the "right to die" or the "right to an assisted suicide." For thirty years (at least) we have been debating the issue, and we appear to be no closer to a resolution than we were at the start. This situation is perhaps not surprising, given that the subject raises all sorts of legal, ethical, religious, and moral questions, none of which is capable of a quick resolution satisfactory to all. Of all these questions, one of the most troubling is the notion of "informed consent," the idea that a terminally ill patient with her mental faculties intact should be allowed, under specified conditions, to set in motion a process that will end her own life. It is easy enough to appreciate the argument that people should be given the freedom to control their

own destinies as they see fit, but at the same time one has to wonder whether the power to make a decision to terminate one's life can in most cases be entirely free and autonomous. In fact, given the practical realities of many (perhaps most) terminally ill patients and their families, the very idea of informed consent, an essential element in any argument advocating a right to die, is open to serious doubts. For that reason alone, we should insist that helping a terminally ill patient commit suicide remain an illegal act.

Introduction B

Shakespeare's *Hamlet* is, by common consent, an ambiguous play, with many conflicting interpretative possibilities. At the heart of many disputes about the play is the character of the hero himself. Just what sort of person is Prince Hamlet? The play puts a lot of pressure on us to explore this question, simply because the motivation for Hamlet's actions and inaction is by no means clear, and yet it is obviously important. A comprehensive answer to this issue is beyond the scope of a short essay. Nevertheless, whatever Hamlet's character adds up to exactly, one very curious feature of it is his attitude toward and relationships with women. For there is a clear pattern in Hamlet's language and behaviour whenever he is thinking about or talking to Ophelia and Gertrude. This pattern is so distinctively aggressive and (at times) cynical, bitter, and insulting that we can reasonably assume it indicates something important about the prince. In fact, Hamlet's attitude to these two women and, beyond them, to women in general, is an important indication of the general psychological unhealthiness of Hamlet's character.

Notice carefully how these introductions proceed. The writers open by announcing a general subject (assisted suicides, Shakespeare's *Hamlet*). In the next few sentences the introductions narrow the focus, that is, restrict the subject matter to something very specific (the notion of "informed consent" and then the problem with that idea; the question of Hamlet's character and then the question about his relationship to women). And the introductions end by establishing a firm opinion about this focus (we should keep assisted suicide illegal; Hamlet's attitude to women is an important symptom of his emotional ill health). By the end of each introduction the reader is fully aware of what the writer is trying to argue (both the particular subject matter and the opinion about that subject matter).

4.1.2 | *General Features of an Introductory Paragraph*

This structure illustrated above is really useful if you are uncertain how to set up the opening to an essay or research paper. Notice the pattern:

1. The opening sentence announces the general subject (a public health issue, a particular work of literature, a political or historical event, a social problem, a technological development, and so on). The general subject matter will usually be contained in the topic for the essay that the instructor has set. The function of this sentence is to get the reader, who at this point has no idea what the essay is going to be about, to direct his attention to a particular area.

   If the essay is on a particular work of literature, then the opening sentence should normally identify it by indicating the author and the title. Do not confuse the reader by failing to identify the specific work you are dealing with (for example, by using a phrase like *this book* or *this work* instead of the specific title).

2. The next two or three sentences narrow the subject matter down to one particular aspect, so that the reader understands clearly that you are not dealing with any and all

questions arising from that subject but only with one particular question or area of concern.

3. Finally at the end of the introduction, the last one or two sentences announce the opinion about that focus—the thesis
of the essay—so that the reader understands what you are
arguing in the essay.

You need to do this even if the essay is a response to a very specific
topic that establishes, not merely the general subject area, but also
a very narrow focus. Notice the following sample introduction to
an essay topic that already stipulates a precise focus.

TOPIC: Discuss three scientific objections to Darwin's theory
of natural selection raised by Darwin's contemporaries.
Why were these significant? Note that this assignment does
not require you to consider how these objections were
answered by later scientific discoveries.

INTRODUCTORY PARAGRAPH: Charles Darwin's *Origin of Species*,
as is well known, got a very hostile reception from some
leading members of the religious establishment in England
and from elements of the press. Less well known perhaps
is the fact that the book also offended many well-known
and respected scientists, including a number of Darwin's
colleagues. No doubt, the attitude of many of these scientific
critics was prompted by their religious convictions. But that is
by no means the entire story, for there were also a number of
scientific objections to Darwin's account of the evolutionary
process, and some of these criticisms were by no means trivial. Indeed, given the fact that at least three of these scientific
objections struck at the very heart of Darwin's theory and
that neither Darwin nor anyone else could provide satisfactory answers to them, one might well wonder why anyone
continued to take the theory seriously.

Notice how this introduction still follows the general pattern: introducing the general subject (*Origin of Species*), narrowing that down to a specific focus (objections and then scientific objections and then three scientific objections), and establishing an argumentative opinion (that these objections were sufficiently important to cripple Darwin's theory). Even though the language in the assigned topic defines the subject matter and the focus precisely, the writer has still provided a full introduction. Someone who has read this introduction does not need to know anything about the assigned topic in order to understand what the essay will be arguing.

What you should *not* do in writing an essay on the above topic is plunge right way into the argument requested, for example, by starting the essay as follows: "Well, one important scientific objection to Darwin came from...." Take the time to produce a coherent introduction.

To recap, by the end of the introduction the reader must have clear answers to some very specific questions, as follows:

1. What is the general subject matter of this essay?

2. What particular part of this general subject is the writer focusing on? Is there any particular aspect of that subject which the writer is clearly *not* discussing?

3. What opinion about that focus is the subject matter of the argument? What does the writer want me to believe?

If the reader cannot answer these three questions clearly by the end of the introduction, if there is any confusion about them, then there is something wrong with the paragraph. If you find yourself concerned about whether or not you have set up a good introduction to your own essay, get someone to read the paragraph and then answer the three questions above. If she cannot answer them correctly or is confused, you need to rewrite the opening definition of the argument.

Notice also what the sample introductions in 4.1.1 and 4.1.2 above are *not* doing. They are not offering us huge generalizations about Shakespeare or Darwin, or about society or the world or the meaning of life. They begin by defining a subject and then continue by narrowing down that subject to a particular focus.

4.2 | The Importance of Identifying a Focus

In setting up your own written arguments, you need to pay particular attention to defining very clearly the particular part of the general subject matter you will be concentrating on, the *focus*. Remember that you are the one in charge of the argument; you can shape it in any way you like, indicating what you are looking at and what you are not looking at. Doing this properly will make constructing the argument very much easier. If you fail to sharpen the focus, then the reader may legitimately ask why you have not looked at some things included in the general subject.

The assigned essay topic may already define a focus for the argument, in which case you do not need to think of how you might restrict that part of the essay any further. If the language of the essay topic clearly stipulates what you are and are not to examine, then you should not seek to change that focus. However, to repeat myself, you should in your introductory paragraph still indicate what the focus of the essay is. Do not rely on the language of the assigned essay topic to convey that information to the reader.

Suppose, however, that the essay topic permits you some latitude in what you choose to look at in your argument and that, for example, you need to write an essay on a long work of fiction (play, novel, epic poem, film, or television series). There are a number of things you could discuss and perhaps want to discuss, but for the purposes of the essay you have to choose. You might begin by jotting down various possibilities, thinking about and discussing them with friends, but at some point you need to make a decision. The focus of the essay will be some aspect of the fiction: perhaps a single character, a particular relationship, a recurring theme, one feature of the setting, the role of the narrator, the cinematic style, or something else. Normally what you choose should be a particular part of the work you find intriguing and significant, an element that really helps to shape your response to the fiction and that you think anyone wishing to understand the work better could benefit from considering closely.

Similarly, if you are organizing an essay about a complex social or political issue, then isolate a very particular aspect of that issue, rather than trying to tackle an unmanageably large subject. If the essay is interpreting a long argumentative work (e.g., in philosophy or political theory), select a very particular part of the argument—if possible, one you find interesting, challenging, problematic, or even, in some cases, distasteful—and focus the essay exclusively on that. What you choose to look at should be something that will enable you to present an argument giving the reader of your essay some insight into that focus and, beyond that, into the general subject as well.

By going through this process, you have taken a complicated subject and selected from it a very specific part that will be much easier to deal with. In fact, as a general rule, the more narrowly and clearly defined the focus is, the easier the essay will be to write and the more persuasive the argument will be. Notice, too, that in defining the focus clearly, you are also indicating to the reader and, most importantly, to yourself the *scope* of your argument, that is, what it will and will not include.

Students are frequently reluctant to narrow the focus because they are worried about not having enough to say. Thus, they set themselves from the start a very difficult task by choosing an argument on a very wide topic. This mistake you should avoid at all costs. It is much better to argue in detail about a more narrowly defined topic than to offer a superficial look at something much wider. Make sure you understand this point.

By way of reinforcing this suggestion, let me return to some remarks I made in the introduction to this book. The purpose of the essay is to communicate your perceptions about something significant to the general subject. The essay will be successful if it helps the reader go back to that general subject with more insight, so that he recognizes and appreciates something that he had not noticed before or that he had noticed but not thought much about. Providing that insight about a relatively small part of the matter at hand can make your argument a very helpful contribution to his understanding of much wider issues. In fact, your detailed exploration of a single element will almost certainly be more useful to him than any attempt to offer a more comprehensive but shallower argument about a complex subject, particularly in a relatively short essay.

Here are some examples (in point form) that illustrate the transformation of a very large general subject, through a series of steps, into a sharp and particular focus.

Essay 1
GENERAL SUBJECT: The television series *Breaking Bad*
FOCUS 1: *Breaking Bad*: the importance of the setting
FOCUS 2: *Breaking Bad*: the importance of the setting: the desert

Essay 2
GENERAL SUBJECT: Lyme disease
FOCUS 1: Treatment of long-term Lyme disease
FOCUS 2: Treatment of long-term Lyme disease: problems
FOCUS 3: Treatment of long-term Lyme disease: problems with the medical establishment

Essay 3
GENERAL SUBJECT: Illegal immigration
FOCUS 1: Illegal immigration: the economic impact
FOCUS 2: Illegal immigration: the economic impact on the hospitality industry
FOCUS 3: Illegal immigration: the economic impact on the hospitality industry in California

Essay 4
GENERAL SUBJECT: John Stuart Mill's *On Liberty*
FOCUS 1: The importance of free competition
FOCUS 2: The importance of free competition in education

Essay 5
GENERAL SUBJECT: The French Revolution
FOCUS 1: The causes of the French Revolution
FOCUS 2: The immediate causes of the French Revolution
FOCUS 3: The immediate causes of the French Revolution: the economic problem

Essay 6
GENERAL SUBJECT: Ibsen's play *A Doll's House*
FOCUS 1: The sense of a corrupt middle-class society
FOCUS 2: The sense of a corrupt middle-class society: the significance of Dr. Rank

Essay 7
GENERAL SUBJECT: Conrad's *Heart of Darkness*
FOCUS 1: Conrad's descriptive language
FOCUS 2: Conrad's descriptive language: the jungle
FOCUS 3: Conrad's descriptive language: the jungle in Marlow's trip upriver

Essay 8
GENERAL SUBJECT: Religion in schools
FOCUS 1: School prayer
FOCUS 2: School prayer: the *Engel v. Vitale* case in New Hyde Park, New York

Notice what is happening in these lists. The opening subject, a very large and complicated topic, is being transformed into a very specific and much narrower sub-topic, which the essay is going to look at closely. You should always end up with a focus that is much more restricted than the general subject and that is manageable in the space available.

An examination of the examples above indicates some of the ways in which you can narrow down the general subject. In dealing with a work of literature, for example, you can limit the focus by looking at a particular character or a particular scene or a particular pattern in the descriptive language in one or two selections or in a particular section of the text. If the general subject is a social issue, you can restrict the focus geographically (by looking only at California) or demographically (by considering only the medical establishment), or by considering a single instance (the legal case in New Hyde Park). In an essay on a historical event where you are to argue about causes or effects, you can select one particular cause or effect and focus exclusively on that, rather than trying to account for a great many more.

At first, of course, you may not be certain just what you wish your argument to focus upon. You may well need to do some research and talk the matter over with others. But the time spent on this process is very worthwhile—it will clarify what you are trying to do (and not trying to do) and remind you that your essay is not about everything you might want to discuss. But the sooner you select the focus, the easier it will be to carry out detailed research into the subject matter.

Once you have determined and defined the focus of the essay, of course, you will not be able to introduce into your argument anything outside that focus, and thus you may have to remove from your list of possibilities some things you would dearly love to write about. In the interests of organizing the essay, however, you have to be ruthless: get rid of whatever is irrelevant.

4.3 | The Importance of Establishing a Thesis

After you have determined a specific focus for the argument, then you need to develop an opinion about that focus. In other words, you need to present a focused claim or statement about the narrowly defined subject matter you have selected. This point is crucial. You cannot base an argument merely on the focus you have defined. You must present an *opinion* about that subject and focus, something we can debate about. This opinion is usually called the *thesis*, the single most important sentence or series of sentences in the entire argument.

You cannot, for example, base an argumentative essay on the attitude of the medical establishment to chronic Lyme patients— or on Dr. Rank in *A Doll's House* or on the legal case in New Hyde Park or on Conrad's descriptive language in Marlow's trip upriver or on the economic causes of the French Revolution or on what Mill says about education. You must base the essay on an *opinion* (an argumentative position) about one of those. And, in general, the sharper the opinion and the more energetically you express it, the clearer the thesis will be, both to you and to the reader.

The thesis should answer the question: What precisely is the presenter of this argument trying to persuade me to believe? If that is not clear, then the argument's central purpose is fuzzy or missing. So you need to take particular care to conclude the introduction with an unambiguous statement and clarification of your thesis, which must be an assertion that someone can dispute (i.e., argue about).

When you set out to do this, remember what we discussed previously (in section 2.2 above), namely, that certain statements do not make a good thesis, because they do not offer anything we can argue about or disagree with. Make sure your thesis does not fall into this category. Notice, for example, that the following statements would make very poor thesis statements, because, although they have a very particular focus, they are not sufficiently argumentative; they state matters which we can quickly confirm by an appeal to the text or to an existing authority:

1. Dr. Rank is suffering from an incurable fatal disease he inherited from his father.

2. Long-term sufferers of Lyme disease often complain about the treatment they receive from doctors.

3. In his discussion of the importance of maximizing freedom in society Mill turns his attention to education.

4. The French revolution had numerous causes, long-term and short-term, and the economy was one of them.

5. Illegal immigration is a widespread problem.

These sentences are useless as thesis statements, because they present nothing we can usefully argue about. They are matters of fact. If that's all you offer at the end of your introduction, then the reader is going to be very puzzled why you are striving so hard to argue about something obvious. Notice the difference between the above statements and the following.

1. Dr. Rank's presence in the play is a repeated reminder of the deadly corruption, both moral and physical, infecting the apparently comfortable middle-class society in which the action takes place.

2. The attitude of the medical establishment (doctors and hospitals) towards long-term sufferers of chronic Lyme disease is often disgracefully callous and dismissive. This situation needs to change.

3. Mill's remarks on education are especially challenging: they take issue with some of our most cherished notions of the role of government in a liberal society and are all the more valuable because of that.

4. Of all the causes of the French revolution, the most significant was the disastrous state of the French economy.

5. Illegal immigration is the economic mainstay of the hospitality industry in California. Any serious attempts to limit the employment of illegal immigrants would be financially crippling to the industry.

These statements put something argumentative on the table. We can easily disagree (or be reluctant to be persuaded), and the writer is going to have to work to convince us. Such statements do not simply announce a matter of fact about which no dispute is possible.

If you do not set the essay up with a clearly argumentative thesis, then the logic of the argument will be defective, because the reader will not be clear about what you are trying to establish. Please make sure you understand this key point. The failure to establish a good thesis is the single most important logical error in student essays.

One final point about thesis statements. I mentioned above (in section 3.3) that in an argumentative essay the writer needs to be careful about letting personal feelings carry too much of an argument in which the challenge is to present a rational case advocating a particular opinion. This point is especially important in formulations of the thesis, where statements of one's personal feelings or beliefs, no matter how sincere and interesting, are generally inappropriate, as in the following examples:

1. As a devout Christian I find the modern biological account of evolution unacceptable.

2. *The Matrix* was just too confusing and ambiguous for me. I found that really frustrating.

3. To a socialist like myself, what Mill has to say about education smells too much like liberal propaganda.

4. Rousseau's recommendations in *Emile* about educating women really offend me.

To opinionated assertions like this, a reader might well be tempted to respond, "All right, but so what? What does your personal opinion have to communicate that will help me understand debates about the modern biological account of evolution or *The Matrix* or Mill's argument or Rousseau's views on educating women?" Notice the difference between these statements of personal opinion and more useful argumentative assertions about the same subject:

1. Some modern religious objections to the scientific account of evolution are more substantial than many people recognize. If we all understood the full implications of that theory many of us might well share some of the same objections.

2. *The Matrix* is, in places, very ambiguous and confusing. These characteristics contribute to the film's portrayal of life in a digital age as an experience of constant change in which the lines between the real and the imagined are blurred.

3. Mill's argument about education is an eloquent statement of liberal principles at work, but from a socialist perspective his recommendations look suspiciously like a blueprint for the enshrinement of social inequality.

4. Rousseau's recommendations about educating women arise logically out of his conception of gender roles. However, his argument in defence of these recommendations leads him inescapably into logical difficulties that undermine the entire educational program he is proposing and encourage one to raise serious questions about his original assumptions regarding gender.

The above statements are not merely expressing a personal opinion. They are setting up an argument, and the writer is going to have to persuade us with a detailed look at particular evidence.

4.3.1 | *Forming Good Thesis Statements*

Given the crucial importance of setting up a good thesis that will define the central claim of the essay, you should not rush this part of the argument. Here are some points to consider in selecting and refining the thesis:

1. The thesis must present your opinionated engagement with the focus you have defined. So it's a good idea to base it on an examination of why you find what you have selected as the focus particularly important. As I mentioned above, that interest might well be initially aroused by a particular response (e.g., to a character you find fascinating, an argument you don't agree with, a writing style you think is wonderfully evocative, a conclusion you find problematic, and so on), but remember that the thesis should focus, not on how you feel about that particular element, but rather on why it is significant for an understanding of the subject under discussion. For example, an essay on, say, the descriptive power of Conrad's writing about the jungle in *Heart of Darkness* should be based on an opinion about why looking closely at his style in these passages provides a significant analytical insight into something important to the story, not just on why you find particular passages marvellous pieces of writing.

2. A claim that arguments about a particular subject are difficult to sort out expresses an opinion and often makes a good thesis: e.g., "The debate about giving people a legal right to an assisted suicide is impossible to resolve because there are such cogent arguments on both sides," "Given the arguments and counterarguments about fracking, the issue remains incapable of clear resolution." Such statements are opinions, which you will have to argue; as such, they are useful thesis statements. Here again, however, remember that the essay is not primarily an argument about your own confusion;

you are arguing that, if we look at the evidence, there is no immediately obvious resolution to the public debate. Your essay will then supply an argumentative analysis of the reasons why that opinion is worth attending to.

3. Similarly, a thesis statement can be a mixed opinion, in which you call attention to conflicting judgements of a particular subject: e.g., "The film has excellent acting and some superb cinematography. Unfortunately, the script in places is very poor. Hence, the experience of viewing it is not as enthralling as it might be." Such mixed opinions are quite common as thesis statements in essays reviewing fine and performing arts events.

4. Do not rush the thesis. If necessary take two or three sentences to get the clearest possible statement of the precise opinion you are presenting and defending in the argument. Do not proceed with the argument until you have defined your thesis as precisely as possible. The clearer and more explicit you are at this point, the easier the rest of the writing process will be. In your thesis statement, don't say "Hamlet's dilemma is interesting" when you can say "Hamlet's dilemma reflects a dilemma at the centre of human experience: whether to accept injustice or act decisively in the face of it." Don't say "This poem's portrayal of x is complex" when you can say "This poem presents two competing visions of x, each of which ultimately undermines the other."

This issue of making the thesis explicit is particularly important because a clear and specific thesis adds clarity and energy to the opening of the argument. So, for example, you should try to avoid a thesis which ends with a rather vague adjective (like "interesting" or "complex" in the above examples). Here are some more examples of this habit:

Conrad's descriptive prose in the passages describing Marlow's trip upriver is remarkable.

The effects of any concerted attempt to restrict illegal immigration would be harmful.

The question of whether terminally ill people should have the legal right to an assisted suicide is problematic.

These thesis statements express opinions, but they are imprecise and limp. To make them more energetic, specific, and interesting, you can add a "because" clause after them.

Conrad's descriptive prose in the passages describing Marlow's trip upriver is remarkable because it brings out so well Marlow's sense of the fascinating mystery and the almost overwhelming fecundity of the jungle while at the same time conveying his growing sense of the potentially lethal physical and psychological danger it poses.

The effects of any concerted attempt to restrict illegal immigration would be harmful because they would severely limit the availability of farm labour (thus leaving farmers incapable of harvesting their crops) and significantly raise food prices for the consumer.

The question of whether terminally ill people should have the legal right to an assisted suicide is problematic because the legal and moral issues involved admit of no easy resolution.

Alternatively, of course, you could leave out "because" and simply make the reasons part of the main clause in the thesis:

Conrad's descriptive prose in the passages describing Marlow's trip upriver brings out remarkably well Marlow's sense of the fascinating mystery and the almost overwhelming fecundity of the jungle while at the same time conveying his growing sense of the potentially lethal physical and psychological danger it poses.

The effects of any concerted attempt to restrict illegal immigration would severely damage our economy: they would limit the availability of farm labour, thus leaving many farmers incapable of harvesting their crops, and would significantly raise food prices for the consumer.

The question of whether terminally ill people should have the legal right to an assisted suicide raises legal and moral issues that admit of no easy resolution.

5. Try not to be too timid in presenting the thesis. Often it's a good idea to overstate the opinion (i.e., really go out on a limb), so that you know you have a real job to do in making the case. At any event, make the thesis as bold and assertive as you dare. If it looks too aggressive once you have written the essay, then you can moderate it. In fact, it is always a good idea, once you have finished the first draft of an essay, to revisit the thesis statement and make sure that it matches the argument you have actually made; then you can moderate, expand, or alter your statement as necessary.

If you wish to express your thesis as forcefully as possible, remember that there is an important difference between an energetic thesis and an exaggerated one. Do not let your desire to offer a strongly assertive thesis lead you to make a claim that is excessive, especially one based on a sweeping generalization that the reader may feel you are not qualified to make. There is an important difference, for example, between the following claims:

The book is an enthralling exploration of modern combat, a fascinating and compelling vision of the glory and horror of war.

The extraordinary quality of this novel makes it quite simply the best story of combat ever written.

Both of these statements are strong, energetic opinions, but the second invites the reader to wonder whether you are not simply exaggerating for effect. The claim might well prompt the obvious question: Have you read every story of combat ever written?

4.3.2 | *Exercise: Recognizing Potentially Useful Thesis Statements*

Comment on each of the following statements as a useful thesis, that is, as something that might form a clearly opinionated basis for an effective argument. Note that this exercise is not asking whether you agree with the statement or not but whether you think it clearly defines an argumentative position.

1. Beth Henley's wonderful play *Crimes of the Heart* was turned into a commercially successful film.
2. *The Duchess of Malfi* is a vastly overrated play, contradictory in its presentation of characters, ambiguous in its literal details, and excessively melodramatic in many crucial scenes.
3. Modern North Americans spend a great deal of money on supplies, veterinary medicine, and food for their pets.
4. Modern North Americans spend far too much money on supplies, veterinary medicine, and food for their pets.
5. McIntyre and Robinson, two medical researchers at McGill University, conducted five separate studies of

fetal alcohol syndrome. They concluded that it is a serious problem in modern society.

6. The study by McIntyre and Robinson, two medical researchers at McGill University, which concluded that fetal alcohol syndrome is a serious problem, is a badly flawed study that produced very misleading conclusions.

7. Frost's poem "Mending Wall" is constructed around a central image of two men repairing a wall between their two properties.

8. In Frost's poem "Mending Wall" the central image of the two men repairing a wall brings out the paradoxical feelings of the speaker regarding figurative boundaries in human relationships. In doing so, the poem captures the ways in which fear of otherness interferes with the development of mutual understanding on both personal and political levels.

9. In *A Vindication of the Rights of Woman*, Wollstonecraft devotes considerable time to discussing the education of women.

10. I quite enjoyed the film *Titanic*.

11. *Titanic* is such a sentimental and poorly scripted and acted work that one wonders what on earth our public standards had come to in 1997, such that the film won so many awards and so many people all over the world flocked to see it several times. Whatever the sociological explanation, the film is undeserving of the accolades it received.

12. We should be paying more attention to dealing with spousal abuse in our society.

13. Violence against women is a common problem in modern society.

14. Violence against women is, quite simply, the most serious crime in our society.

15. New Cadillacs are more expensive than new Honda Civics.

16.   A new Cadillac is, in the long run, a much better investment than a new Honda Civic.

4.3.3 | Thesis Statements with a Scientific or Historical Focus

A particular subject area that can cause trouble for those setting up an argument is one which appears, at first glance, largely factual. This can be a problem in essays with a strong scientific or historical focus (e.g., a discussion of a nuclear reactor, or Galileo's astronomical observations, or Gandhi's campaign against the British in India). You need to remember that essays on historical or scientific events are not asking for a summary of those events (i.e., a rehash of the facts) but an argument about why those events matter.

You can do this by setting up the thesis as a statement about the *significance* of the focus: e.g., "Galileo's astronomical observations were a breakthrough in the history of science; they effectively challenged the traditional views of the universe and introduced a bold new method of understanding the heavens." In the course of the argument which follows, you will provide details of Galileo's work, but the central point of the essay will be an argument that this work was a significant breakthrough (which is an opinion about the focus).

Here are some examples of effective thesis statements about subjects which, at first glance, might seem purely factual:

1.   Nuclear power is the most effective and practical way to generate the electrical power we need in the coming decades.

2.   Marie Curie's pioneering work in physics and chemistry is one of the most significant achievements of modern science; it made a major contribution to revolutionary changes in the way scientists think about the atom.

3. The early and unexpected death of Alexander the Great quickly led to a major transformation of the political order in the Near East, an important factor in the early development of the Roman Empire.

4. Gandhi's successful tactics against the British in India were brilliantly conceived and courageously carried out, so much so that the British authorities found they had no effective answer to them.

In essays based on these thesis statements, the writer will, of course, discuss facts regarding nuclear power, Marie Curie's work, events following Alexander's death, and Gandhi's actions. But the emphasis in the essay will fall, not on these facts, but on the *significance* of these facts (i.e., the Main Body of the essay will be interpreting the facts to argue for the opinionated claim in the thesis, in answer to the questions: Why is nuclear power the most effective and practical way to generate our electrical power? Why was Marie Curie's scientific work so significant? What was so important about the effects of Alexander's death, especially in relation to the development of the Roman Empire? Why were Gandhi's tactics so brilliant and courageous?). The reader will not just be learning *what happened*, but, more importantly, will be finding out *why it matters*.

When your essay is focusing on a single historical person, be careful that you do not turn it into a review of the biographical information, so that instead of offering an argument it becomes simply a regurgitation of facts. Of course, you will have to offer biographical details in places, but only when those details contribute something to your argument—and the central thrust of the argument should be an evaluation of the significance of those facts. How did this person's achievements challenge his contemporaries and why was that important? Turning arguments about historical figures or events into long factual summaries (i.e., into little more than condensed accounts of what happened) is a very common mistake in undergraduate essays and research papers.

If all else fails, then you can try applying the following formula. Write out a sentence of the following form: "*In this essay I am going to argue the single opinion that* X (the particular focus of the essay) is very significant because (give your reasons for thinking the focus important)." Then get rid of the words in italics.

4.4 | The Start of an Outline for the Argument

Together, your subject, focus, and thesis make up the beginning of an outline for your essay. The initial setup for the argument (which may take considerable time to prepare) should result in something written down under the following headings:

GENERAL SUBJECT:
FOCUS 1:
FOCUS 2:
(FOCUS 3, IF NECESSARY):
THESIS:

Here are some examples of the start of such an essay outline:

GENERAL SUBJECT: The Affordable Care Act
FOCUS 1: The Affordable Care Act: benefits
FOCUS 2: The Affordable Care Act: benefits for the working poor
THESIS: (*In this essay I am going to argue the single opinion that*) While the Affordable Care Act is far from perfect, it does offer tangible, necessary, and long-overdue benefits to the working poor. This fact alone makes it a major improvement to health care in America.

GENERAL SUBJECT: Warfare and Technology
FOCUS 1: The machine gun
FOCUS 2: The machine gun: its impact on forms of combat

THESIS: (*In this essay I am going to argue the single opinion that*)
No modern weapon has had such a revolutionary impact on the conduct of warfare as the machine gun. It has transformed not only the nature of combat but the way we think about battle.

GENERAL SUBJECT: The James Bond film *Skyfall*
FOCUS 1: The portrayal of women in the film
FOCUS 2: The portrayal of women in the film: the character of M
FOCUS 3: The portrayal of women in the film: the character of M: a feminist analysis
THESIS: (*In this essay I am going to argue the single opinion that*)
While the portrayal of M in *Skyfall* is a great improvement compared to the portrayal of women in earlier Bond films, it is nonetheless not as feminist as it may first appear. M's character exists merely to provide Bond with a surrogate mother, and once her purpose is served she is immediately and violently eliminated from the story.

Such outlines look easy enough, but you may have to take time with them. And the time is worth spending, because if you do not clearly sort out for yourself and the reader just what you are arguing (the subject, focus, and thesis), then it is not going to matter very much what you do in the rest of the essay. If the opening does not set out the argument properly, then there is usually no recovery.

4.5 | Writing Introductory Paragraphs

Once you have an outline for an opening paragraph similar to the examples immediately above, transforming that outline into a coherent introductory paragraph is usually straightforward if you remember to move from a statement of the general subject, through a narrowing of the focus, to a clear and energetic thesis statement. This sounds simple enough, but there are a few common problems you should take care to avoid.

1. Do not make the opening of the argument too abrupt and awkward. Take the time to go through the steps outlined above. If you are doing that properly, then the introduction should be a fairly substantial paragraph of between 150 and 200 words (at least). Never offer as an introduction a one-sentence paragraph something like the following: "In this essay I am going to discuss how the heroine is a fascinating character." That is much too rushed.

2. In the introductory paragraph, the sentences should normally become increasingly specific. The opening statement will probably be something quite general; its purpose is merely to alert the reader to the general subject of the argument. The sentences immediately following should be narrowing that general opening down to something more particular, so that just before you state the thesis of the argument, the focus of the argument is clearly defined.

3. Do not stuff the introduction with irrelevant detail (e.g., about the biography of the writer, the historical details of the book, sweeping generalizations about human beings, and so on, unless these are essential to the argument you will be developing). Keep directing the reader to the particular focus and thesis you wish to concentrate upon. Stay directly on the content of the discussion you wish to present.

4. Do not make the thesis a promissory note which lacks an argumentative edge: for example, something like the following: "This essay will discuss how domestic violence is a serious problem." Establish clearly the opinion about subject matter that you wish the reader to accept as persuasive. "Domestic violence, especially against women and children,

is a much more serious crime than current law enforcement practices reflect."

5. Make sure that the argument is clearly established by the end of the introduction. By that point the reader must be able to answer the following two questions accurately: What is this argument focusing on? What specific opinion about the focus does the arguer wish me to believe by the end? If you are not sure whether the opening paragraph does that clearly enough, give the paragraph to someone else to read and ask him to tell you what your essay is going to be about. If he cannot provide a clear answer, then revise the paragraph.

4.5.1 | Exercises in Opening Paragraphs

Exercise 1

Here are some sample opening paragraphs to an argumentative essay reviewing a film (the film and its details are fictional). Comment briefly on the quality of each paragraph as the introduction to an argument. If you think it is inadequate, then indicate why (give *specific* reasons that would help the writer correct what is wrong).

Example A

The film *To Rangoon on a Trading Ship* tells the story of Martin, a teenage runaway on a cargo boat which sails from London to the Far East. On board the ship are two other stowaways, Gumby and Sian, two friends, who know nothing about Martin's presence. The ship is called the *Narnia*. The captain is called Fred Jones. He hates stowaways and is keen to punish them whenever he finds them. Rangoon is in the Far East. The story is set in the early 1900's. Pirates chase the ship at one point. At another time, the ship joins a group of navy ships sailing off to a war in the Pacific. Martin is nineteen years old. He is played by Adam Blimph.

Example B

The film *To Rangoon on a Trading Ship* came out in 2014. It is the best film I have ever seen. Everything about it was splendid. Everybody should see it.

Example C

To Rangoon on a Trading Ship, a recent adventure film, tells the story of some young stowaways on a cargo vessel going to the Far East in the early years of this century. Martin, a young London boy, and two other teenagers, Gumby and Sian, escape from oppressive situations at home by stowing away on the *Narnia*, a vessel bound for exotic places. The ship and the young stowaways encounter all sorts of adventures, but ultimately the story resolves itself happily. The work contains many predictable elements, including a wicked captain, some pirates, brave teenagers who help each other, a storm at sea, a mutiny, and so on. These scenes are quite familiar to anyone who has ever seen or read many sea yarns aimed at a young audience. However, for a number of reasons, particularly the script, the direction, and the acting of the lead characters, this is not just another conventional romantic adventure aimed at the younger set. It is in many ways a mature, amusing, and inventive reworking of a traditional genre, well worth the price of admission, even for skeptical adults.

Example D

To Rangoon on a Trading Ship is a recent film directed by Sue McPherson. I really like her films because they usually combine a good script with some excellent camera work. Her first film, *Manhattan by Night*, won several prizes at film festivals, and in 2010 another work won her an award for best screenplay. McPherson is a filmmaker from Canada. She attended film school in New York and was in the graduating class that produced a number of excellent Canadian filmmakers, including Alice Jackson and Terry Bright. I really like all their films. I think it's a shame that more Canadians don't support Canadian filmmakers by paying more attention to their work. That's why so many good directors go south to the United States. Anyway, McPherson's film is another excellent example of the high quality work that can be done by Canadians.

Exercise 2

Below are two pairs of opening paragraphs, the first pair on the *Odyssey* and the second pair on the Book of Genesis. Compare the two members of each pair. Which do you think is the more effective opening? Why? If you were in a position to recommend revisions to the writers of these paragraphs (especially the paragraphs you find less effective) what would you say?

Paragraph A

Homer's *Odyssey* recounts the adventures of the Greek hero Odysseus, in his return home from the Trojan War. In fact, much of the book is taken up with various tests of this epic hero, encounters in which he has to demonstrate his ability to overcome obstacles of various kinds. In the process of following Odysseus through these adventures, we, as readers, come to recognize many important qualities of the central character. We also learn a great a deal about what he values and about the nature of the world he lives in. There are many episodes in this exciting story which might serve to introduce us to these issues, for in virtually every adventure we learn something important about the hero and his values. One obvious and famous example is the story of his encounter with Polyphemos, the Cyclops. A close inspection of this incident tells us a great deal about what is most important in the poem. In fact, if we attend carefully to what is going on here, we come to understand some central features of Odysseus' character: his insatiable curiosity, his daring, his cunning, his ruthlessness, and his very strong, even egotistical, sense of himself.

Paragraph B
Homer's *Odyssey* recounts the adventures of the Greek hero Odysseus, in his return home from the Trojan War. This is a very old story, composed by the poet Homer at some point in the eighth century BCE and passed on for many generations before it was written down. At first the poem existed only as an oral composition; it was recited by bards. Only later was it put into the form in which we have it today. No one really knows whether or not a poet named Homer actually existed. Homer also composed the *Iliad*, the story of Achilles. Both of these books played a central role in Greek religion and education, and they have been important parts of the tradition in Western literature ever since. The *Odyssey* was probably written after the *Iliad*. The *Odyssey* is a much easier poem to read than the *Iliad*. The story moves much more quickly, and there are a lot more adventures. One adventure that is particularly well known and important is the encounter with Polyphemos. This essay will discuss this episode, focusing on its importance.

Paragraph C
The Bible is one of the most important texts in Western society. Christianity has helped lay many of our moral foundations, and these are still an important part of modern society. For instance, many people still follow the Ten Commandments. However, not all of Christian beliefs still fit into our modern world. So the Bible is a source of oppression. There are many examples of this. For example the creation story clearly is oppressive to women. The dominion of people over nature also endorses oppression of non-human animals. And there is lots of killing of people by the Israelites in the name of the Lord. This also

is oppressive. And the story of Abraham and Isaac is oppressive as well.

Paragraph D

One of the central issues of the book of Genesis is the relationship between particular characters and the Lord. Repeatedly in the narrative, God selects an individual for special attention, and that individual becomes, in effect, an example of the appropriate relationship between God and humanity, a role model for the faithful. An obvious example of this point is Abraham, one of the most important of the patriarchs. He displays complete faith in God, and God rewards him with the Covenant. But Abraham's faith makes large demands on him, and we are forced to recognize in him just what a truly meaningful relationship to the Lord demands. Many places in the Abraham story bring out this point, but we can best appreciate it by exploring in detail the famous account of Abraham's sacrifice of Isaac. This section of Genesis explicitly and compellingly offers us an insight into the religious life defined and illustrated in the Old Testament, an apparently harsh but passionate and compelling belief. Abraham's sacrifice of Isaac illustrates a paradoxical conception of relationship to God in which total sacrifice is required—even the sacrifice of moral principles—but in which everything an individual sacrifices is returned to him.

Exercise 3

Here is another pair of opening paragraphs, this time not on literary topics. Evaluate them as introductions to an argument.

Paragraph E

There's a lot of talk these days about how we just have to do something about guns. Guns have always been a part of civilization. Human beings have used guns for hunting and for sport for centuries. A gun is also an expression of human creativity. Many guns are fine objects of art. And anyway if we don't have guns the government will control us even more than they do now. Besides, the right to protect ourselves is obviously important. And guns don't kill people; people kill people. If we cannot have guns then how are we going to fend off the police when they start attacking our homes? Are we supposed to use kitchen utensils? So I say we should forget about any further gun control legislation. That's what this essay will argue.

Paragraph F
The question of increased governmental control over guns raises a number of important issues that the public seems eager to discuss. In fact, few subjects stir more passionate and widespread national debates than the issue of gun ownership and gun legislation. Every story about someone running amok with a gun—and these, we know, are frequent enough—has a lot of people calling for more regulations and restrictions on the sale of guns. In some quarters to oppose such legislation is seen at once as a sign of one's right-wing, red-neck credentials. So anyone who wishes to argue reasonably that those opposing more gun legislation may have a good case, or at least a case worth paying attention to, is unlikely to get a proper hearing in many forums. However, the attempt to present such a case must be made, because bringing down more restrictive legislation on guns will not merely do nothing to deal with our concerns about lethal weapons in the wrong hands, but will also threaten a number of other important personal rights which we take for granted.

Look very carefully now at the various reasons you found one member of each pair better as an introduction to an argument. Then look at those reasons again. Remember these criteria when you have to evaluate your own introductory paragraphs.

5.0

Explaining Key Terms

Often an important part of setting up an effective argument is the establishment of clear, precise, and effective definitions for key terms in the argument, so that everyone is in agreement from the start about what is under discussion. And the analysis of an argument requires you to pay the closest attention to any definitions, simply because a devious or inadequate or misleading definition can produce something that looks plausible but which is, in fact, problematic because the initial definition is self-serving or ambiguous.

Hence, once you have organized the opening paragraph clarifying what the argument is, you need to think carefully whether there is any information the reader needs to understand before you begin stating your case and, if there is, how detailed that information should be. The answer to that will depend, first, on the requirements of the assignment (How specialized and complex am I expected to be?) and, second, on the nature of the readership (How much specialized knowledge will my readers already possess?).

In most undergraduate assignments the readership you should keep in mind is the one composed of those in your class. If you are confident that they all share an accurate understanding of the subject matter, then you can in most cases dispense with the need to define any key terms and move to starting the argument immediately after the opening introductory paragraph. If, however, you are not sure about that shared knowledge or if there is a chance that a key term might be misunderstood, then a paragraph dealing with that term will probably be in order.

Let's take an obvious example. Suppose I wish to present an argument that we must do something at once to alleviate the growing poverty in American society. An essential prerequisite here will be defining just what I mean by *poverty*. That is, I shall have to make sure that everyone following my argument shares the same definition. If I simply let each reader bring to bear her own understanding of that term, then I am inviting confusion. And the plausibility of my argument is going to depend upon the adequacy of that definition. If, for example, I set a higher income level than normally recognized as the defining line, then I can easily show that poverty is much worse than others have claimed; if, by contrast, I set a lower income level, then I can show that poverty is decreasing or is not as widespread as other people state.

Similarly, if I am writing an essay on a subject that my readers may not fully understand (e.g., bacteriophage treatments for infection, the Affordable Care Act, cloning, the North American Free Trade Agreement, Freud's concept of the uncanny, and so on), I had better make sure early in the essay that we all share the same understanding of the key term.

5.1 | Organizing Definitions

Where does one find satisfactory definitions? Well, the most obvious places are those texts recognized as authoritative in a particular area, that is, dictionaries or specialized handbooks. An important part of study in an academic discipline is learning where one finds the most current and acceptable definitions for that subject area.

Sometimes you are going to have to adapt such definitions or else come up with one of your own. If that is the case, there are some important principles to keep in mind:

1. Fit the descriptive detail in the definition to the knowledge of the people who will be attending to your argument and to the requirements of your argument. The definition of, say, *Lyme disease* for a general readership will be different from the definition for a group of medical specialists (the latter will be much more technical).

2. Make sure in the definition you focus on what something is, not just on what its effects are, what it is used for, or how common it is. For instance, a definition of, say, *fetal alcohol syndrome* that says only that it is "a condition that affects many pregnant mothers and that can have very harmful effects on the children, including alcoholism, brain damage, behavioural problems, and stunted growth" or a definition that reviews how widespread the condition has become is not immediately very useful, since it has not said exactly what the condition is.

3. Extend the definition so that it exactly covers what you want the reader to understand. This may mean that you will want to expand on the dictionary definition (most definitions from standard language dictionaries are too short to serve

by themselves). Make sure definitions are full and complete. Do not rush them unduly.

4. It is often useful to include in a definition what a key term does *not* mean, especially when the term you are defining is commonly misunderstood.

5. Making the definition sufficiently detailed is important, but do not provide more detail in the definition than is necessary for your argument. In an essay about nuclear power generation, for example, you do not need to provide a full description of all the details of a nuclear reactor. Confine your definition to a succinct explanation of the essential details relevant to the essay.

6. Normally, you should not invent a definition for anything which already has a clear and accepted definition in place (but see the paragraphs below on disputed definitions). This is particularly important when there already is a specific authoritative definition that deals with a term in the context you are discussing it. For instance, if you are writing an essay about *endangered species* or *obesity* or *surrealism*, work with a definition provided by a recognized authority on the subject.

7. Definitions should normally be presented in an impartial tone. That is, you should not load them up with words which indicate to the reader your judgement about what you are defining (even if the purpose of the essay is to evaluate some aspect of that term). The definition is a prerequisite to the argument, which has not yet started. So keep the language of the definition neutral.

8. Once you establish a definition, do not change its meaning in the middle of the argument (another common and misleading fallacy). So make sure, when you initially establish

the definition, that it states exactly what you mean for the purposes of the entire argument, and then stick to that meaning of the term.

5.1.1 | Sample Definition Paragraphs

Below are some examples of paragraphs offering definitions as part of the introduction to an argument:

Definition Paragraph A
Before discussing the notion of a right to die, we need to review precisely what the term *right* means. In common language, the term *right* tends to mean something good, something people ought to have (e.g., a right to a good home, a right to a meaningful job, and so on). In law, however, the term has a much more specific meaning. It designates something to which people are legally entitled. Thus, a legal right also confers a legal obligation on society to make sure the right is conferred. For instance, in all Western countries, children of a certain age have a right to a free public education. This right confers on the government the obligation to provide that education, and the government cannot refuse to do so without breaking the law. Hence, when we use the term *right to die* in a legal sense, we are describing something to which a citizen would be legally entitled, and, in arguing for this right, we are insisting that people in society would have an obligation to respect that right, to permit an individual to exercise it, and, in some cases (depending upon the language in the law conferring the right) to provide the services which would guarantee that right to anyone who wanted it.

Definition Paragraph B
We need first to clarify the term *evolution*, particularly since the word is commonly misunderstood and misused

by scientists and non-scientists alike. The root biological meaning of the word, the one I am using in this essay, refers simply to the notion that animal and plant species develop, over time, out of species unlike themselves and that these new species will, in their turn, change, over time, into different forms. It is extremely important to note that this definition has nothing to say about *how* evolution proceeds (i.e., the processes creating the changes). Whatever is driving it—Darwin's natural selection, or Gould's punctuated equilibrium, or Lamarck's inheritance of acquired characteristics, or divine intervention, or something else—is completely irrelevant: all the word designates here is *change*.

Definition Paragraph C
Let me begin by explaining what I mean by Romantic irony, an elusive term often defined in different ways. For the purpose of this essay, I am using the following definition from Alper Erdogan (6):

> Romantic irony is characterized by the spirit of romanticism: a conception of "[a] universe founded in chaos and incomprehensibility rather than in a divinely ordained teleology" (Mellor 1980: vii). This conception, however, is not nihilistic, as it may sound. Although the romantic has lost faith in the traditional morality and believes that everything is in vain, he still preserves a belief in a final reconciliation. He "feels" that there is a way out, thus a romantic ironist employs irony to constantly undermine given meanings, with the hope that this undoing will eventually result in a state of privilege and security he has been longing for. (Lang 1996: 576)

I particularly wish to focus the meaning of the term on that notion of an irony that works "to constantly undermine given meanings," the idea that when Romantic irony is present whatever sense of purpose, hope, stability or emotional certainty is evoked by the language is quickly cancelled out, so that the irony establishes a recurring rhythm of rising energy constantly collapsing, usually very quickly. Romantic irony, one critic has remarked, is like writing a series of immediately cancelled cheques.

Notice that these definitions are extensive and precise. They provide all the information that the reader will need to understand how the key term is being used in the argument. In the first definition, the writer has used an example to clarify the key term; in the second she has taken time to explain what the term does not mean; and in the third she has borrowed a definition from a secondary source and highlighted the aspect of it she wants to use in her argument. Notice also that there is nothing argumentative in the definitions—the tone is neutral and matter-of-fact.

5.1.2 | Disputed Definitions

Sometimes you will have to deal with a disputed definition, that is, a term for which there are different or even conflicting explanations. In such a case, it is often useful to review the existing definitions and then to stipulate the definition you are going to use in the argument.

For instance, suppose you are constructing an argument about how we should deal with a particular problem of rights for aboriginal Americans. You will probably have to define precisely what you mean by the term *aboriginal American*. Does this term include all people who call themselves aboriginal Americans? Is the term restricted to those whom the governing bands or the federal government or the census designate as aboriginal Americans? Is an aboriginal American anyone who is married to or descended from an aboriginal American? Is there a legal definition of the term? And so on. In such a case, it is a good idea to indicate that the term is disputed and perhaps briefly to review some of the options. Then for the purpose of your argument you stipulate the particular definition that you are going to use.

Similarly at the start of an argument about, say, the number of people for whom religious values are important, you should indicate that this term *people for whom religious values are important* may mean different things to different readers and then clarify what you mean by the term (Does it mean people who attend church or those who describe themselves as religious people? Does the term in your essay designate only traditional religions or all varieties of religious spirituality? And so on). Do not assume that every reader brings to the essay the same understanding of the term as you do. And, of course, if you are going to be using statistical results in your argument (as you probably will), then the reader will need to know what exactly you are measuring in order to fully understand the statistics.

5.1.3 | *Self-Serving Definitions*

When you construct an argument and especially when you analyze someone else's argument, be very careful about definitions which may be twisted to support a particular opinion, a very common tactic in misleading arguments. Often, the entire logic of an argument depends upon a particular definition, so if you accept it too casually, then you may find it difficult later to avoid conclusions which do not sound plausible but which do seem to arise logically from the points made. And if you deliberately use a self-serving definition yourself, then your entire argument may well be doomed from the start. Normally, if you rely for your definition on a reliable and respected source, this problem should not arise.

Getting readers quickly to accept a loaded definition is one of the commonest methods of sounding reasonable and yet playing a subtle logical trick. Here is an example of a two-paragraph argument, which begins with a definition and moves from that to a conclusion.

What is science? Well, we all agree that science is an activity in which we observe and measure a natural occurrence. We carry out this process repeatedly until we have a sense of how this process might work mechanically. On the basis of this sense, we construct a theory and a mechanical model, and this theory will enable us then to predict various things about the process under observation. Once this theory is in place, we proceed to test it by further observation and experiment involving the process we are explaining. At the heart of the scientific endeavour is this constant return to detailed observation of the natural process under investigation. Unless the process is observed directly, the study of it is not scientific.

Now biological evolution is obviously something we cannot observe. By the evolutionists' own admission, the time spans involve millions of years—far beyond the capacity of any single human being or of any collection of human beings to investigate according to the very processes which science itself requires. Thus, while evolution is clearly a theory, an idea, it cannot be scientific. It cannot be tested because it cannot be observed. So clearly evolution, no matter what its supporters might claim, has no scientific validity.

This argument, you will notice, works by applying a general principle to a specific case. It begins by setting up a definition of science that, it claims, is shared by everyone. Then, in the second paragraph the writer applies this definition to the modern theory of evolution, in order to conclude that evolution does not fit the definition and, therefore, is not scientific.

Is this argument persuasive? Well, if we accept the definition of science in the first paragraph, then the conclusion given at the end of the second paragraph would seem inescapable. So the key question here is this: How adequate is that definition of science? If it is inadequate or simply wrong, then clearly the argument collapses.

The short answer to the above question is, of course, no, that definition is not adequate. The writer has defined science in a very misleading manner. Science is better characterized, in brief, as the construction of theories (often involving things we cannot observe), deriving predictions from those theories, and then testing and observing to see whether those predictions confirm or contradict the theory. What matters is our observation, not of the process described in the theory, but rather of the predictions which arise logically out of the theory. By that standard, the modern theory of evolution has proved to be a spectacularly successful scientific achievement.

When you are analyzing an argument, you may need to exercise some care in dealing with initial definitions, for there is an important difference between deliberately misleading definitions (like the one above) and definitions with which you do not agree. Many philosophical works, for example, begin with a definition of the nature of a human being (or of different groups of human beings) and then, on the basis of those initial definitions, proceed to construct an argument about how human beings should behave or organize society. In many cases, these opening claims will jar with modern sensibilities, for they may be quite different from (and sometimes contradictory or offensive to) modern beliefs. You should never reject such arguments out of hand simply because their opening assumptions are not agreeable or different or (in your view) wrong. You should begin your analysis of the argument by provisionally accepting those definitions and seeing what the writer does with them. If the writer's argument based on his initial definitions leads to a contradiction or to a recommendation that is unacceptable, at that point one might want to go back and challenge his initial definitions (for a more detailed consideration of this point see Section 8.3.1).

5.2 | Descriptive and Narrative Background

The need to define the terms central to an argument may also sometimes include a requirement to provide a *descriptive* or *narrative* definition of a term that refers to a particular place, institution, person, or event. In other words, you may need, as a preliminary step in an argument, to provide the reader an accurate explanation of who or what you are discussing.

For example, if you are writing an argument about a particular political protest, it is important that the readers fully understand what you mean when you refer to the incident. So, unless you are certain that the readers of your essay already possess enough information, you will need to provide a descriptive definition of the key term (in this case, an explanation of where and when the protest occurred, what it was about, and what happened there). This will normally be a brief factual geographical or historical description sufficiently detailed to give the reader, who may have no knowledge of the event, an understanding of what you are talking about. Since you cannot assume that all readers will have accurate information about these matters, you will need to provide them.

For instance, if you wish to argue that the attack on the US consulate in Benghazi in 2012 prompted a massive cover-up which has never been properly investigated, then before you begin the argument, you should devote a paragraph to providing details about the incident that the reader needs to understand in order to follow the essay. Similarly, an argument about the construction of a particular oil pipeline will require, as part of the introduction, some description of what that project is. An essay arguing for the significance of an unjustly neglected thinker or artist should provide a paragraph of biographical facts.

Similarly, an essay presenting an argument about a particular judicial decision should normally give the reader the facts of the case before launching the argument: When and where did the court hearing occur, who were the plaintiff(s) and defendant(s), and what was the key question the court had to resolve?

If in your essay you are applying a particular psychological, philosophical, or historical concept to a work of literature, you will almost certainly have to offer a descriptive definition of that concept in some detail before launching the argument. For example, in an essay arguing that, say, Freud's notion of the Oedipus complex provides useful insights into the character of Hamlet or that a Marxist approach to Kafka's *Metamorphosis* helps to make sense of a very puzzling story, you should first give the reader some idea of what you mean by *Freud's Oedipus complex* or *a Marxist approach*. The following outline illustrates the point:

THESIS: If we explore Kafka's mystifying tale from a Marxist perspective we can see one important interpretative possibility: Gregor's transformation is a direct result of the oppressive capitalist conditions of the society in which he lives and works.

DEFINITION: Let me begin by clarifying what I mean by the phrase "from a Marxist perspective." Obviously there is no time here to outline Marx's theory in any detail, but it is worth stressing two of his key insights....

ARGUMENTATIVE POINT 1: With this in mind, we can recognize that one way to understand Gregor's transformation is to see it as the result of what he does for a living—of the nature of his working life.

Providing a quick review of the analytical concepts you are using in the argument is common in a number of essays and research papers. But there is one important danger: you must not overload these paragraphs, letting the background information run away with the paper. If the purpose of the essay is an argument, then the introduction to it must focus succinctly *only* on those matters essential for an understanding of that argument. You have to be careful not to let the introductory material grow so long that it takes over the paper.

For instance, in the above sample outline for the opening of an essay on a Marxist approach to Kafka's *Metamorphosis*, the writer does not overwhelm the reader with a comprehensive outline of Marxist theory. If he had done that, he would have risked the paper becoming an outline of Marxist theory with the story serving merely as an example of that theory. Instead, the writer isolates the two features of the theory that he is going to use as analytical tools for a discussion of the story. Once these have been described briefly, he moves on to the argument. For a further discussion of this point see Section 8.2.7.

Be careful, however, of providing unnecessary narrative or descriptive summaries. If there is no need for such background, do not provide it. For instance, in a normal academic essay on a particular fiction, film, or philosophical argument, you should *always* assume (unless informed otherwise) that the readers of the essay are quite familiar with the work you are discussing. Hence, you have no need to provide detailed information about its contents (e.g., summarizing the story, describing the argument at length, and so on). Writing lengthy summaries in such essays (either in the introduction or elsewhere) is often popular because doing so is very easy and can use up a great many words. However, descriptive summaries are not arguments: if they are merely telling the reader what he already knows, then they are a waste of time.

Remember, incidentally, that any background information you do provide is part of your preparation to launch the argument. So keep the language in such paragraphs neutral: you are providing necessary facts, not pushing the reader to accept an opinion about those facts. Do not, for example, write something like the following:

> First we need to understand what the proposed legislation states. It stipulates that in twelve months the already excessive state sales tax will be increased by 1 per cent and that the number of necessary items exempted from the sales tax

will be reduced, so that everyone will be paying more for
their essential requirements (clothing, food, school supplies,
various services, and so on). In other words, this arbitrary
legislation, which is little more than a tax grab, imposes an
additional burden on all citizens resident in the state by
making them send even more of their hard-earned money
to that sink-hole bureaucracy in Providence.

Your essay may be an argument striving to persuade the reader of
this very unfavourable view of the increase in the sales tax, but do
not impose that opinion on the definition. Keep that part of the
essay impartial.

5.3 | Extended Definitions

Definitions can sometimes be quite extensive, when you need to
make sure that the readers have a full grasp of all the necessary
details of a particular topic. So in some cases you may need to
take more than one paragraph to include all the facts you want
readers to know. While such extended definitions are not really
common in a short essay, they are often a key part of the introduction to a longer research paper.

Suppose, for instance, that you are writing a long argument
(in the form of a research paper) about the dangers of cloning technology. Before going into the argument, you want people to have
a very clear understanding of the factual background to this topic.
In other words, you have to clarify a few matters. Depending on
the nature of your argument, you might want to include a number of paragraphs defining and describing the issue of cloning in
various ways, as follows:

PARAGRAPH 1: Introductory Paragraph, setting up the subject,
focus, and thesis of the research paper (an argument that
we need to impose some strict regulations on research into
cloning techniques).

PARAGRAPH 2: Formal definition of cloning: What does the term mean, what are key elements in the process? (From this the reader should derive an accurate sense of what cloning is, what you mean by the term in the rest of the essay.)

PARAGRAPH 3: Description of the development of cloning, in the form of a narrative: When did it start? What were the key experiments in the history of the process? Where are we now? From this the reader should derive an idea of the developing history of the process.

PARAGRAPH 4: Descriptive definition of the present laws on cloning: What is the legal status of the process right now? Are there any challenges to the law before the courts? (From this the reader should understand exactly what the present law does or does not say about the procedures.)

PARAGRAPH 5: Start of the main part of the argument.

The first four paragraphs, you will notice, are not arguing anything. After the introduction, which sets up the argument, the next three paragraphs are providing the key factual background upon which your argument will draw once you launch it. Their purpose is to give all readers a shared sense of the necessary facts, without which they may become confused once the argument begins.

Extended definitions are often very important in setting out the full factual context for an argument about the historical significance of an event or a discovery. If, for example, your paper is arguing that Galileo's experiments marked a decisive shift in the way science was conducted, then you will need to inform the reader (briefly but usefully) of the state of affairs in scientific thinking when Galileo began his work. Similarly, if your essay is arguing that the truth about the assassination of President Kennedy was not fully explored in the official inquiry, then before the argument starts, you will need a paragraph providing details of the assassination and another describing the work and the conclusions of the Warren Commission. Then you can start presenting the details of your argument.

Hence, you should observe three principles in such extensive definitions: (1) only include matters relevant to what you are going to say later, (2) provide the needed factual description quickly and clearly, and (3) keep the tone neutral (don't launch the argument in this section of the introduction).

5.4 | Summary Points on Establishing the Argument

Let us pause to review briefly the main points made in the past two sections of this handbook about setting up the argument in the opening paragraph(s).

The first task in any argument is to define it properly, so that the reader clearly understands what the debate is about, what is not being included, and what essential information is required to follow the argument.

In most cases, the argument will be defined in the opening paragraph (the Introduction) and, if any factual information is needed, it will follow in one or two subsequent paragraphs. Here, for example, are some sample outlines for the opening paragraphs of a longer argument in which some definition is necessary before the main argument commences.

Example 1
GENERAL SUBJECT: Unnecessary drugs
FOCUS 1: Ritalin and Attention Deficit Disorder
FOCUS 2: Ritalin and Attention Deficit Disorder in North American Public Schools
THESIS: The present use of Ritalin in public schools is a major scandal. Though it enriches drug companies and perhaps makes the lives of school teachers less troublesome, it is turning thousands of children into addicts unnecessarily.

PARAGRAPH 1: What exactly is Ritalin? (The paragraph goes on to define what Ritalin is chemically, giving an idea of what it is and how it works.)

PARAGRAPH 2: Ritalin is routinely prescribed for a condition known as Attention Deficit Hyperactivity Disorder (ADHD). The standard definition of this condition is as follows. (The paragraph goes on to define ADHD and indicate the widespread use of Ritalin to cope with it.)

PARAGRAPH 3: The widespread use of Ritalin to treat students may not seem like a major issue, but in fact there are several serious problems associated with this trend. First of all.... (The argument starts here with the first point in support of the thesis.)

Example 2

GENERAL SUBJECT: Modern poetry

FOCUS 1: The Imagist Movement

FOCUS 2: The Imagist Movement: Stylistic Innovations

FOCUS 3: The Imagist Movement: Stylistic Innovations: Their influence on the work of Amy Lowell

THESIS: A comparison of Amy Lowell's work from the years immediately before and the years immediately after she became involved with the Imagist Movement in 1913 clearly illustrates the importance of the stylistic innovations associated with Imagism. Where Lowell's pre-1913 poetry is dull, wordy, and unfocused in content, her post-1913 poetry is vibrant, concise, and clear in content.

PARAGRAPH 1: Lowell first met Ezra Pound, a leader of the Imagist Movement, in London 1913 ... (The paragraph goes on to give a narrative description of the facts surrounding the Imagist Movement and Lowell's involvement with it.)

PARAGRAPH 2: The basic principles of this new movement were few and easy to understand. (The paragraph goes on to define in further detail just what the Imagist Movement consisted of.)

PARAGRAPH 3: These principles are clearly absent from Lowell's early work, but begin to appear in her poems immediately after her discovery of Imagism. (Argument starts here with attention to the first point in support of the thesis.)

Example 3
GENERAL SUBJECT: Natural Science
FOCUS 1: The Development of Modern Science
FOCUS 2: The Development of Modern Science: The Importance of Descartes' *Discourse on Method*
THESIS: Descartes' new method for investigating nature was a revolutionary challenge to traditional science and led to a significantly different way of thinking about and studying nature, including human nature.
PARAGRAPH 1: In order to assess the significance of Descartes' ideas, we need to consider briefly a few salient characteristics of what I am calling "traditional science." (The paragraph defines a few key characteristics of science in the fifteenth and early sixteenth centuries.)
PARAGRAPH 2: What Descartes proposes in his new method is something very different. (The paragraph briefly describes a few major features of Descartes' argument in his *Discourse on Method*.)
PARAGRAPH 3: Not surprisingly, Descartes' ideas introduced a radical shift in how scientists viewed the relationship between the world of nature and the human mind. To begin with ... (The argument starts here with the first point about one effect of this new method of enquiry.)

To repeat a point made more than once in this section: not all essays will need definitions of this sort, and the arguer can launch the argument immediately after the introductory paragraph.

This will normally be the case in short essays, especially those on literature. But in a longer research paper, it is frequently essential to provide definitions of key terms, especially when you are writing for a general audience that has no expert knowledge of the subject matter you are looking at.

Sometimes, as we shall see, a paragraph defining or describing a key term can be deferred until later in the argument and inserted at the point where it first becomes necessary (more about this later).

6.0

Organizing the Main Body of an Argument

6.1 | General Remarks

Once an argument has been defined in the opening paragraph(s), so that the reader fully understands what is at issue, then the argument can proceed with what is called here the *Main Body*. This section consists of a series of points the arguer makes in support of the position advanced in the thesis. An important quality of this part of the argument is *clarity*: the reader must always understand precisely where she is in the context of the total argument.

While there are a number of ways you can organize the presentation of the argument in order to make it as clear as possible, here are a few basic principles which apply to all arguments. We will start with some simple principles and, in later sections, consider more sophisticated structures for written arguments.

1. The Main Body of an argument must proceed *one point at a time*. The writer introduces the point, discusses it so as to bring out its relationship to the thesis, and then moves onto the next point. Normally each point will take at least one paragraph, sometimes more. The important things to remember here are that you should never try to deal with more than one point at a time and that you should say what you have to say about that single point and then move on. Do not jump back and forth to and from the same point in different paragraphs.

2. In most arguments you can never include everything that you might want to include. You have to select the best points you can muster in support of your thesis and present those thoroughly, leaving the others out of the essay. A few points thoroughly discussed are almost always more persuasive than a great many more points dealt with casually.

3. Once the Main Body of the argument starts, you should not digress from the line established in the thesis. Everything in the essay must be directly relevant to what you have set up as the argument. Do not change horses in mid-stream.

We will be looking at these matters in more detail below.

6.2 | Selecting the Topics for the Main Body

Once you have estimated how many paragraphs you have at your disposal for the main body of the argument (see Section 3.2 above), you then have to select the points you are going to include. Remember this important and obvious priority: you cannot include everything you might want or be able to say in support of the thesis; you have to reduce the argument to the few best points so that you have space to argue each of them in detail.

Let's take a particular example. You wish to write an essay of up to 1000 words on a short story. This means you will be constructing an essay of about five paragraphs, with an introduction (Paragraph 1) and a conclusion (Paragraph 5). The main body of the argument will thus be three paragraphs long. You need to select the three most important things that will make your argument about the short story persuasive. Do not be too quick to determine those three things. Pause to reflect on what you might include.

The first stage in the selection is usually a brainstorming session in which you jot down all the things you might say. Such a list would cover a wide range of different possibilities. Then, by a process of elimination, you select from this list of elements the ones that, in your view, are the most important for the purposes of your argument. The best way by far to go through this process is a discussion with other people who have also read the story. They may not share your view, but the conversation will clarify for you more quickly than anything else what you most need to say in order to support your point of view (and the other people will also be the source of some interesting topics you may wish to incorporate).

Whether you discuss with other people or brainstorm on your own, you should at the end of this process have a list of the three items which will form the core of your argument, the key elements that you want the reader of your essay to think about and accept. By offering a detailed discussion of each of these in turn, you will be trying to persuade the reader that your interpretation of this work is worth attending to.

The process is the same for a research paper, except that you have more paragraphs to deal with. This enables you not only to include more points in the argument but also, as we shall see, to give the argument a more complex structure.

6.3 | Rethinking the Focus and Thesis of the Argument

You will be able to organize the main body of your argument well only if you have a very specific idea of what you are setting up as the main argument and if that argument is manageable within the space available. It is almost impossible to develop a sense of the structure of an argument if you do not have a very specific focus and a clear thesis or if these are too unwieldy for the space available. Thus, if you find that you simply cannot decide what to leave out and that there is just too much you might say on the topic, then you should go back to the definition of the argument and restrict the focus further and/or make your thesis statement more precise.

For instance, suppose you decide you want to write an essay on, say, the importance of nature in *Huckleberry Finn* or on the abuses of the present government programs for immigrants. In the planning stages you get hopelessly bogged down because there seems to be far too much material for you to cover and you simply cannot decide. In such a case, you should rethink the definition of the essay. Instead of writing something on the importance of nature in *Huckleberry Finn*, restrict the essay to an argument about the importance of the river (i.e., narrow the meaning of *nature*); similarly, instead of writing about government programs for immigrants in general, restrict the meaning of that wide topic to something much more specific (e.g., education initiatives).

6.4 | Developing an Outline: Argumentative Topic Sentences

Once you have a sense of the three or four main points you would like to make (assuming we are still dealing with a relatively short argument), you need to frame those points in the form of topic sentences. A *topic sentence*, as the name suggests, announces to the reader a particular topic (or stage) in the essay, a new point that you are now going to present. As such, it is a key signal to the reader, indicating the direction of the argument.

The topic sentences you draw up will introduce each argumentative paragraph in the main body of the argument. They will declare to the reader the point you are now starting to make in support of your thesis. The clarity of the argument in the main body of the essay is going to depend, more than anything else, on the clarity of these topic sentences.

In framing a good topic sentence, you should strive to answer these questions: What exactly am I arguing in this paragraph? What argumentative point do I want the reader to accept? A sentence in answer to those questions will usually provide a helpful and energetic opening to a new stage of the argument. Here are some examples:

Example A
(In an essay exploring the deficiencies in the present system of welfare in a particular jurisdiction)
The present system by which welfare deals with rental payments to landlords invites dishonesty on the part of the welfare recipient and has created widespread abuse of the system. In fact, the present system encourages such fraud.

Example B
(From an essay arguing that there is too much emphasis on academic research and publication in our colleges)
Academics often seek to justify the emphasis on research and publication by appealing to a cherished but misleading faculty myth: the assertion that such research and publication activity is essential to good teaching. This claim is without foundation.

Example C
(From an essay reviewing a particular poem)
The images in the poem are very unsatisfactory. They are

constantly presented in vague, imprecise language appealing to a warm sentimentality rather than to clear vision, not unlike a commercial for some product involving intimate personal hygiene.

Example D
(From an essay arguing that a recent zombie movie offers a critique of modern capitalism)
The film first puts forward zombies as a symbol of mindless consumption in the opening mall scene, in which a crowd of teenage zombies raid a Wal-Mart. The chaos and violence created by the zombie attack is portrayed to resemble the chaos and violence that often occurs surrounding Black Friday and other extreme sales.

Example E
(From an essay arguing that the use of Ritalin is a dangerous trend that should be stopped)
The widespread use of Ritalin in the schools also indicates a massive failure on the part of our education system to deal properly with the way the setup of the typical classroom makes it nearly impossible for teachers to offer sufficient help to struggling students.

Here are some important things to notice about these topic sentences:

1. First, and most important, they all express argumentative opinions. They put on the table some specific points related to the thesis and thus advance the argument in the essay. They are not stating matters of fact. This, as we shall see, is crucial.

2. Second, the writer takes time to establish the topic firmly, if necessary taking two (or perhaps three) sentences to get the argumentative point across to the reader.

3. Thirdly, they all announce single, specific points. There is no doubt about the one issue that this paragraph is now going to deal with.

4. Finally, they are not putting particular evidence into the argument (that is about to come). They are setting up a new point, indicating to the reader what this paragraph is now going to turn to.

6.4.1 | A Common Error in Argumentative Topic Sentences

It is particularly important to notice what the topics sentences listed in the previous section are not doing: they are not stating matters of fact. That is, they are not simply stating something obvious about which there is no disagreement.

This is a crucial point, because one of the most frequent stylistic weaknesses in student arguments is a series of topic sentences that are not argumentative opinions but statements of the obvious. Notice the difference between the above sentences and the following:

Example 1
(From an essay on the abuses in a government welfare program)
Under the present scheme of welfare, the monthly government cheque pays for rental expenses.

Example 2
(From an essay arguing that there is too much emphasis on academic research and publication in our colleges)
Academic faculty are always claiming that their research and publishing activities are essential to good teaching. Without such research and publishing, so they say,

instructors and professors will be uninformed, out of date, and unsatisfactory in the classroom.

Example 3
(From an essay reviewing a particular poem)
This poem contains a lot of images. Some of these are images of natural scenes, and others are dream images.

Example 4
(From an essay arguing that a recent zombie movie offers a critique of modern capitalism)
The film's opening scene takes place in a mall.

Example 5
(From an essay arguing that the use of Ritalin is a dangerous trend that should be stopped)
Ritalin is prescribed by doctors for many young school children, and the drug is administered with the parents' consent. This has been going on for many years.

These sentences do not express argumentative opinions. They express facts. There is nothing to argue about here. Hence, as topic sentences they are inherently unsatisfactory, because they do not indicate to the reader where the argument is going. And they threaten to derail the whole paragraph because they invite the writer to abandon the argument and to devote the paragraph to a lot of obvious facts (that is, to write a paragraph that summarizes factual material rather than presenting an argument), a serious flaw in many essays.

6.4.2 | *Exercise in Argumentative Topic Sentences*

In the light of the remarks given in Sections 6.4 and 6.4.1 above, indicate which of the following statements would make a good topic sentence or sentences and which would not. Remember the key point: the topic sentence(s) should announce an argumentative point and not a statement of fact about which there is no dispute.

1. The language the judge used in his ruling illustrates that he did not take the plaintiffs' concerns seriously because they were teenagers.
2. Later in the novel Huck meets up with two confidence men. Together they plan a number of tricks on the citizens of small towns along the river.
3. Some of the salaries paid to average professional athletes are very high. It is not uncommon to read about a journeyman player receiving a salary of several millions of dollars a year.
4. The poem repeatedly describes the narrator's anger with visceral, gory language that links her past trauma to the violence she witnesses in the slaughterhouse.
5. A second major erroneous claim made by the proponents of the Keystone pipeline in order to "sell" the project to the general public is that it will create a number of well-paying, long-term jobs. Such a claim is dubious at best.
6. Robert de Niro has appeared in many different films. He has been a leading actor for many years. He has received a number of prestigious awards for acting.

Make sure you understand this point about how topic sentences must advance an argumentative opinion relevant to the thesis and not just offer a statement of fact. If you have trouble formulating a proper topic sentence, then try to set it up by completing the following sentence: *In this paragraph I wish to argue in support of my thesis the single point that ...* If you complete the sentence with something we can argue about and then get rid of the above introductory clause, you should have a workable opening to an argumentative paragraph.

6.5 | Drawing Up a Simple Outline (For a Short Essay)

You have completed your preliminary organization for an argumentative essay when you have a relatively detailed outline which does two things: first, it defines the argument (with a clear focus and thesis) and, second, it sets down the series of topic sentences that you intend to follow in developing the argument. These you may wish to adjust in the course of writing the essay, but you should not start on the writing phase until you have an outline in place, so that you know where you are going, stage by stage, in the total argument.

Below are two sample outlines for a short essay (about 1000 words). At this point there is no need to worry about the conclusion (we will be dealing with that later). The abbreviation TS indicates "Topic Sentence," the opening sentence(s) of each paragraph.

ESSAY 1: On *Hamlet*
GENERAL SUBJECT: *Hamlet*
FOCUS 1: Polonius
FOCUS 2: Polonius's treatment of his family
THESIS: Polonius is particularly important in the play because his attitude to his family reveals to us very clearly the emotional sterility of the court in Elsinore.
TS 1: Polonius, an important court official, is so addicted to lying, manipulation, and routine deception, especially in his family life, that he has no understanding of emotional honesty.
TS 2: The relationship between Polonius and his son, Laertes, provides a clear sense of Polonius's priorities, especially the way in which his values are dominated by his desire for practical worldly success rather than by genuine feelings of love.
TS 3: In his dealings with Ophelia, Polonius is a cruel bully.

ESSAY 2: On Illegal Drugs

GENERAL SUBJECT: Illegal Drugs

FOCUS 1: Illegal drugs and the law

FOCUS 2: The need to legalize drugs

THESIS: The only appropriate solution to our present drug problem is to decriminalize all derivatives of marijuana, heroin, and cocaine immediately.

TS 1: The present situation, in which so many drugs are illegal, is the major cause for a much bigger problem than narcotic use: violent crime.

TS 2: Since we have many harmful narcotics legally available throughout the country, making less harmful substances illegal is foolish.

TS 3: The idea that the police and the courts, given plenty of money, can somehow prevent or even reduce the supply and the consumption of illegal drugs is wholly misguided.

Notice how such an outline provides a very clear sense of what the essay is focusing upon, what the thesis is, and how each paragraph of the argument will start. Pay particular attention also to how the key elements here are complete sentences (the thesis and the topic sentences) rather than just jotted-down points. While you might well begin to organize an outline by drawing up a list of abbreviated comments, you should always strive to convert these into clear and complete topic sentences, so that you have a firm sense of the argumentative thrust of each paragraph and can easily inspect the overall structure of the argument. Organizing an essay on the basis of a series of short, point-form phrases may lead to difficulties (you may, for example, forget why you included a particular point or what specific argumentative opinion it is referring to). If you have a series of topic sentences, on the other hand, you know how you are going to start each paragraph, before you set out to write the first draft.

The above outline may look simple enough. But it will usually take a good deal of thought and discussion. For some arguments you may have to do some research in order to determine just what main points you wish to include, so drawing up such an outline may be quite time consuming. But you should not start the first draft of the essay until you have something like this in place. The time you spend working on a useful outline will save you a great deal more time in the writing of the paper.

6.5.1 | Checking the Outline

Once you have an outline like one of the above samples, review it carefully with the following points in mind:

1. Is the thesis a clearly assertive argument, something we can dispute? Is it clear in your mind precisely what you are arguing and what you are not arguing? Can you make it any more specific and clear?

2. Is each topic sentence an opinionated assertion, something we can argue about? Are you certain that the topic sentence is not just making an obvious statement of fact?

3. Does each topic sentence state very clearly just one important and specific opinion in support of the thesis? Is the point stated in the topic sentence one that you can adequately cover in just one paragraph? Are there any ambiguities or contradictions in the topic sentence which you might clarify?

4. Are the topic sentences in the most persuasive order? If parts of your argument are much stronger than others, then normally you should put the most persuasive point last, the second most persuasive point first, and the least persuasive point in the middle.

6.6 | Some Sample Formats for Topic Sentences

Topic sentences form the major framework of the argument—its logical spine, as it were—and thus you need to pay particular attention to framing them appropriately. The following notes offer advice on some of the ways in which you might like to formulate and vary the topic sentences in the essay.

Standard Format: Interpretative Assertion (Opinion)
A common form of topic sentence is a statement of the assertive opinion you are now going to deal with in the paragraph. The following examples illustrate the style:

1. The store itself plays an important role in Sammy's decision to leave, for his walking out is a rejection of what it stands for.

2. The crucial factor in the economic crisis was the inability of the government to repay its debts.

3. Capital punishment does not, as many of its supporters claim, deter crimes of violence.

4. Odysseus's defining characteristic is an insatiable curiosity which overcomes all thoughts of potential danger to himself or his men.

Standard Format Emphasized
Here the topic sentence is basically the same in form as the first, except that the writer expands on the opening sentence, making it more emphatic and clear. This is a particularly useful and common style for a topic sentence.

1. The store where he works plays an important role in Sammy's decision to leave, for his walking out is a rejection of what it

stands for. In fact, if we attend carefully to the language of Sammy's descriptions of where he works, we come to understand his feelings about the life he faces if he remains in the job.

2. The crucial factor in the economic crisis was the inability of the French monarchy to repay its debts. For years the king had insisted on borrowing money to conduct expensive foreign wars and glorify the court; now the money urgently needed to address social problems was not available.

3. Capital punishment does not, as its supporters claim, deter crimes of violence. There is, in fact, repeated evidence that imposing capital sentences for murder has no effect whatsoever on the frequency of such crimes.

4. Odysseus's defining characteristic is an insatiable curiosity which overcomes all thoughts of potential danger to himself or his men. When he encounters great dangers, such as the Cyclops or the Sirens, Odysseus places himself and others at risk in order to experience them firsthand.

Simple Direct Question

An alternative approach is to set up the topic sentence as a question. The paragraph will then become an answer to the question. This is a good way to add emphasis and variety to your style, but be careful not to overuse it, so that it becomes a repetitive habit.

1. What exactly is the importance in the story of the main setting of the store?

2. Why was the economy in such difficulty at this stage?

3. Does capital punishment effectively deter crimes of violence?

4. Why is Odysseus so curious about the world?

Double Question

A really emphatic way to open a paragraph is to set up a double question, the second emphasizing the point raised in the first.

1. What exactly is the importance in the story of the main setting, the store? What significant role does it play in Sammy's decision to leave?

2. Why was the economy in such difficulty at this stage? Why was a country as rich and powerful as France unable to meet the financial demands of the new situation?

3. What about the argument that capital punishment deters crime? Is it not the case that the threat of a lethal punishment makes potential criminals more reluctant to commit murder?

4. Why is Odysseus so dangerously curious about the world? Why, that is, does he never temper his thirst for new experience with some common-sense prudence which might lead him to avoid dangers rather than embrace the risk they pose to him and his men?

Statement of Fact and a Question or Interpretative Assertion

Earlier in this section, I stressed repeatedly that a paragraph should never open with a statement of fact, and that principle is still an important one. However, the style is sometimes acceptable, but *only* if you immediately direct the reader's attention to an argumentative point about that fact.

1. Sammy works in a standard supermarket in a small town. This store plays an important role in Sammy's decision to leave, for his walking out is a rejection of what it stands for.

2. By the mid-1780s the poverty of the agricultural classes and the poorest groups in the major cities had reached critical proportions. Why had this come about, especially in a country apparently so economically well off?

3. Supporters of capital punishment often claim that it is an effective deterrent for some people who might commit murder. But is this true?

4. Odysseus has no particular need to visit the Cyclops, but he places himself and his men at risk in order to encounter it firsthand. This decision illustrates an insatiable curiosity that is Odysseus's defining characteristic.

Statement of Fact and a Double Question

Again, one can make the previous style of topic sentence more emphatic by including two questions instead of one:

1. Sammy works in a standard supermarket in a small town. What is significant about this fact in the story? What role, if any, does the store play in Sammy decision to leave?

2. By the mid-1780s the poverty of the agricultural classes and the poorest groups in the major cities had reached critical proportions. Why had this come about, especially in a country apparently so economically well off? What was it about this particular moment that turned a widespread social problem into the fuse that lit a revolution?

3. Supporters of capital punishment often claim that it is an effective deterrent for some people who might commit murder. But is this true? Does a statistical analysis of murder rates bear out this common contention?

4. Odysseus has no particular reason for visiting the Cyclops.

So why then does he incur the risk, especially against
the wishes and entreaties of his men? What qualities in
his character almost require him to undertake whatever
adventures this island will bring?

Notice that these different ways of framing topic sentences are
all doing the same thing: they are alerting the reader to the argumentative point that will be discussed in the paragraph. The
reader thus has a clear sense of the direction of the argument.

6.6.1 | *Topic Sentences to Avoid*

The following are some common forms of ineffective topic sentences. They are not immediately useful in an argumentative
structure because they do not alert the reader to anything directly
relevant to a new development in the argument. You should check
to make sure that you are not offering up as topic sentences statements which fall into one of the following categories:

1. Statements of fact which stand by themselves (i.e., which are
   not immediately followed by something of interpretative
   interest or a question, as in the examples above).

2. Major generalizations about life, liberty, morality, the nature
   of the world, or anything not directly related to the details
   of the focus you are considering (e.g., "Absolute monarchies
   tend to be unjust and extravagant"; "Curiosity is a trait we
   always admire, especially in children"; "Working in a small
   store is a depressing experience"; and so on).

3. A sentence which expresses a simple personal feeling, belief,
   or response to the subject matter ("I myself have no difficulty
   with capital punishment"; "I was happy when Sammy walked
   out of the store; it made me feel good"; "I find it confusing
   that Odysseus went to visit the Cyclops in the first place").

4. Any sentence which introduces a point not directly relevant to the thesis you have established.

6.7 | More Complex Structures

In this section so far we have been looking at the structure of topic sentences for a simple additive argument, in which each paragraph of the main body of the essay introduces a separate point in support of the thesis. Such a structure is relatively common in short essay assignments.

Now we will turn our attention to more sophisticated structures in which major points in the argument are dealt with in a sequence of two or three (or more) paragraphs, what we can call a *paragraph cluster*. This technique enables the writer to establish an argumentative point in much greater detail and is thus a useful way of adding depth and persuasiveness to an argument.

6.7.1 | *Depth versus Breadth*

When you are organizing an argumentative essay, remember this important principle: *depth is almost always preferable to breadth*. What that means, in practice, is that an argument with a few well-argued points (even just one or two) is generally more persuasive and interesting than an argument which offers a cursory review of many more. Make sure you understand this principle. Your argument is not necessarily a good one simply because you include a great many different items supporting your point of view. What matters is the persuasiveness of those topics you do introduce.

Does this mean that no one should ever include a number of different topics in a relatively short argument? No, not at all. It simply means that such an argument, especially by an inexperienced essayist, runs the risk of being superficial, simply because there is insufficient space to go into the detail necessary to make the points included in the argument convincing.

Of course, some argumentative points can be well presented in a single paragraph, and a series of such paragraphs can make a good essay. But usually a more thorough discussion of a limited number of topics central to the argument makes the essay more persuasive, as we shall see from the examples in the sections which follow.

6.7.2 | *Interrupting the Argument*

In order to construct an argument made up of paragraph clusters, the writer needs to understand the importance of interrupting his sequence of argumentative paragraphs in order to further emphasize a point he has just made. Suppose, for example, you are writing an essay on a serious social problem—say, heroin addiction among adolescents in our cities—and you begin the essay as follows:

> INTRODUCTION
> THESIS: Heroin addiction among urban adolescents is far more serious than we have been led to believe. It is having a devastating effect on young people in our inner cities.
> ARGUMENTATIVE POINT 1: Young people's use of heroin has led to a staggering increase in urban crime and that, in turn, has created a crisis in the lives of many adolescents. (The paragraph goes on to present evidence to support this assertion and discusses it.)

Having argued that first point, you now face a choice. In the simplest additive structure you could move onto your next argumentative point. But in order to consolidate what you have just argued, you could introduce an *illustrative paragraph* to provide a detailed example of what you have just been talking about. Such a paragraph would not advance the argument (by introducing something new), but it would put a human face on the facts you have presented in the first paragraph of your argument.

INTRODUCTION

THESIS: Heroin addiction among urban adolescents
is far more serious than we have been led to believe.
It is having a devastating effect on young people in our
inner cities.

ARGUMENTATIVE POINT 1: Young people's use of heroin has led
to a staggering increase in urban crime and that, in turn, has
created a crisis in the lives of many adolescents.

ILLUSTRATION PARAGRAPH: Consider, for example, the life of
Henry Tyler and his sister Alyma, both teenage residents of
the north-east section of the city. (The paragraph goes on to
describe details of Henry's and Alyma's life.)

In the illustrative paragraph you would provide evocative descriptive detail of these teenagers' experience (a brief case study, if you
will), in order to underscore vividly the point you have been previously arguing. In other words, the first stage of your argument
is a paragraph cluster of two paragraphs: the first establishes the
argumentative point and offers statistical evidence, and the second provides a detailed example or illustration. You will have
added depth to the argument by supplementing the evidence of
the first paragraph with particular examples of the issues as they
affect named human beings in the second.

6.8 | Organizing Paragraph Clusters

There are a number of ways a writer can organize his argument in
paragraph clusters. The following sections illustrate some of the
options available.

6.8.1 | Inserting a Detailed Illustration or
Example into the Argument

As we have just seen in Section 6.7.2 above, a really useful way of
making an essay more interesting and bringing it closer to the

reader is to stop the argument somewhere in the middle to dwell in detail upon a single specific illustration or example.

Suppose, for example, you are writing an argumentative interpretation of a work of literature or an artistic style. You have made one or two argumentative points. You might now insert into the argument a detailed look at one particular passage from the text or at a single painting, something that will illustrate the points you have been making.

Essay A
(The opening two paragraphs discuss T.S. Eliot's use of Romantic irony in "The Love Song of J. Alfred Prufrock.") ILLUSTRATION PARAGRAPH: The impact of this technique is clear enough if we take a close look at the following lines in the poem: (The paragraph offers a quotation from the poem and a detailed analysis of this one passage in order to emphasize points made earlier about Eliot's use of Romantic irony.)

Essay B
(The opening paragraph of the argument discusses the significant features of Alfons Mucha's Art Nouveau style.) ILLUSTRATION PARAGRAPH: These characteristics of the new style are clearly present in many of Mucha's famous posters. Consider, for example, the following advertisement. (The paragraph offers a reproduction of a poster and discusses in detail how it illustrates the points made in the previous paragraph.)

Similarly, as we have seen, in the middle of an argument about a social issue you can often provide a useful illustration:

Essay C
(The opening paragraph of the argument discusses why the North American Free Trade Agreement [NAFTA]

has had deleterious effects on the local economy of many communities.)

ILLUSTRATION PARAGRAPH: We can appreciate what these grim statistics really mean to our communities by looking at what happened in the once-prosperous middle-class town of Podunk. (The paragraph illustrates the problems discussed in the previous paragraph by focusing on a single example.)

Illustrative paragraphs are extremely useful in any essay interpreting the style of a literary or artistic work (as in the examples Essay A and Essay B above), because they enable (and require) the writer to move from a consideration of matters of importance in the style generally to a very close look at a particular part of the text.

Here are a few more examples in outline of illustrative paragraphs.

Example A

(From an essay arguing that Descartes' skepticism is flawed but nonetheless extremely useful)

ARGUMENTATIVE POINT 1: Descartes' argument creates difficulties when he tries to connect the "proven" world of the mind with the external world of the body. (The paragraph describes and discusses the difficulties.)

ILLUSTRATIVE PARAGRAPH: To illustrate this problem, consider the following passage in detail. (A detailed examination of a particular spot in Descartes' text which illustrates in his own argument the point made in the previous paragraph.)

ARGUMENTATIVE POINT 2: This difficulty aside, however, we need to note the great strength of Descartes' logic in approaching questions of knowledge in this way: his skeptical approach discourages us from acting on unjustified beliefs. (Argument resumes on the next point.)

Example B

(From an essay arguing that the Chipko movement is a significant indication of the power of uneducated women to affect government policy)

ARGUMENTATIVE POINT 1: The Chipko movement won popular support among a wide variety of women because it addressed their concerns directly. (The paragraph goes on to discuss the appeal of the movement.)

ILLUSTRATIVE PARAGRAPH: To appreciate this point more fully, we can examine the case of Gaura Devi. (The paragraph goes on to illustrate the point in the previous paragraph by a particular case study of a single woman involved.)

ARGUMENTATIVE POINT 2: But the movement was significant for reasons other than its popularity. (The paragraph resumes the argument with the next point.)

Example C

(From an essay arguing that Thoreau's *Walden* exemplifies a distinctly American form of Romanticism)

ARGUMENTATIVE POINT 1: Thoreau's attitude to nature is clearly what we might characterize as intensely Romantic and spiritual. (The paragraph goes on to explain what these terms mean with reference to Thoreau's *Walden*.)

ILLUSTRATION PARAGRAPH: This point is made over and over again in Thoreau's text. The following passage brings out eloquently his characteristically intense sense of the spiritual value of the woods around his house. (The paragraph goes on to examine in detail a particular example.)

ARGUMENTATIVE POINT 2: But there's more to his views than this. For there is also a shrewd Yankee element at work in his imagination which sees things from a different perspective. (The paragraph goes on to consider the next point.)

ILLUSTRATION PARAGRAPH: This quality is nowhere more evident than in Thoreau's attitude to the railway.

(The paragraph goes on to illustrate the point of the previous paragraph by examining a single passage dealing with the railway.)

Example D
(In an essay arguing that a particular legal judgement was correct)
ARGUMENTATIVE POINT 1: An important principle, crucial to the plaintiff's case, was the controversial issue of family assets. (Paragraph goes on to discuss why this was important.)
ILLUSTRATIVE PARAGRAPH: The significance of this point emerged clearly in the summing up of one of the judges, in the following remarks. (Paragraph goes on in detail to examine one portion of the remarks of one judge, a close reading of part of his judgement.)
ARGUMENTATIVE POINT 2: Another determining factor in the judgement was the definition of work on the farm. (Paragraph resumes the argument with a new point.)

Notice again in these examples how the illustrative paragraph works. It follows a paragraph which is making an argumentative assertion and serves to provide an in-depth analysis of a particular section of the text, of a case study, or of a personal example. The illustrative paragraph thus does not advance an argument, for it is introducing nothing new. Its purpose is to consolidate a point already made, to make sure that the reader understands the point by being confronted with a detailed look at a specific example.

It is possible to use more than one illustrative paragraph to consolidate a point. This is particularly common in essays which are interpreting an aspect of a work of literature such as style, character, or imagery, or any essay that requires you to take a very close look at a particular text. Notice the following example.

ARGUMENTATIVE POINT 1: Nora's behaviour constantly suggests that she is a very self-centred person, interested only in herself. (The paragraph goes on to argue this point, using small pieces of evidence.)

ILLUSTRATIVE PARAGRAPH: We can see this aspect of her character very clearly in her first conversation with Mrs. Linde. (The paragraph gives a detailed look at parts of this scene.)

ILLUSTRATIVE PARAGRAPH: Another place where Nora's egocentricity manifests itself is the curious scene in which she and Dr. Rank discuss her silk stockings. (The paragraph goes on to show how parts of this scene illuminate the point introduced two paragraphs before.)

ARGUMENTATIVE POINT 2: But there is considerably more to Nora than this self-centredness. For she is a genuinely intelligent and courageous person striving to deal with an intractable problem. (The paragraph goes on to discuss the next point.)

An illustrative paragraph is also a convenient place to provide a summary of research studies which endorse a position you have already introduced into the argument, a useful step in an essay in which you are expected to demonstrate that you have conducted a significant amount of reading in secondary sources. Here is the outline of an example:

ARGUMENTATIVE POINT: The Warren Commission into the assassination of President Kennedy was particularly cavalier about answering some pertinent questions arising out of evidence provided by the analysis of ballistics experts. (The paragraph goes on to discuss this point.)

ILLUSTRATION PARAGRAPH: Many other studies by academics and lay experts have reached the same conclusion. (This paragraph provides a survey of some of the studies into the question discussed in the previous paragraph.)

Notice in this example that the second paragraph is not advancing the argument; it is, by contrast, reinforcing a point already made in the first paragraph by adding a good deal of scholarly weight to the writer's argument.

Illustrative paragraphs do not have to be based on a real person or place. Sometimes you can supplement your argument by making up a detailed case study to illustrate a point you have been making. Suppose, for example, you are presenting an argument about the growing debt crisis among university graduates who have had to take out massive student loans. You have given a survey of the numbers and now want your reader to understand what those numbers mean in a particular case. Well, you could choose real people and outline their situations, but you could equally well focus on one you have made up yourself.

> To appreciate how acute this problem is, consider the following hypothetical case of a student I will call Terry, whose student loans and debt load reflect what are rapidly becoming normal practices…. (The paragraph goes on to describe "Terry's" situation in order to illustrate in a personal way the growing problem.)

While using illustrative paragraphs like this really illuminates an argumentative point, you should be careful not to overuse the technique. Once the point has been illustrated, the argument is not usually helped by multiplying illustrations unnecessarily, since that tends to turn large sections of the essay into a mere list of examples.

6.8.2 | Acknowledging Alternative Arguments

One of the most useful, persuasive, and sophisticated techniques for amplifying an argumentative point is incorporating into it a position which does not agree with the thesis you are presenting (or which provides an alternative view). Notice the following sample outline:

GENERAL SUBJECT: Pollution

FOCUS 1: Industrial Pollution

FOCUS 2: Industrial Pollution in the Fraser River

THESIS: We must act immediately to deal effectively with industrial pollution in the Fraser River. If we fail to do this, we will soon have no fishing available there for native bands, tourists, or commercial fishers.

TS 1: Many people do not have the faintest idea just how seriously the present levels of industrial pollution are threatening the sustainability of salmon populations in the Fraser River. (The paragraph launches the argument by presenting evidence to argue that the present situation is critical.)

TS 2: According to many spokespeople, the cost of doing anything effective about this problem is prohibitive; we simply cannot afford the sorts of measures that will significantly affect the problem for the better. (The paragraph presents an argument opposing the thesis of the essay.)

TS 3: But these views about the expense of addressing this issue seriously misrepresent the problem and the real costs involved. (The paragraph answers the objection raised in the previous paragraph.)

TS 4: Besides, we cannot afford to quibble about the price; what we stand to lose is priceless. (The paragraph resumes the argument with the next argumentative point.)

Notice that in this essay, which is arguing that we must do something right away about a particular environmental problem, the organization makes room in the second paragraph of the main body (TS 2) for an opposing point of view. The argument is here going to call attention to something that people who oppose the thesis will bring up (i.e., the essay is *acknowledging an alternative argument*).

Notice, too, that in the paragraph immediately following

this introduction of an alternative argument, the writer answers that point; in other words, the paragraph counters the opposition's point. He has introduced the counterargument in order to refute it or to display its weaknesses.

Here are some more examples of this technique. Note how the second outline uses the technique twice in a row.

Essay A
GENERAL SUBJECT: Criminal Justice System
FOCUS 1: Capital punishment
THESIS: There is no acceptable reason why any state should punish a criminal with death. Capital punishment should be universally illegal.
TS 1: The first cogent argument against capital punishment is that it does not deter future crimes of violence.
(The paragraph establishes the first argumentative point.)
TS 2: Supporters of capital punishment often point to the enormous expense of keeping murderers incarcerated for years, arguing that this is an unnecessary expense.
(The paragraph introduces an alternative argument, one arguing against the thesis.)
TS 3: However, this cost analysis is seriously misleading. (The paragraph answers the alternative argument in the previous paragraph.)
TS 4: Moreover, there is always the horrible possibility that an innocent party will be convicted of a capital offence and executed. (The paragraph argues the next point.)

Essay B
GENERAL SUBJECT: Machiavelli's *Prince*
FOCUS 1: The *Prince* as a satire
THESIS: The best way to make sense of this often puzzling work is to accept that it is, first and foremost, a satire attacking the very things that Machiavelli seems to be endorsing.

TS 1: The most obvious suggestions of a satiric intention emerge from the words of moral approval and disapproval Machiavelli inserts into the argument. (The paragraph introduces the first point in defence of the thesis.)

TS 2: A number of writers, among them James Johnson, ignore or downplay these satiric possibilities and argue instead that Machiavelli's recommendations are to be taken quite literally as a hard-headed expression of the amoral realities of political life. (The paragraph introduces and reviews an alternative argument challenging the thesis of the essay.)

TS 3: Such an interpretation, however, is difficult to sustain. (Paragraph answers the alternative argument.)

TS 4: Some of those who take Machiavelli's language literally argue that he is, in fact, a utilitarian advocating a firm moral position. (The paragraph introduces and summarizes a second alternative argument.)

TS 5: This view that Machiavelli is a utilitarian is interesting but ultimately unpersuasive. (The paragraph answers the alternative argument presented in the previous paragraph.)

TS 6: The satiric possibilities of the text also manifest themselves in many of Machiavelli's historical examples. (The paragraph advances a new argumentative point to advance the thesis.)

Notice that when you are answering an alternative argument you do not have to dismiss it out of hand. You can, for example, acknowledge that the point of view is interesting or has some merit (as in TS 5 in the last of the above examples), before you move on to explain why it is nonetheless unsatisfactory or inadequate.

This technique of admitting into the argument opposing or alternative opinions so that you can answer them is very useful for a number of reasons. It is a way to respond to certain arguments that are likely to form in the reader's mind as she proceeds through your essay. It also shows the reader that you are aware of views different from your own and are prepared to meet them. As such, it really helps to enhance the persuasiveness of your case. Such a technique is particularly helpful in essays where you are encouraged or required to do a certain amount of research and incorporate that research into your argument, a very common requirement of History essays, for example, or any essays where you have to offer a review and an evaluation of what a number of other people have said about a particular issue.

Acknowledging alternative arguments in this way is not always necessary or possible, but it is almost always strongly advisable when you are dealing with a topic that is well known as disputatious and for which there are recognizably different interpretative possibilities. In long papers where you are expected to incorporate a great deal of research material, such a technique is usually essential (because it enables you to review and deal with a range of scholarly studies of the issue you are dealing with). Such a structural technique is almost always required, too, if you are writing an argument and there is an obvious objection or challenge to the position you are advancing, one so obvious that the reader of your essay will be expecting you to deal with it (for example, an essay arguing against the death penalty will almost certainly have to deal with the claim that capital punishment is necessary because it deters certain crimes). Your argument will be far less persuasive if you simply avoid the point.

As a result, when you are organizing an essay, and especially when you are dealing with a long argument in a research paper, ask yourself the following question: "What are the most important points someone who does not agree with my thesis is likely to bring up against my position?" If there are such opposing arguments, you might think about acknowledging one or more of them in the essay in the above manner. And when you are conducting your research, remain alert to such arguments; do not simply discard them because they do not support the thesis you are advancing.

However, if you are going to apply this structural technique in an argument, make sure you observe the following principles. Otherwise you may end up weakening your case.

1. Make sure that the counterargument you introduce is significant and that you represent it fairly. Do not create the logical fallacy of a *straw-figure argument*; that is, do not set up a simplistic, trivial, fictional, or obviously erroneous point just so that you can knock it down.

2. Where possible identify the source of the counterargument by naming a person or study advancing that view. Avoid rather weak phrases such as "Some people claim …," "There is also the view that …," and so on, unless you are going to identify the source more precisely later on.

3. Do not introduce the opposing point of view unless you are prepared to answer it in the paragraph immediately following. Obviously you cannot end the essay with a view opposing your own, so you have to make room in the essay for a proper reply to your opponent. Since a short essay has relatively few argumentative paragraphs, the technique is not nearly so common there as in a longer paper, where you have room to use it repeatedly.

4. Do not introduce the opposing viewpoint unless you really can answer it convincingly. If you end up making an opponent's case sound much more logical and persuasive than your own, then the purpose of the technique is defeated. This does not mean that you have to demolish a counterargument. It is quite all right to acknowledge that the counterargument has some value (if you think it does), but in your answer to it you have to show why your viewpoint is preferable.

6.8.3 | *Introducing Analogies*

You can often amplify an argumentative point by introducing after it a paragraph dealing with a comparison or an analogy that either reinforces the point you have just made or offers a contrast to it. Notice the following example:

> *Essay A*
> (on *Macbeth*)
> ARGUMENTATIVE POINT 1: A particularly significant aspect of Macbeth's character emerges from his response to the first prophecy of the witches. His imagination evidently cannot resist the prospect of becoming king. (The paragraph discusses this point by exploring Macbeth's speeches about the witches.)
> COMPARISON PARAGRAPH: One way of appreciating this aspect of Macbeth's character is to compare Banquo's reaction to the same prophecy. He, too, is clearly fascinated by what the future may hold, but he checks his imagination from drifting too far. (The paragraph looks closely at Banquo's response to the witches' prophecy, comparing it with Macbeth's.)

The first paragraph is an argumentative claim about Macbeth's character. The second invites the reader to compare that aspect of Macbeth's character with the response of another character in the same play. The purpose of that second paragraph is to clarify and underscore the claim made in the previous paragraph by providing a contrasting example.

Here are two other examples:

> *Essay B*
> (On the need to curb municipal spending in Seattle)
> ARGUMENTATIVE POINT 1: One important step we need to undertake is to reduce our enormously expensive

commitment to providing generous pensions to
municipal employees.

COMPARISON PARAGRAPH: Consider, for example, the dire situation in which Detroit finds itself, largely as a result of public
service pensions. (The paragraph reviews how public service
pensions contributed to the bankruptcy in Detroit.)

Essay C
(On the need to legalize certain drugs)
ARGUMENTATIVE POINT 1: Our attempts to curtail the use of
illegal drugs with harsh laws have been counterproductive.
They are producing more serious problems than the one
they are attempting to solve.

COMPARISON PARAGRAPH: The situation is not unlike the
notorious experiment with Prohibition, a disastrous
attempt to make alcoholic drinks illegal. (The paragraph
establishes a comparison between Prohibition and present
drug legislation in order to emphasize the futility of
both endeavours.)

Such comparisons and analogies are often useful for illuminating
an argument and reinforcing a point you have made earlier. But
there are some things to be careful about.

1. Never introduce a comparison unless you are well informed
    about the details of the example you are calling attention
    to and are prepared to defend the similarity between the
    two things being compared. The argument will suffer if the
    reader fails to see the similarity and sees only differences.
    This is particularly true if you are going to use historical
    analogies (e.g., "What is going on in the Ukraine today is just
    like the earlier situation in Kosovo").

2. Be very careful of extreme analogies, that is, bringing into
    the argument an example of something so extraordinary

that the comparison is suspect. For example, be extremely cautious about comparing anything with Nazi Germany's treatment of the Jews. That may be rhetorically powerful, but unless the situation you are describing is as horrific as the original event, the analogy simply indicates to the reader that you do not understand what you are talking about or are exaggerating wildly for the sake of it.

3. In general, stick to analogies which bring together things which are, indeed, very similar. No two situations are identical, and sometimes in a careless comparison the differences will undermine its effectiveness (for example, in Essay B above, someone might argue that the situation in Seattle is not at all like the one in Detroit and therefore the argument is suspect). In an argument that the high salaries of NBA players are spoiling the game, you might want to make an analogy with what is happening with high salaries in the NFL. Those situations are close enough to make the comparison carry some persuasive weight. But if the analogy involved, say, the Premier League (PL) football teams in the United Kingdom, then the obvious differences between the NFL and PL might diminish the effectiveness of the comparison. Similarly, if you are arguing about an educational issue in Oregon, you might want to draw an analogy with what is happening in, say, Washington State or California, rather than moving too far away (e.g., to a European country, where the education situation is very different).

4. If you are not sure whether to introduce an analogy or not, you probably should leave it out. Analogies are not all that persuasive most of the time, and if they are stretched or inappropriate they weaken the argument. If there's any doubt that the reader might not see or might challenge the similarity between the two cases, then you might have to argue it.

For example, if you wanted to make the argument that the prohibition of alcohol was just like the prohibition of narcotics, then you might have to make that point in detail, rather than just assuming that the reader sees it clearly.

6.8.4 | Paragraphs of Narration, Description, and Definition

We have already talked about using paragraphs of narration, description, and definition as part of the introduction to the argument. Sometimes it is preferable to hold back on such background information until the appropriate point in the argument (i.e., when the reader first needs it). In other words, instead of giving the reader right at the start of the argument all the background facts he is going to need to understand every part of your argument, you reserve some of the information that you might put in the essay as part of the introduction and insert it where it is first needed.

Suppose, for example, you are writing an essay on a particular environmental issue and, halfway through the essay you wish to point out that a proposed course of action violates the Precautionary Principle (something you have not mentioned so far). You cannot assume that all your readers will be familiar with the term, as they need to be in order to understand this stage of your argument. At that point, you should interrupt the argument and in a new paragraph define the term in detail. Then you can resume your argument.

Similarly, if you are creating an argument on a historical event, you may need to interrupt the argument in order to supply some background information about a particular person or place you are now going to discuss. Here is an example of such an insertion into the middle of an argument. Here the thesis of the essay is that the death of Alexander the Great precipitated a crisis that transformed the Hellenistic world. The introductory paragraphs have been omitted.

ARGUMENTATIVE POINT 1: The first crisis provoked by the unexpected death of Alexander in 323 BCE was confusion in the leadership of the Macedonian armies, largely because the traditional method of determining a successor did not work. (The paragraph argues this point.)

DESCRIPTIVE DEFINITION: Of all the generals who rose to sudden prominence at this juncture one of the most interesting was Ptolemy, son of Lagus. His association with Alexander went back many years. (The paragraph goes on to give biographical details of Ptolemy; it is not advancing the argument, but it is making sure that the reader has the necessary background details to understand who Ptolemy was.)

DESCRIPTIVE DEFINITION: Ptolemy's immediate response to the crisis was a decision that the most important part of the Empire was Egypt. At the time, Egypt.... (The paragraph goes on to describe some background details of Egypt; here again, it is not continuing the argument, but it is providing necessary background details.)

ARGUMENTATIVE POINT 2: To gain this prized territory, Ptolemy carried out a bold, aggressive, and successful military strategy. (The paragraph resumes the argument by trying to persuade the reader that Ptolemy's tactics were bold, aggressive, and effective.)

Pay close attention to what is going on here in the second and third paragraphs above. The writer has stopped the argument to provide background information: in the first, some biographical details of Ptolemy, in the second, some geographical and economic facts about Egypt. Once these have been dealt with, the essay resumes the argument.

This is an important and useful technique, especially in longer research papers. You should use it with care, however, making sure that you introduce only narrative or geographical or analytical details essential to the argument. Do not use it simply to pad the essay (i.e., to add irrelevant material).

Here is another example from an essay arguing that we should not be developing any more nuclear reactors to cope with our energy needs.

> ARGUMENTATIVE POINT 1: The major danger of a reactor is, of course, the risk of something going dreadfully wrong, either from a malfunction in the reactor, a natural disaster, or a terrorist attack. (The paragraph argues about the dangers.) DESCRIPTIVE DEFINITION: We also need to remember that a nuclear reactor produces radioactive waste products. These are an unavoidable part of the process itself. (The paragraph goes on to explain briefly how a reactor produces such waste; this section is not continuing the argument but making sure that everyone understands how the waste product is produced and what the waste product is.)
>
> The fact that nuclear reactors produce potentially harmful waste that is difficult to dispose of is another serious problem. (The paragraph resumes the argument by discussing how disposing of waste products is an important reason for not building any more nuclear reactors.)

In the above paragraph cluster, the second paragraph interrupts the argument to provide an analytical description and definition, so that the reader has a clear sense of what that phrase *nuclear waste* means. Once that is taken care of, the argument resumes.

6.8.5 | Setting Up a Narrative or Descriptive "Hook"

In a longer paper, you can sometimes add variety and interest to the paper by starting with a narrative or descriptive paragraph which draws attention to a particular example in a graphic way and enables you to lead into the introduction after you have seized the reader's attention.

Notice the following example; these are the opening paragraphs to an essay on acid rain (the example is fictional, here to illustrate the style):

Paha Lake is situated about fifteen miles north of Laketown in a beautiful forest. The lake, about ten miles long and half a mile across at its widest, is justly celebrated as one of the most beautiful in the entire region, with moderately steep sides of granite interspersed with lower regions often covered with wild flowers. There are many places on the lake which make good natural campgrounds providing easy access to the water and panoramic views of the much of the shoreline. A visitor today also notices immediately the wonderful clarity of the water, which seems to catch the sun in unusual ways and, when the light is at the right angle, to shimmer invitingly. Only gradually does one get the sense that there is something odd about the scene. At first, there no clear indication what that might be. And then one realizes—there are no birds around, none of the usual crowd of gulls or loons or ducks. And there are no other people, no avid fishers out for a weekend's adventure. And then the reason dawns: Paha Lake is a dead lake. Its waters support no life at all, because Paha Lake has become one more victim of a silent killer of our forests, acid rain.

There are many Paha Lakes in Northern Lakeland, and their number is increasing every year. Where only a few decades ago, in a single afternoon one could catch one's limit of pike, pickerel, lake trout, or bass, there are now no fish at all. The water is too acidic to sustain life. We have all heard about this problem, of course, and we probably know about some of the steps various governments and industries have taken to meet it. What we may not realize as urgently as we should is how serious the problem still is and how quickly it is growing in Northern Lakeland. In fact, it seems evident that if we do nothing more against the threat than we are presently doing, huge areas of our nation may soon have no fresh water fish; the life which those fish sustain will then leave; and sooner or later the acidic waters will destroy much of the forest life. It is thus imperative that we make dealing with the causes of acid rain in our northern forest a top priority, no matter what the economic cost.

Notice here how the first paragraph does not introduce any argument. It serves to catch the reader's attention with an example. The point of the example is not revealed until the last line. Then the writer moves directly into the introductory paragraph, which announces the subject, focus, and thesis. Such an opening paragraph could equally well be a short narrative, designed to arouse the reader's interest, before the main introduction.

This technique of opening an argument with an illustration or narrative is very common in journalism, where the technique is known as the hook. In many essays you do not have the space to try it, but in longer research papers, you might want to experiment with such an opening.

If you are going to use a narrative or descriptive hook, then make sure you observe the following principles:

1. The hook should not be too long. You should be able to present it in a single paragraph. If the hook starts getting too long, it will overwhelm the introduction.

2. Try to structure the hook so that the main point of the illustration or narrative does not emerge until the very end (as in the above example). That makes it inherently more interesting. The technique loses much of its effect if the reader gets the point of the example in the very first or second sentence.

3. Follow the hook immediately with the standard introduction in which you announce the subject, focus, and thesis of the essay in the usual manner (as in the above example).

4. Do not provide more than one narrative or illustrative hook. If you have a number of examples, select the best one. Remember the purpose of this technique is to arouse the reader's interest, not to carry any of the argument.

6.9 | Guiding the Reader through a Paragraph Cluster

If you keep these possibilities in mind, then you can appreciate how organizing an argumentative essay involves a series of decisions about what you want to do, stage by stage in the argument: What exactly do I wish to argue in this essay? Do I need to provide any initial background (definitions, descriptions, narratives)? How do I wish to start the argument? Once I have that first argumentative paragraph, do I want to offer a detailed illustration, a comparison, an alternative argument, additional background, or something else, or do I wish to continue the argument with the next point? Is what I want to do now an important contribution to the argument, or am I digressing into something unnecessary?

Once you have made these decisions, it is vitally important you inform the reader of what you are now intending to do. Normally you will do that in the opening sentence of the paragraph. Do not just plunge into the task you wish to perform in the paragraph without giving the reader a clear indication of where the essay is now going.

Notice, for example, how the following opening sentences accomplish this task.

1. We can appreciate the severity of these problems by looking closely at what happened in Harrisburg, Pennsylvania.

(This announces we are now about to read a specific example of the issue discussed in the previous paragraph.)

2. The critic P.D. Harding has offered an alternative explanation for this phenomenon. (This announces that the paragraph is going to discuss an alternative viewpoint, something challenging the argument made in the previous paragraph.)

3. Before advancing this argument, it is important to clarify just what I mean by the term Romantic irony. (This sentence alerts the reader that this paragraph is offering a key definition.)

4. These criticisms, however, are all ill-founded. (The paragraph is going to refute or challenge the alternative viewpoint offered in the previous paragraph.)

5. What is Ritalin exactly and what condition is it supposed to treat? (The question introduces a paragraph that will define Ritalin and discuss why it is prescribed.)

6. A second serious problem exacerbated by these new voter identification laws is that they further disenfranchise many poor people. (Paragraph is resuming the argument with a new point.)

The important principle here is that you must inform the reader early in the paragraph (normally in the opening topic sentence) about what you are now doing. Do not expect her to understand what is happening if you do not tell her.

6.9.1 | An Example

Here is a sample outline for a longer essay. Notice how the writer has organized her argument in paragraph clusters, how she has indicated the function of each paragraph in the opening sentence, and how, in that opening sentence, as well as announcing the topic of the paragraph, she has also alerted the reader to the direction the argument is now taking.

RESEARCH PAPER: Modern Medicine and the Law
SUBJECT: Modern Medicine
FOCUS 1: The Terminally Ill
FOCUS 2: The Right to Die by Assisted Suicide
Thesis: We should not alter the legislation concerning assisted suicides, and we should certainly not press for any legislation which might confer on citizens what has been called the "right to die."
TS 1: What exactly do people mean when they encourage us to demand the right to die or the right to die with dignity or the right to an assisted suicide? (The paragraph goes on to define in detail a key element in the argument, so that everyone will share the same idea of what the "right to die" phrase means, at least for the purposes of this argument.)
TS 2: We also need to clarify what the term *right* means in law. Many of those demanding the right to die seem unaware of the legal meaning of what they are seeking. (The paragraph goes on to define the concept of a legal right.)
TS 3: Given this legal meaning of the term *right*, many doctors are justifiably worried about conferring the right to die on citizens generally. (The argument starts here by showing how any change in the law will make the situation difficult for doctors.)
TS 4: In addition, there is the problem of what has been called the "slippery slope." Once we admit legal killing into our hospitals openly, then where will that process end? (The paragraph argues a second point in support of the thesis.)
TS 5: Many people, however, are not convinced by these arguments. They believe that citizens should have the right to die with dignity. (The paragraph here acknowledges

a counterargument by reviewing one view of those who would not support the thesis.)

TS 6: Supporters of this position often cite the case of Sue Rodriguez, a terminally ill woman whose case was decided by the Supreme Court. (The paragraph goes on to provide an illustration of the opposition's point by giving details of a single well-known example.)

TS 7: But Sue Rodriguez lost her legal battle, and for good reason. The Supreme Court justices were quite correct in their assessment. (Paragraph uses some details of the legal judgement to support the thesis and answer the counterargument above.)

TS 8: But many do not agree with this court decision. They point to the example of Holland, where assisted suicide is legal. (Paragraph gives the opposition another hearing, this time using a comparison from another country.)

TS 9: Those who make this argument, however, overlook some of the problems with this policy that the Dutch themselves have acknowledged. (Paragraph answers the opposition's point in the previous paragraph.)

TS 10: Any legal right to an assisted suicide will place undue pressure on the many terminally ill patients who do not have the resources they need to make an independent, informed decision. (The paragraph presents a final argumentative point.)

TS 11: Consider for example, the case of Alice Brown. (The paragraph provides a close look at a particular example in order to consolidate the point made in the previous paragraph.)

TS 12: Concluding paragraph, summing up the argument and looking ahead.

The important point to notice in this outline is the way in which the writer uses a mixture of paragraph functions: argumentative paragraphs advancing the thesis, paragraphs acknowledging a counterargument, paragraphs providing illustrations, definitions, comparisons. These papers will be quite long, but they do not make a great number of different points. However, they really go into detail about the points which they do mention.

Here, for example, are sample outlines for two essays both on the same topic and making the same argument with the same points. The first, however, is considerably shorter than the second.

Essay A

THESIS: The theory of evolution is a firmly established scientific truth—every bit as true as Newton's Theory of Universal Gravitation.

TS 1: First, let me explain what I mean by the term *evolution*. (The paragraph defines the concept central to the argument.)

TS 2: The proof of evolution starts with the widely acknowledged fact that life must come from life (i.e., life cannot spontaneously emerge from non-living material).

TS 3: The second point is that we know that some animal and plant species now alive on earth were not present here in past ages.

TS 4: Now, if we put the two previous assertions together— that life must come from life and that some species now alive on earth were not there in past ages—then the conclusion is obvious: the animal and plant species now alive must have come from species unlike them (i.e., they must have evolved).

CONCLUSION

Essay B

THESIS: The theory of evolution is a firmly established scientific truth—every bit as true as Newton's Theory of Universal Gravitation.

TS 1: First, let me explain what I mean by the term *evolution*. (The paragraph defines the concept central to the argument.)

TS 2: The proof of evolution starts with the widely acknowledged fact that life must come from life (i.e., life cannot spontaneously emerge from non-living material).
TS 3: A common objection to this claim is that, since we do not know how life first started and since it must have started from non-living material, then we are not entitled to assert that life must come from life. (The paragraph goes on to outline this alternative view.)
TS 4: This objection, however, is clearly spurious. (The paragraph goes on to argue this point, in order to answer the alternative view explored in the previous paragraph.)
TS 5: The second point is that we know that some animal and plant species now alive on earth were not present here in past ages. (The paragraph argues this point by discussing the fossil record.)
TS 6: A number of people have also challenged this point as well, arguing that the geological and fossil record is not a reliable indication that the world was created over a long period of time. (The paragraph presents another alternative view point.)
TS 7: However, this argument is hardly convincing because it rejects the most basic principles of geology and violates common-sense experience. (The paragraph answers the alternative viewpoint in the previous paragraph.)
TS 8: Moreover, how do those advocating the theory that the world and all living species were created in a matter of days or weeks account for the clear patterns of fossils in layers of sedimentary rock and the absence of any human fossils except in the most superficial layers? (The paragraph introduces a single illustration to discuss its criticisms of the alternative viewpoint presented in TS 6.)
TS 9: Now, if we put the two previous assertions together—that life must come from life and that some species now alive on earth were not there in past ages—then the

conclusion is obvious: the animal and plant species now alive must have come from species unlike them (i.e., they must have evolved).
CONCLUSION

The second essay will probably be more than twice as long as the first one, although the main argumentative points are the same. Essay B has amplified the argument, providing alternative viewpoints, responses to those viewpoints, and an illustration. Which organization the author chooses will depend upon the length of the essay he wishes to write.

I include this example to point out that longer essays do not necessarily need a great many more argumentative points than smaller ones—not if they concentrate on organizing the argument in paragraph clusters and on deepening the argument, rather than just adding more argumentative points.

7.0

Paragraph Structure

Up to this point we have been concentrating on the overall logic of an argument (the introduction and the sequence of paragraphs). The emphasis has been on developing a clear logical framework for the argument, in the form of a detailed outline, so that you and the reader know from the start the central claim of the essay and can easily follow the way in which each paragraph contributes to that argument.

If you can now formulate a focus, thesis, and sequence of topic sentences, then your essay will have a logical framework. What you are trying to achieve and how you are proposing to structure the essay will be perfectly clear. No matter what you write further, if you stick to the outline you have proposed and if it is a good one, the reader will understand the purpose and direction of the argument. Now, we must turn to the specific details of the argument that will help you turn that framework into a convincing essay.

7.1 | Argumentative Paragraphs in the Main Body of the Essay

Argumentative paragraphs are those which advance new points in the argument (as opposed to illustrative or definition or comparison or counterargument paragraphs, which amplify or clarify argumentative points). The argumentative paragraph will be either a deductive argument, an inductive argument, or a combination, and the structure of the paragraph will reflect the structure of the argument being made in that paragraph. Here, we will discuss two common and useful methods of structuring argumentative paragraphs: paragraphs that establish a common and agreed-upon general principle or shared truth and apply that to a specific case, and paragraphs that reach a conclusion by means of evidence, such as facts, research data, or quotations from the text.

Here are two examples of paragraphs taken from the main body of an argument against capital punishment. Each has a clear topic sentence, and each conducts the reader to a conclusion that reinforces the point made in the topic sentence. Notice that the first reaches its conclusion by applying general principles to a specific case, while the second reaches its conclusion by providing and interpreting evidence.

Sample Paragraph A

The first compelling argument against capital punishment is that it is morally indefensible. If we consider the argument from a Christian standpoint, we have the prohibition on killing in the Ten Commandments. In addition, we learn from the Bible that vengeance belongs to the Lord. However we describe capital punishment, it clearly involves killing another human being and, in many cases, assuming responsibility for avenging the death of someone else. From the point of view of secular human rights, too, it is widely acknowledged that the death penalty violates fundamental human rights, for the deliberate taking of a human life, especially in circumstances where the person killed is defenceless against the invincible power of the state and where the state's action constitutes cruel and unusual punishment, is morally wrong. It may well be that our feelings are often outraged at the particular barbarity of the original murder, that the guilt of the murderer is beyond doubt, that he or she shows no signs of remorse, and that society incurs a considerable cost by incarcerating a murderer for life—all that may be true. None of it, however, removes from us the awareness that for a group of rational human beings to sanction ritual state killing of an individual, especially when there is no immediate threat to any other individual or to the state collectively, is never morally justifiable.

Sample Paragraph B

The argument that we need capital punishment in order to reduce the cost of maintaining the penal system is misplaced. There is no evidence that executing criminals will save us money. Quite the reverse is true: having the death penalty in place imposes massive additional costs upon the state. For example, according to a 2008 report from the *California Commission for the Fair Administration of Justice*, in California the existing system with the death penalty cost roughly 137 million dollars per year; it would cost 11.5 million dollars without it. A study by the Urban Institute (2008) revealed that in Maryland death penalty cases cost three times more than non-death-penalty cases. A study by Philip J. Cook (2009), an economist from Duke University, concluded that if North Carolina dropped the death penalty, the state would save 11 million dollars per year. Moreover, study after study reveals that, as Amnesty International reports, "The greatest costs associated with the death penalty occur prior to and during trial, not in post-conviction proceedings. Even if all post-conviction proceedings (appeals) were abolished, the death penalty would still be more expensive than alternative sentences." One doesn't have to read very many of these studies (and there are plenty of them) to realize that if we really want to save money in our prison system or allocate it more usefully, we should get rid of capital punishment immediately.

Both of these paragraphs are opposing capital punishment. The first appeals to agreed-upon principles, which it applies to the example of capital punishment. The second presents information, data, and statistics gathered by research.

Notice that each paragraph begins with a clear topic sentence which announces the opinion being presented in the paragraph, and each finishes by bringing the reader back to that opinion. Moreover, each paragraph is substantial, more than 200 words, and deals with the point thoroughly.

7.1.1 | *Paragraphs Arguing from General Principles*

A paragraph arguing from general principles will normally follow the most obvious outline of such arguments:

> TOPIC SENTENCE (asserting the argumentative claim);
> [FIRST ESTABLISHED TRUTH]: Since we agree that this principle or this fact is true ... [SECOND ESTABLISHED TRUTH] and since we agree that this second fact is true, [CONCLUSION] then this conclusion follows.

So long as the writer follows this basic pattern and does not introduce anything irrelevant to the three-part argument, then the paragraph should remain unified and coherent. Here is an example of the above outline fleshed out into a paragraph:

> [TOPIC SENTENCE] The proposed law that will permit the recitation of prayers in the classrooms at the beginning of the school day in government-funded high schools in this state is unacceptable. [FIRST ESTABLISHED TRUTH] To begin with, the Establishment Clause of the First Amendment prohibits the government from enacting any legislation "respecting an establishment of religion" or from favouring one religion over another. This requirement has been repeatedly cited by the Supreme Court as a reason to strike down state laws requiring or permitting certain forms of prayer in public schools, even if participation by students is not mandatory: e.g., *Abington Township v. Schempp* (1963), *Wallace v. Jaffree* (1985), *Lee v. Weisman* (1992), among others. [SECOND ESTABLISHED TRUTH] Now, the legislation proposed by our state legislature explicitly requires schools to offer or to allow prayers and religious readings with a distinctly Christian emphasis in the school classroom and, so it appears, makes no provision in its list of recommended texts for prayers and readings by many other religious, spiritual, or secular groups (Muslims, Unitarians, Native Americans, Hindus, pagans, Wiccans, Satanists, or atheists, for example). [CONCLUSION] One does not need a law degree to recognize that the proposed legislation violates the First Amendment and goes against a long history of legal precedents. Thus, the State Assembly should withdraw the proposed law or vote it down.

Notice here how the writer first establishes in the opening sentence the opinion she is advancing (the topic of the paragraph). Then she appeals to the First Amendment as a principle we all agree with (or as an authority the readers, as citizens of the

United States, must defer to) and to a number of legal judgements interpreting that First Amendment. Then she describes certain features of the proposed legislation which establish its connection to First Amendment issues. And finally she draws a conclusion that re-emphasizes the opinion with which she began.

Here is another example of a paragraph that follows this structure:

> Dr. Williams's actions in this case raise serious ethical and legal questions. The confidentiality provisions established by the College of Physicians and Surgeons of Ontario clearly state that "A physician may not provide any information concerning the patient to a third party unless the patient or the patient's authorized representative consents to this disclosure, or the physician is required by law to disclose the information" (Policy Statement #5-05, published March/April 2006). In addition, according to Part III (Section 18.3) of the *Personal Health Information and Protection Act* (2004) "A consent to the disclosure of personal health information about an individual must be express, and not implied, if (a) a health information custodian makes the disclosure to a person that is not a health information custodian...." Now in this case, Dr. Williams was under no legal compulsion to reveal the information about Helen Jackson's medical condition to her employer, School District 68, and he never received permission from Helen Jackson or her authorized representative to do so. His claim that he thought Jackson might want him to convey the information to the school superintendent obviously does not meet the legal requirement that the patient's consent "must be express, and not implied." As a result, Dr. Williams's actions, however well intentioned, were clearly unethical and illegal.

The paragraph begins with a Topic Sentence introducing the argumentative point of the paragraph. It then appeals to two general principles—a policy of the College of Physicians and Surgeons of Ontario and a section of a provincial law. Then the argument considers how these general principles apply in the particular case under discussion and reaches a conclusion that echoes the claim made in the opening sentence.

Notice, incidentally, that the appeals to the general principles in the above arguments are *specific*: they identify the source of the principle and quote the wording. This makes the argument much more persuasive than something vague, like "The US Constitution obviously does not allow such a law" or "The doctor's conduct violates confidentiality provisions in the ethical and legal code physicians are expected to follow." As a general rule, if you are going to appeal to a principle of professional ethics, law, or right, you should follow a procedure like this and identify the source of the principle, law, or right you are appealing to and, in most cases, offer a quotation from an authoritative source providing a precise definition.

The most important danger in this type of argument, as I have already mentioned (in Section 2.8.3 above), is that the writer makes some logical error in combining the general principle and the details of the particular case (e.g., invoking the First Amendment in a case where that constitutional provision does not apply).

7.1.2 | *Paragraphs Providing and Interpreting Evidence*

Most of the argumentative paragraphs you write will resemble the second example in Section 7.1 above, that is, they will be presenting arguments based upon evidence. Thus, the strength of the argument is going to depend, in large part, on the nature of the evidence you present. No inductive argument which lacks reliable evidence will be persuasive.

Evidence comes from many places, depending upon the nature of the argument you are making. Here is a partial list of the principal sources:

1. In essays on literature (where you are arguing about the interpretation of a book), the evidence often comes almost entirely from the text of the work you are evaluating, that is, from the words on the page. In some essays, of course, you may have to introduce evidence from elsewhere (for example, if you are linking what is going on in the text with details of the author's life and times, you will be using factual evidence from biography and history).

2. Essays about films or the fine and performing arts normally get their evidence from what the work itself contains. For instance, a review of a film or musical performance usually focuses directly, often exclusively, on what people can actually see and hear in the film, play, ballet, recital, and so on, just as a review of a painting or an art exhibition will in most cases concentrate on what one can see in the works themselves. Once again, however, the essay may at times introduce into the essay biographical or historical evidence from beyond the work, if that is germane to the argument.

3. Evidence can also come from your own research, that is, from data you yourself have collected as part of field work (e.g., questionnaire results, field measurements, photographs, interviews, and so on) or experimental data you have collected in the laboratory.

4. Evidence also comes from secondary sources, that is, from books, articles, and reports about the subject you are discussing. This is particularly the case in social science and science arguments (like the second example in Section 7.1 above) and in research papers generally.

5. Evidence should not come from sources which cannot be checked (for example, imagined details of a fictional story, unacknowledged secondary sources or subjective recesses of the writer's memories) or appeals to unspecified authorities. Nor should evidence be gathered from sources that do not have established credibility (e.g., many internet sources).

7.1.3 | *Interpreting Evidence*

A really important principle of arguments based on evidence is the following: evidence by itself is rarely sufficiently persuasive; the writer has to *interpret* the evidence in order to point out its precise significance. What this means, in practice, is that filling the argumentative paragraph with facts (i.e., quotations, statistics, and empirical results) is, in most cases, not enough. The writer has to interpret the facts, that is, show how these facts establish the argumentative point she is making in the paragraph.

This is a crucial point, especially in arguments about literature. It is never enough in a paragraph arguing about a point in a literary work simply to offer a quotation from the text or a series of such quotations. While such evidence is essential, it is unpersuasive unless the writer then interprets the evidence, that is, offers a discussion of what it is about the quotation or passage referred to that supports the point of view advanced in the paragraph.

The same point holds for statistical evidence. Simply presenting a table of data, for example, or a graph or a list of facts in support of an argumentative point is not very persuasive unless, immediately after the table or graph or list, the writer then directs the reader's attention to those details in the table or graph which are relevant and explains how they support the argumentative point which the paragraph is trying to make.

Here, for example, is an argumentative paragraph from an essay on the European voyages of exploration in the fifteenth and sixteenth centuries.

Given that we nowadays consider lengthy trips everyday occurrences, we may well forget just how extraordinary the explosion of expeditionary voyages that started at the end of the fifteenth century truly was. As soon as monarchs became willing to sponsor such endeavours, sailors began lobbying for patronage, and the results were astonishing. Here, for example, is a list of the best known early voyages (the name of the sponsoring country is in brackets at the end of each entry):

Dias, around Africa, into the Indian Ocean, 1487–88 (Portugal)
Columbus, voyage to West Indies, 1492–94 (Spain)
Cabot, voyage to Newfoundland, 1497 (England)
Columbus, voyage to Venezuela, 1498 (Spain)
Vasco da Gama, around Africa to India, 1497–99 (Portugal)
Ojeda and Vespucci, to South America and the Amazon, 1499–1500 (Spain)
Cabral, to Brazil, around Africa, to India, 1500 (Portugal)
Corte-Real, voyage to Greenland, 1500 (Portugal)
First Portuguese voyage to Malacca, 1509
Abreu, voyage to Malacca, 1512–13 (Portugal)
First Portuguese visits to Canton River, 1514
Ponce de Leon, voyage to Florida and Yucatan, 1512–13 (Spain)
Magellan and Elcano, first voyage around the world, 1519–22 (Portugal).

The most significant feature of such a list, apart from the sheer number of expeditions, is the ambition of these early voyagers. All of a sudden, small groups of ships sent out from Europe were reaching places no one had ever heard of or dreamed about a few years before. If we remember that sailors at that time had no accurate maps, no way of knowing where they were on the open sea, and sometimes no idea where they had arrived, the achievement is all the more remarkable. In addition, the list inevitably makes one wonder why, all of a sudden, European monarchs, especially those of Spain and Portugal, were willing to patronize such expensive enterprises. What was it that sparked this remarkable phenomenon?

Notice that the writer has not just deposited the list of facts as a piece of evidence and moved onto the next point. He takes the time to call attention to what is significant about the list and finally to raise a question that the next part of his argument will answer.

Similarly with any illustrative material (maps, graphs, charts, photographs) you introduce into your argument as evidence, make sure you discuss how that material helps to establish the point you are making. Do not expect the reader of your essay to make the necessary interpretative connections between the evidence and the argument.

For example, here is a paragraph from an essay about the effects of varying grading standards in college courses:

One of the most alarming aspects of college grading systems is the significant disparity between the grades given by different professors teaching the same course. One might reasonably expect that the standards in different sections of the same course would be quite similar, so that a student's grade would not be significantly affected by the particular section she is enrolled in. However, the reality is that her success in the course may well depend on that factor more than on anything else. Here, for example, is a table showing the results of a study tracing the different grades awarded by ten English professors in the same department, all teaching the same compulsory course, first-year English Composition (the results are based on a study of grades over a period of three consecutive years).

Professor	Percent As (80–100)	Percent Bs (70–79)	Percent Cs (60–69)	Percent Ds (50–55)	Percent Fs (below 50)
AB	3	33	52	8	4
CD	32	48	17	3	0
EF	23	55	16	4	2
GH	62	33	5	0	0
IJ	2	13	67	8	10
KL	13	31	48	6	2
MN	43	41	16	0	0
OP	0	17	56	9	18
QR	15	36	35	11	3

The disparity in the grades is clear enough. Professor OP, for example, awarded no A grades; whereas, 62 percent of Professor GH's grades were in the A category. The A grades awarded by other professors range haphazardly between these two extremes. The results in the column of B and C grades looks almost equally scattered. The failure rate ranges from 0 percent F grades awarded to 18 percent. When one considers that these instructors, all in the same department at the same institution, are teaching the same course and that the grading system is supposed to be reasonably standard (as outlined in the college calendar), something appears seriously amiss. It would seem that a student's success in this particular course might well depend, more than anything else, on the class she is assigned to by the random process of registration. Given that a student's future academic choices depend, in part, on her success in first-year English, this situation seems all the more serious.

The writer has not placed the table in the argument and left it for the reader to interpret. She has pointed out certain features of it and linked them to the claim made in the topic sentence.

This point is particularly important in essays on literature, where interpreting the evidence is a crucial part of the argument. Here is a paragraph from an essay on *Hamlet* in which the writer is presenting an argument using details from the text to support a claim about the play. Notice that the argument does not just offer evidence; it *interprets that evidence* to show how it helps to endorse the claim made in the topic sentence:

> Hamlet's opening soliloquy in 1.2 reveals immediately that he is in a very peculiar emotional state, in contrast to everyone else at court. The prevailing sense is clearly that of a character morbidly obsessed with death and preoccupied in a most unhealthy way with female sexuality. The emphasis on death comes out clearly in Hamlet's references to suicide (129–32). There also runs throughout the speech a sense of hatred for fertility and sexuality in the world. Notice especially the following lines:
>
> > 'Tis an unweeded garden
> > That grows to seed; things rank and gross in nature
> > Possess it merely. (135–37)
>
> Here we see what later emerges as a characteristic tendency in Hamlet to reduce human experience to the lowest, most unsatisfactory terms. For him life is a "garden," but he rejects all the conventionally pleasant associations of that term, by seeing the place as "unweeded," a place where vigorous and unchecked wild nature has taken over in a riot of reproductive energy. The adjectives "rank" and "gross" convey a strong sense of disgust, with marked sexual undertones, and the last word in the sentence, "merely,"

sounds almost like a sneer. If we recognize from his refusal to participate in the action at the court a sense that he is, right at the start of the play, alienated from the social life of the court, then his manner of expressing himself to himself—that is, of thinking aloud—creates the sense that Hamlet is cultivating his own overreaction as a result of some desire to see the worst. It is true that Hamlet has just lost his father, and his mother has remarried his uncle, but these events do not appear to upset anyone else unduly. The very strong language he uses in his first soliloquy to express his deepest thoughts immediately conveys to the reader the suggestion of an unhealthy and excessively morbid response to both his father's death and his mother's sexual relationship.

In the above paragraph the writer has selected relatively few details from a particular part of the text and drawn the reader's attention to them. But he has not simply left the evidence there for the reader to figure out or offered more. He takes almost all the second half of the paragraph to comment on the evidence he has introduced, explaining to the reader how it brings out the point he has announced as the topic for the paragraph.

Here is another example, from an essay arguing that Machiavelli's *Prince* should be read as a satire. Notice how much of the paragraph is taken up with interpreting the evidence derived from the text.

One feature of Machiavelli's style which exerts a certain ironic pressure on the reader is the yawning gap he creates between a conventional moral language and the immoral activities he is proposing. This is a common satiric technique. Notice, for example, the following passage:

I believe that this depends upon whether cruel deeds are committed well or badly. They may be called well committed (if one may use the word 'well' of that which is evil) when they are all committed at once, because they are necessary for establishing one's power and are not afterwards persisted in, but changed for measures as beneficial as possible to one's subjects. Badly committed are those that at first are few in number, but increase with time rather than diminish. Those who follow the first method can in some measure remedy their standing both with God and with man.... Those who follow the second cannot possibly maintain their power. (33)

There's an inherent tension here between the actions he is analyzing and the words indicating his approval or disapproval ("well" and "badly"), words which, in common speech and writing, tend always to have important moral connotations. The style calls attention to the moral absurdity of Machiavelli's universe (as his parenthetic comment makes clear). If people can break God's laws in the most serious way and later "remedy their standing with God," then the notion of taking one's standing with God seriously, by any Christian orthodoxy, makes a mockery of religion or, alternatively, the phrase is a way of mocking the suggestion. In a society in which one's standing with God is, for many people, more than one more political strategy, the phrase carries significant satiric weight. Machiavelli rubs our noses here (and elsewhere, although not so clearly) in the moral absurdity of what he is proposing. It would have been relatively easy to avoid using moral language altogether (as he does in much of the text) by using, instead of words like "well" or "badly," words like "efficient," "inefficient," "prudent," "imprudent," and so on. To allude to moral concerns in the vocabulary is to do more than merely state that efficiency is more important in politics than morality: it reminds the reader of the satiric point that the literal recommendations empty the world of any significant moral value.

Make quite sure you understand this point: the use of evidence requires interpretation which links the facts to the point being made in the topic sentence of the paragraph. It will not satisfactorily carry the argument unless the writer makes this connection for the reader. Thus, if your arguments merely present evidence, with no interpretation, they will probably not be very persuasive, no matter how much evidence you introduce, because the reader will fail to understand the ways in which the evidence substantiates the points you are trying to establish.

Here is another example of a paragraph presenting an inductive argumentative, this time in an essay on a non-literary topic:

> Academic faculty routinely proclaim that conventional research and publication are essential to maintaining a high quality of instruction in the university. This claim, however, is dubious at best, because it has never been substantiated in a convincing manner. There have been a number of reputable attempts in recent decades to explore the issue, and none of them has confirmed what faculty so confidently urge us to believe. For example, studies in the last twenty years indicate that claims about the creative links between academic research and teaching have no basis in fact. Rushton, Murray, and Paunonen (1983) make the point unambiguously: "being good, bad, or indifferent at one activity [research] has very little implication for performance at the other [teaching]." Later studies by Feldman (1987) confirm the point: "an obvious interpretation of these results is either that, in general, the likelihood that research productivity actually benefits teaching is extremely small or that the two, for all practical purposes, are essentially unrelated." Summaries of research by Webster (1985) and later by Neill (1985; 1989) stress the conclusion reached by every reliable study of this matter in the past thirty years: there is no evidence whatsoever to support the view that academic research and publication have a beneficial effect

upon instruction. Given such studies and the unanimous conclusions of the researchers who conducted them, the widespread claim that faculty need to carry out research and to publish in order to be good teachers of undergraduates looks increasingly like a myth designed to cater to faculty priorities rather than to student needs. When one remembers that a major aim of undergraduate courses is to help students understand the difference between good and bad arguments, this situation becomes all the more remarkable.

Notice how the writer here has appropriated the conclusions of some of his source material (by quoting them directly) and then added some interpretative comments of his own.

Once you begin to grasp and to practice this principle of interpreting the evidence you introduce, you should be using up a significant portion of the paragraph for this purpose (as in the above examples). And your argumentative style will begin to change, so that you introduce less evidence but discuss in greater detail the evidence you do introduce.

When students complain, as they often do, about having said all they have to say and still falling short of the word requirements of the assignment, the reason is almost always the same: there is insufficient interpretation. The essay may be establishing good topic sentences and putting useful evidence on the table. But a main part of the argument, the interpretation of evidence, is missing or inadequate. By contrast, students who learn to interpret properly often face the problem of not having enough space, since thorough interpretation takes up so much of the essay.

In general, the best essays tend to be those with a relatively narrow focus, in which the evidence presented is good evidence but not overwhelming in volume and the interpretation of the evidence is first-rate and thorough. The quality of the interpretation, in fact, is one of the key features characterizing an exceptionally good essay.

Given the points mentioned above, you can often recognize quite easily whether your paragraphs are fulfilling the requirements of a good evidence-based argument. The following are some characteristic symptoms:

1. If the paragraphs are quite short (i.e., less than, say, 150 words), then they are almost certainly not doing everything they should be. As is evident from the various examples given above, introducing the topic sentence, presenting evidence, and interpreting the evidence in detail should take up a substantial amount of space. So if, when you look at the visual appearance of your essay, you notice that the paragraphs are changing every five or six lines, then something is wrong. It most cases, the problem will be that you are not doing enough interpretation.

2. As you review your essay, look carefully at those places where you have quoted or referred to some material, and ask yourself this question: What is going on in the sentences immediately after that material? If you are not at that point discussing the significance of what you have called attention to (i.e., interpreting the evidence), then you are probably neglecting an essential part of the argument.

3. How much of each paragraph is taken up with quotations from the text or from secondary sources? If these make up the major part of the paragraph, then you are probably overloading the argument with evidence and not providing sufficient interpretation of it. As a general rule, select the best evidence available, and interpret it thoroughly, rather than stuffing the essay with quotations.

   Remember that, in order to call attention to a portion of the text, you do not need to quote extensively. Assume that the reader of your essay has the relevant book in front of her and can easily locate the quotation if she wishes, so that you simply have to give a short reference to the precise location of the material. Notice the following examples:

> For example, in the first paragraph of the Second Part of his argument (46), Descartes uses a curious expression ...

> Nora's conversation with Torvald in the opening scene of the play is revealing. Notice especially ...

If you call attention to the location of the material you wish to look at you do not need to quote the entire passage or provide a prose summary of what is going on in the story or the argument. The first example provides a page reference, because the writer has earlier identified the appropriate edition of the work under discussion.

Similarly when you introduce evidence from secondary sources, particularly when these are research results, you do not need to go into excessive detail about the source of the results. Normally, it is enough simply to provide a reference. If you wish to include a very brief description of the study, that is acceptable. But do not go into excessive detail, so that the description of the study overwhelms the argumentative point you are making.

> A study by J.R. Smith and L. Robinson (2010), which surveyed 250 households in rural Texas, came to a similar conclusion.

This style is acceptable (the description of the method is sufficiently brief). Do not, however, go overboard in describing the study, as in the following example.

> A study by J.R. Smith and L. Robinson (2010) surveyed 75 households (selected at random) in rural Texas in a telephone poll, followed that up with written

> questionnaires and a second telephone poll, and then
> conducted personal interviews with a representative
> sample of the original 75 households. That study came to
> a similar conclusion.

The detail provided here about the research method is unnecessary and excessive. If the reader is interested, she can locate the study from your reference to it and read about the research method herself.

I mentioned above that a writer should normally be careful about quoting material from a text too frequently or at excessive length. One exception to that general principle is an argument in which you wish to build a significant part of the argument on a close look at a particular passage, in other words, when you wish to discuss a particular quotation at great length (over several paragraphs). Here is an example (from an essay on Virginia Woolf's style in *To the Lighthouse*):

> [ILLUSTRATIVE PARAGRAPH INTRODUCING THE QUOTATION]
> In order to explore the importance of Woolf's writing
> style, we need to take a close look at a particular exam-
> ple. Here is one passage, selected almost at random,
> from an early part of the book; it is a description of
> Mrs. Ramsay:
>
> > All she could do now was to admire the refrigerator, and
> > turn the pages of the Stores list in the hope that she
> > might come upon something like a rake, or a mowing
> > machine, which, with its prongs and its handles, would
> > need the greatest skill and care in cutting out. All these
> > young men parodied her husband, she reflected; he said
> > it would rain; they said it would be a positive tornado.
> > But here, as she turned the page, suddenly her
> > search for the picture of a rake or a mowing-machine

was interrupted. The gruff murmur, irregularly broken by the taking out of pipes and the putting in of pipes which had kept on assuring her, though she could not hear what was said (as she sat in the window which opened on the terrace), that the men were happily talking; this sound, which had lasted now half an hour and had taken its place soothingly in the scale of sounds pressing on top of her, such as the tap of balls upon bats, the sharp, sudden bark now and then, "How's that? How's that?" of the children playing cricket, had ceased; so that the monotonous fall of the waves on the beach, which for the most part beat a measured and soothing tattoo to her thoughts and seemed consolingly to repeat over and over again as she sat with the children the words of some old cradle song, murmured by nature, "I am guarding you—I am your support," but at other times suddenly and unexpectedly, especially when her mind raised itself slightly from the task actually in hand, had no such kindly meaning, but like a ghostly roll of drums remorselessly beat the measure of life, made one think of the destruction of the island and its engulfment in the sea, and warned her whose day had slipped past in one quick doing after another that it was all ephemeral as a rainbow—this sound which had been obscured and concealed under the other sounds suddenly thundered hollow in her ears and made her look up with an impulse of terror. (15)

The first thing we notice about this style, I suspect, is the extraordinarily complex sentence structure, which is extremely significant because of what it reveals about the meandering, multivalent nature of Mrs. Ramsay's thoughts. (The paragraph calls attention in detail to the structure of the sentences in the quotation.)

The structure of the sentence, of course, does a good deal more than simply describe the inner life of Mrs. Ramsay. It also characterizes that inner life as having multiple layers, with pleasant, everyday thoughts covering over negative ones, especially an underlying dread of death. This emphasis on layered consciousness is sustained for all of the characters in the novel. (The paragraph continues to discuss the quotation in order to make a second point about the significance of Woolf's sentence structure.)

Woolf's style thus contributes to offering the reader a particularly challenging vision of life....

This essay has based an entire argument on a very close and lengthy look at a single point in a long story. Because the point is so central to the argument (which makes frequent references back to the quoted material) and the essay takes so much time examining it, the writer has decided to include the relevant passage in the essay.

7.2 | Paragraph Unity

A key characteristic of good paragraphs is *unity*—that is, everything in the paragraph should be linked directly to the main point announced in the topic sentence. There are no digressions into other subjects or additional points introduced in the middle of the paragraph. Everything is relevant to the single argumentative point of that paragraph.

Notice in the following paragraph how the logic of the argument announced in the topic sentence begins to go astray as soon as the writer introduces another point, not directly linked to the topic:

The first impression we get of Elisa from the description of her clothing suggests that she is uncertain about or afraid of her femininity. Her figure looks "blocked and heavy."

She wears a man's hat pulled low over her face. She does wear a dress, but that is almost totally concealed under a heavy apron, so that we sense she is a woman who is hiding something, an impression strongly reinforced by the narrator's description of her clothes as a "costume," a word which refers to actors impersonating someone else. The setting also sounds quite isolated and lonely, as if there is no daily human contact with a community of friends. And the fact that the story is set at a time when the fields are "brown" and without a crop evidently coming to fruition, a time of "waiting," creates a sense that Elisa has no immediate fulfilment in her daily life. Elisa's conduct when the stranger arrives is thus quite understandable; she is uncertain about how to deal with a sudden intrusion, especially a strange man. All these details reveal clearly that Elisa is suffering from significant emotional insecurity.

This paragraph begins by announcing a very specific topic, the relationship between the description of Elisa's clothing and our sense of her uncertainty about her femininity. And the first few details focus on that well, with evidence and useful interpretation. But then the writer switches to something else (the setting) and then, a bit later, to something else (the arrival of the stranger). Hence, by the end the reader has lost contact with the specific point announced at the start. Thus, the unity of this paragraph has disappeared.

It is important to concentrate on paragraph unity and to keep out of a paragraph things not immediately relevant to the point the topic sentence announces. If you suddenly realize that there is another important point you must include in the argument, make it in a separate paragraph. For example, if you are writing a paragraph arguing that fracking poses dangers to our domestic water supply, then do not introduce into that paragraph anything that is not directly connected with that particular danger (such as the destruction of animal habitat or the release of excessive amounts of methane into the air). If those are topics you wish to pursue, then devote a separate paragraph to each of them.

One way in which inexperienced writers commonly interrupt the unity of a paragraph (and the argument) is suddenly to stray into large questions far outside the scope of the focus you have defined. Once you start the argument, you should stay focused specifically on that, without invoking generalizations which lie outside the specific area you have defined. If you want to link the argument to bigger questions, then do that in the conclusion.

For example, if you are writing an argumentative essay about the significance of Hamlet's treatment of women, then stay on that particular subject. Do not stray into generalizations about men and women or about Shakespeare's life and times or about gender-based violence. If you find yourself writing about something *in general*, something not directly pertinent to the specific details of the argument as you have defined it, then you are almost certainly weakening the unity of the paragraph.

7.3 | Paragraph Coherence

A second important characteristic of argumentative paragraphs is that they must be *coherent*, that is, the argument going on in each of them must flow logically from sentence to sentence, so that the reader moves from the opening declaration of the topic (in the topic sentence), through the evidence and interpretation, to the conclusion of the paragraph in a clear linear fashion, with no erratic jumps or confusing interruptions.

7.3.1 | Achieving Paragraph Coherence

We have already briefly considered the coherence of an argument that applies general principles to a specific case. If the writer sticks to the basic pattern of such an argument and does not interrupt it, then the resulting paragraph will almost certainly be coherent:

Topic Sentence(s).

We all agree on this point (first agreed-upon truth).

(Optional) We all agree on this next point (additional agreed-upon truth or truths).

This particular example is clearly covered by that principle/these principles.

Therefore, this conclusion follows.

The most logically coherent form for a paragraph presenting an argument based on the interpretation of evidence is somewhat more complicated, as follows:

TOPIC SENTENCE, an argumentative assertion announcing the main point the paragraph is seeking to make, perhaps followed by one or two sentences reinforcing and clarifying the argumentative stance in this paragraph.

EVIDENCE in the form of direct references to the text, quotations, statistics, summaries of relevant research data, and so on.

INTERPRETATION OF THE EVIDENCE, a section which discusses in detail how the particular evidence you have introduced helps to back up the argumentative point announced in the topic sentence.

(Optional) Steps 2 and 3 repeated (i.e., new evidence on the same point is introduced and interpreted).

(Optional) Any qualifications you want to introduce to limit the argument, and especially to clarify the reliability of the evidence and thus the interpretations you have made of it (for examples, see below).

FINAL SUMMARY point bringing the reader back to the point stressed in the topic sentence.

This is by no means the only possible coherent structure for an argumentative paragraph, but, if you follow it closely, the resulting argument will be coherent, since this follows the standard logic of the argument: "This is what I am claiming"; "Here is my evidence"; "This is what the evidence indicates"; "Here are any reservations I have about the evidence"; and "Thus, I have established the claim I began with."

Notice how this format works in the following paragraph, moving from topic sentence(s) to evidence, to interpretation, to qualification, and finally to a restatement of the original point (note that the references are imaginary, included simply to show an example of the style). I have inserted phrases in square brackets to indicate what the paragraph is now doing.

[TOPIC SENTENCE] To start with, it is clear that our attempts to control the spread of illegal drugs are not producing the results we had hoped for, and it is thus high time we assessed the value of our anti-drug measures.
[EVIDENCE] For instance, as we redouble our efforts and give the police additional powers, the street price of illegal narcotics continues to decline, a sure sign that the supply is becoming more plentiful (Jackson, 2011).
[MORE EVIDENCE] Moreover, a recent study of the street trade in Vancouver confirms our worst fears: addiction is increasing in the city, street prices are falling, and the illegal infrastructure is growing in power (Callows, 2012).
[MORE EVIDENCE] Other studies of the same city have also shown that there is an increasing supply reaching school children (Smart, 2011; Stuart, 2012). Not surprisingly, this increase is producing more young addicts (Thomas, 2010).
[INTERPRETATION OF EVIDENCE] What do these results indicate? It is clear that the war on drugs, for which we are paying so much money, is not having much success, if reducing or eliminating the supply is still a major goal: the supply is still plentiful, drug gangs are more powerful, and addiction rates are growing. [QUALIFICATION] It is true that we have to be careful with the results of some of these studies, for their methods are not always as reliable as they might be, and

there are often political agendas at work in the studies of our problems with illegal drugs.

[REASSERTION OF THE TOPIC SENTENCE] Nevertheless, the fact that none of the recent literature offers any firm evidence that our combat against illegal narcotics is achieving anything other than enriching criminals and empowering police forces must surely give us reason to pause before we hurl additional millions of dollars into these programs. For there is no evidence at all that such an expenditure will achieve anything socially beneficial. The money will largely go to waste.

7.3.2 | Transition Words as Logical Indicators

One key to sustaining the coherence of a paragraph is often the appropriate use of *transition words*. These are words or phrases, usually right at the start of a sentence, which indicate the logical direction of the new sentence in relation to what has just been said.

Here are a few examples (the transition elements are in capital letters).

1. IN ADDITION to THIS point, there are many studies which establish a positive correlation between the income of one's parents and success in school. THIS fact is important to recognize.

2. BY CONTRAST, other passages of the poem suggest a completely different mood.

3. THIS emphasis on pharmaceutical intervention, HOWEVER, brings with it real dangers. FOR EXAMPLE, the medication often has immediately harmful side effects. MOREOVER, it can ALSO create long-term addiction. BEYOND THAT, there is the question of the expense. THIS BEING THE CASE, one wonders why we are so keen to continue with THIS medication.

4. MOREOVER, rock and roll music has exercised an important influence on civil rights in North America. IN FACT, in popular music since the 1950s, more than in any other activity (with the possible exception of professional sports), black people have won fame, fortune, and lasting status among the white middle-class. FOR EXAMPLE, thousands of eager white people all over North America have lined up to attend concerts by Prince, Michael Jackson, Tina Turner, the Supremes, Chuck Berry, Little Richard, Beyoncé, Dionne Warwick, and countless other black performers. IN ADDITION, black musicians have ever since the 1960s been in demand with companies seeking high-profile figures to endorse products aimed at the white middle classes or to star in shows they sponsor for a wide general audience. INDEED, it is now an everyday sight to see white and black musicians working together on prime-time television, without regard to the colour of their skins. THIS phenomenon, we sometimes forget, is very different from the situation before the 1950s. THEN, in some places no white group could appear on stage with a drummer (white or black), because the drum was considered a black instrument. MOREOVER, there was a rigidly enforced distinction between black music and white music. Radio stations, FOR INSTANCE, played one type of music or the other, not both. HOWEVER, since the advent of rock and roll all that has altered. TO BE SURE, many other factors were involved in this important and complex social change. STILL, we should not deny our popular black musicians the credit which is their due. FOR without their pervasive influence and talent, often under very difficult conditions, THIS improvement in race relations would have come about much more slowly than it did.

Look carefully at these words in capital letters. Most of them could be removed from the sentences, without damage to the sense. What would be lost, however, is the constant presence of words and phrases linking elements in the argument and providing the reader a sense of the logical relationship of the element coming up to what has gone before.

An intelligent use of transition words really helps to create and sustain the coherence of a paragraph, enabling the reader to easily follow the logical connections from one idea to the next.

7.3.3 | A Short Catalogue of Transition Words

The list below includes some of the common transition words indicating logical connections between sentences and paragraphs. The words are grouped according to the logical function they carry out. (Note that this list is not meant to be comprehensive.)

1. Words indicating continuity with what has gone before: *and, in addition, also, as well, beyond that, furthermore, moreover, indeed, besides, second, next, similarly, again, as well.*

2. Words introducing an example or illustration or evidence: *for example, for instance, as an illustration.*

3. Words introducing something which is reinforcing or clarifying a previous point: *in fact, in other words, that is, indeed, as a matter of fact, to put it another way.*

4. Words indicating a conclusion from or a result of what you have just been discussing: *thus, hence, therefore, consequently, as a result, accordingly, this being the case.*

5. Words indicating a contrast with what has just been said: *but, however, nevertheless, by contrast, on the other hand, conversely, and yet, notwithstanding, still.*

6. Words indicating a qualification, doubt, or reservation about what you have just been discussing: *no doubt, of course, to be sure, it may be the case, perhaps.*

7. Words indicating a summary statement is coming up:
   in short, all in all, in brief, in conclusion, to conclude.

8. Pronoun and adjectival links to something which has gone
   before: *this, that, the above-mentioned, such.*

9. Words or phrases establishing time relationships (important
   in narrative paragraphs): *after, afterwards, then, later, before,
   while, at the same time, immediately, thereupon, next, subse-
   quently, previously, simultaneously.*

10. Words or phrases indicating spatial relationships (important
    in physical descriptions): *above, beside, next to, on the other
    side, facing, parallel to, across from, adjacent.*

7.4 | Concluding Paragraphs

An argumentative essay should normally finish with a conclusion
and sometimes, depending on the subject matter, with conclusions and recommendations. The conclusions and recommendations (if there are any) should be placed in the last paragraph(s).

7.4.1 | Conclusions

In thinking about how to write a conclusion, you might benefit
from considering the following ideas:

1. The conclusion should not continue the argument by introducing new material. Hence, you should never introduce new
   disputatious points in the conclusion.

2. At the same time, you must try to avoid making the conclusion little more than a limp repetition of the opening paragraph ("And thus we have seen that ..."). Yes, you are leading

the reader back to a reassertion of the thesis of the essay, but that doesn't mean you should pretend that you are a parrot and just repeat the thesis almost verbatim.

3. The main purpose of the conclusion is to sum up the argument, to re-emphasize the thesis, and to leave the reader thinking about the importance of the argument, perhaps in a wider context. In a sense, its purpose is the reverse of the introduction: the conclusion moves the reader from the particular emphasis of the argument and takes it out into a wider context (if this seems confusing, read some of the examples below). In doing this, the concluding paragraph can also establish a certain final tone to the argument:

> Given the above evidence that capital punishment is not an effective deterrent to violent crime, that the procedures in this country for implementing the death penalty are a massive drain on inadequate budgets, and that our system repeatedly executes innocent victims, the widespread popularity and use of judicial executions in the US raise all sorts of troubling questions about the judgement of many of our politicians and the electorate. One wonders why, in the face of so much reliable information about the futility, expense, and barbarity of capital punishment, so many people still insist that this option must remain as some form of ultimate punishment. But that melancholy fact is an issue for another time.

This concluding paragraph is reminding the reader of the major points in the argument and then widening the focus by raising a general question about the nature of a country which still refuses to act on the conclusions reached. Notice how the final tone of the essay becomes more reflective and sad.

4. Sometimes a useful entry into the concluding paragraph is a reminder to the reader that your essay has been looking at only one part of a much greater issue. Having pointed that out, you can then stress once again the importance of the thesis. Notice the following examples of sentences starting a concluding paragraph (to an essay argument about what *A Vindication of the Rights of Woman* has to say about education):

> There is, of course, much more to Wollstonecraft's argument than those parts where she discusses education. These, in fact, form only one part of her case. However, in the context of her total argument, we need to realize that what she has to say about that subject … (The paragraph goes on to re-emphasize the original thesis of the essay.)

Here is another example of the start of a paragraph which concludes an argument about the need to develop alternative sources of energy by reminding the reader that the essay has been discussing only one part of a much wider issue:

> Meeting Canada's energy needs in the coming decades is obviously a more complex matter than the issues I have been discussing here. For one thing, adequate alternatives to petroleum, natural gas, and coal will be difficult, if not impossible, to find in the short term. However, investing our resources in these alternatives must remain an important priority … (The paragraph goes on to re-emphasize the thesis of the argument.)

5. Sometimes it is useful in the final sentences of a conclusion to point the reader to a question arising out of the argument, an issue she might perhaps like to think about or act upon:

a.   Given that research has no relationship to the quality of instruction, we might well wonder why the universities insist that professors teaching undergraduates must spend so much time on academic research. Dealing with that question, however, would require another essay.

b.   There is little doubt that this serious and well-known problem of spousal abuse will remain with us for the foreseeable future. Will we ever take significant steps to address it with the resources an intelligent response requires?

6. Avoid the temptation to disqualify the argument you have just presented with a comment along the lines of "But all this is just my opinion" or "But I really don't know that much about the subject." Make sure the conclusion is a confident reassertion of the main point of the argument.

7.4.2 | Sample Conclusions

Here are some sample conclusions. Notice how the writer does not continue the argument (which is over) but tends to draw back to place the issue in a wider perspective and, at the same time, to reinforce for the reader the central argument which the essay has been presenting.

Conclusion A
(From an essay arguing that Hamlet's character is not that of the ideal prince but is badly flawed)
All of the above points indicate quite clearly that, whatever the origin of the evil in Elsinore, the prince himself is one source of the sickness in the court. As we have seen, again and again in the play Shakespeare brings out Hamlet's essential immaturity, morbidity, aggressive hostility to women, and characteristic duplicity. Of course, there is

more to the man than just these elements and more to the play than just the character of the prince. Moreover, Hamlet's character, like the play, is very complicated and ambiguous. It will always have elusive elements. However, as this essay has argued, the emphasis on the unhealthy aspects of Hamlet's personality is so strong and frequent in the play that, however we finally assess the hero, we must take into account his own obvious inadequacies, all too clearly a source, if not the only source, for the "something ... rotten in the state of Denmark."

Conclusion B
(From an essay arguing that the only rational solution to our narcotics problem is to legalize all drugs)
Surely it's time we recognized the facts: that our efforts to stamp out illegal narcotics are only succeeding in enriching organized crime, providing the police with dangerous new powers, filling our prisons, and encouraging many others to break the law. And, as I have mentioned, we need to remember that the drugs we are trying to stamp out are less dangerous than many legal substances in widespread use. Instead of devising new utopian and increasingly expensive and futile schemes to eliminate drugs, we should move at once to change the law and to make cocaine, heroin, marijuana, and their derivatives as legal as tobacco and alcohol. "Insanity," Albert Einstein once observed, "is doing the same thing over and over again and expecting different results."

Notice carefully what each writer does in the above samples.

Conclusion A (about Hamlet) opens by summarizing the main thrust of the argument throughout the paper, reminding the reader one more time of what each paragraph has been presenting. Then the writer moves back to consider the topic in the context of the entire play, adding a qualification to indicate that she realizes there is more to the topic than one short essay can deal with. Finally, the concluding sentences answer the qualification by stressing the main point: the unhealthy aspects of Hamlet's character are a significant part of the play. This strategy of using the conclusion to place the specific issue of the essay in the wider context of the entire work is often useful in conclusions to essays on literary subjects.

Conclusion B (about narcotics) opens with a quick but very specific summary (almost in the form of a list) of the main points of the essay (each of which has been discussed in detail during the main argument), and finishes with a specific recommendation for future action. Such a structure is quite common in the concluding paragraph of an essay exploring a modern social issue and demanding action.

7.4.3 | More Substantial Conclusions

Sometimes conclusions will have to be considerably more substantial than the examples above, especially if they come at the end of a lengthy argument about a complex event or phenomenon. Suppose for example, that you are writing the conclusion to a lengthy analytical argument about, say, a difficult social problem, a major industrial accident, or a civic riot. At the end you may wish to offer two or three concluding paragraphs, each one summing up a different aspect of the argument.

Here are a series of sentences that illustrate how such a conclusion might work.

> What conclusions can we draw from this event? Well, the most important one is clear: the municipal and provincial police bear a major responsibility for what went wrong. They were poorly trained for such an event and ill prepared for this particular one. (The paragraph goes on to summarize points the argument has already discussed about the conduct of the police forces.)

The municipal authorities were also at fault. They refused to heed warnings about what might happen if the gathering were held at that place and time, especially if the bars were permitted to extend their regular hours. (The paragraph goes on to summarize what the argument had to say about the municipal authorities.)

Outside agitators also played a role. They came deliberately intending to aggravate the situation, if necessary by force. (The paragraph again summarizes details of this part of the argument.)

Finally, the organizers of the rally played a significant role. (The paragraph reminds the readers of this part of the argument.)

This conclusion, going on for two or more paragraphs, is not continuing the argument. All the points mentioned are ones that have already been dealt with in greater detail in the course of the essay. However, the writer is giving a detailed summary of them, focusing on one point at a time. A conclusion like this might be presented as a numbered list.

Such a lengthy conclusion is relatively rare in undergraduate essay writing. However, certain reports require this form of conclusion, because some of the readers will want to focus on the conclusions first, before reading the report. In fact, the nature of the conclusions may well determine whether they read the report or not; in some cases, the only thing they may be interested in is the conclusion.

7.4.4 | Recommendations

Sometimes the argument you are conducting will require recommendations. Such a requirement is quite common in arguments which are urging that there is a need for particular social, political, or economic responses to problems.

The first thing to note is that a recommendation is not the same thing as a conclusion. A conclusion arises, as we have seen, out of a deductive or inductive argument. It is the logical result of a process of reasoning, and it indicates the completion of a thought process. A recommendation is, as the name suggests, a statement urging action (or sometimes inaction). Alternatively put, a conclusion says, in effect, "This is the case" or "This is very probably the case"; a recommendation says "This is what we must (or should) do (or not do) about the case."

Logically speaking, recommendations should normally follow conclusions. That is, the thought process and the argument which result in our understanding a problem better should come before the proposals for how we should address the problem. This, I take it, is generally obvious enough. We cannot review options and recommend a course of action, until we have drawn conclusions about what the problem is.

None of this is something you need worry about, unless the argument is leading up to a series of recommendations— unless, that is, the major purpose of the argument is to urge the readers to think about a series of practical measures which should be implemented. Such a requirement is not uncommon in papers exploring social problems or policy analysis or technical reports, but it is rare in arguments about literature or philosophy. If you are leading up to a series of recommendations as a major purpose of the argument, then separate the conclusions from the recommendations, present the conclusions first, and then in a separate paragraph present the recommendations. Here are a few principles to observe in presenting recommendations:

1. Organize the recommendations as a numbered list introduced by a short comment indicating what you are now doing.

2. Make sure each item in the list is a specific single recommendation. Try not to combine different recommendations under the same number.

3. When you make the recommendation, keep the verbs in the active voice so that you indicate who should be responsible for carrying out the recommendation. Notice the difference between the following two lists:

Recommendations A
Given the above conclusions, this report recommends the following actions.

a. Our present procedures for screening an application to hold a large public event in a municipal park should be reviewed and revised.

b. A deposit should be posted or insurance purchased to cover any unexpected costs arising from public disturbances during such an event.

c. Better training must be provided for police officers who may have to respond to disturbances at these public events.

Recommendations B
Given the above conclusions, this report recommends the following actions.

a. The City Manager should review and, in consultation with the Parks Committee, revise our present procedures for screening an application to hold a large public event in a municipal park.

b. Anyone applying to hold a large public event in a municipal park must be willing to post a deposit or purchase insurance to cover any unexpected costs arising from public disturbances during the event.

c. The police must provide better training for those officers who may have to respond to disturbances at these public events.

In the first list, the sentences do not mention who is to be responsible for carrying out the recommendations; whereas, in the second list (in which there are no passive verbs) the sentences specify precisely who is responsible for the necessary follow-up action.

Such a structure is, as mentioned, of particular importance only in those arguments whose main purpose is to analyze a problem, reach some conclusions about the nature of or reasons for the problem, and make recommendations about how we might deal with it. The essay could very well end without the list of recommendations (i.e., the writer could leave the reader to come up with her own), but if the assignment calls for specific recommendations, then this is the place they belong.

Sometimes, in certain technical reports, conclusions and recommendations are combined, so that the writer offers a single conclusion and follows that with a recommendation addressing that conclusion, before moving on to a second conclusion and recommendation. If you are not sure just how much you are expected to offer by way of conclusions and recommendations, get clarification from the instructor.

7.5 | Structuring a Comparative Essay

Sometimes you may be writing an essay in which you are comparing two or more things. Such an essay is expected to offer a sense of the similarities and differences of the things being compared (A and B) and a judgement about the two of them in relation to each other. In general, comparative essays fall into two groups:

A and B are both very similar, but A is superior to B. (The argument will state a decided preference for A rather than for B.)

Although similar, there are important differences between A and B. An analysis of these similarities and differences reveals that ... (The argument will stress that something interesting can be learned by comparing A and B.)

Your first task in a comparative essay is to establish (usually in the introduction or the paragraph immediately after that) that the two things you are discussing are sufficiently similar so that a comparison is justified. Obviously if the two things are totally dissimilar a comparison does not make much sense.

The following examples show how one can introduce an argument based upon a comparative evaluation. Notice that the introduction follows the customary format (subject, focus, thesis).

Essay 1: A Comparison of the Theories of Karl Marx and Sigmund Freud

Karl Marx and Sigmund Freud, two of the most famous thinkers of modern times, both developed enormously important and comprehensive views of human nature and society, theories which have exerted a major and continuing influence on the way we think about ourselves and our fellow citizens. Of particular importance are the views of these two thinkers about the nature of human suffering. For their theories on the origin of suffering have shaped in large part the way we understand that problem and therefore the methods we use in our attempts to deal with it. And the differences between these two men's ideas have created continuing debates about how we should organize ourselves to mitigate human suffering. Although both men's theories on this subject have been enormously influential, what does seem increasingly clear is that Freud developed a much more subtle and enduring understanding of the issue; Marx's writings on the subject, though complex and still fascinating, now appear by comparison in many respects inadequate.

Essay 2: A Comparison of Two Literary Characters
In many ways Nora in Henrik Ibsen's *A Doll's House* and Elisa in John Steinbeck's short story "The Chrysanthemums" face similar circumstances. Each woman lives with a husband who does not understand her intelligently, in confined circumstances with little prospect for significant change. And in the course of both stories, each woman comes to discover just how much she is being oppressed by men. However, the two women react very differently to the crisis which that recognition brings: Elisa collapses and retreats, and Nora abandons her family for a life on her own. By examining the characters of these two women and their reactions to an important emotional turning point in their lives, we can better understand the very human tensions created by married life and the enormous difficulties of finding a proper response to that situation.

Notice how in the first sample, the writer introduces the general comparison first (Marx and Freud), pointing out the basis for the similarity (two great thinkers with theories of human nature), then moves onto a very specific aspect of that general subject (the different views on human suffering), and finally establishes a thesis by declaring a preference. In the second sample above, the writer again starts with a general point which establishes the similarity between the two fictional heroines. Then the introduction moves to the specific focus of the essay (their response to an emotional

crisis in their lives), and then finally establishes a thesis in an interpretative assertion. This is not the statement of a preference but an
argument about the significance of two different stories.

Once the comparison and the basis of the argument have
been defined, then you need to organize, as before, the sequence
of paragraphs in the main body of the argument. An important
principle to bear in mind is that the comparison must be more or
less balanced and fair. In other words, you should be giving each
element in the comparison roughly equal attention and discussing similar aspects of each of them.

In setting up the sequence of the paragraphs, you have some
options, as follows:

1. You can keep the comparison alive in every paragraph, so
    that the argument discusses each half of the comparison
    in each paragraph. The advantage of this structure is that it
    keeps the comparison between the two subjects constantly
    before the reader and forces you to pay equal attention to
    each side of the comparison.

2. A second method for organizing the sequence of paragraphs
    in the main body of a comparative essay is to alternate
    between the two subjects. The method gives you the chance
    to discuss each point in greater detail, and it also keeps the
    comparison alive for the reader, provided you keep alternat-
    ing and making sure that you continue to discuss the same
    aspect of each subject.

3. The third way of dealing with comparative essays is to say
    all you want to about one side of the comparison and then
    to switch to consider the other side of the comparison. Thus,
    the main body of the essay would tend to fall into two parts:
    in the first you consider the first element in the comparison,
    and in the second half you consider the second element in
    the comparison.

One danger with this method (and it is a common problem) is that the comparison will become lopsided—that is, you will end up writing a great deal more about one of the two items than the other. Another real danger is that you will discuss both elements, but switch the criteria of the comparison in the second half, so that you discuss different features of the second item in the comparison from those you considered in the first. If this happens, then the comparison may fall apart, because you are not comparing the same features of the two things.

Suppose, to take a simple example, I am writing a short argument comparing two different automobiles (Model A and Model B). The structure of my argument (based on the options above) could be any one of the following:

Option 1
PARAGRAPH 1: Comparison of A and B (Highway performance)
PARAGRAPH 2: Comparison of A and B (Styling)
PARAGRAPH 3: Comparison of A and B (Cost: Fuel and Maintenance)
PARAGRAPH 4: Comparison of A and B (Special Features)
CONCLUSION

Option 2
PARAGRAPH 1: Model A (Highway performance)
PARAGRAPH 2: Model B (Highway performance)
PARAGRAPH 3: Model A (Styling)
PARAGRAPH 4: Model B (Styling)
PARAGRAPH 5: Model A (Cost: Fuel and Maintenance)
PARAGRAPH 6: Model B (Cost: Fuel and Maintenance)
PARAGRAPH 7: Model A (Special Features)
PARAGRAPH 8: Model B (Special Features)
CONCLUSION

As I mention above, you should normally avoid Option 3 in a simple comparison of two items. You may, however, have to resort to it if you are comparing more than two items.

Here are two more examples of detailed outlines for essays whose central argument involves a comparison. Notice the different structural plans in the two: the first follows the first structural plan mentioned above (Option 1); the second follows the second structural plan (Option 2).

Comparative Essay A
GENERAL SUBJECT: The Development of Modern Science
FOCUS 1: René Descartes and Francis Bacon:
A Comparison of Their Methods
THESIS: Although Bacon's and Descartes' recommendations for the new science were in many respects very similar, there were significant differences between the methods they proposed, especially concerning the relative importance of deductive and inductive ways of thinking. Both, however, made vital contributions to the development of the new science.
TS 1: In their writings, both Bacon and Descartes repeatedly stressed the need for a radical break with old authorities and traditional methods in natural science. (Paragraph considers an important similarity.)

TS 2: Moreover, in marked contrast to older traditions, both men repeatedly urged that scientific enquiry must be organized as a concerted effort to gain power over nature. (Paragraph considers another similarity.)

TS 3: One important difference between these two thinkers was their starting point. Descartes, the philosopher, began by seeking some way of arriving at knowledge of the truth—clear and distinct ideas more reliable than sense experience. Bacon, a more practical thinker, began with a demand for useful scientific knowledge based on observations of how things worked.

TS 4: As a result of these different purposes, there were some important differences in the methods they proposed: Descartes' desire for certainty led him to emphasize the importance of mathematics and deductive reasoning; Bacon, by contrast, stressed the pre-eminence of empirical demonstrations.

TS 5: One way to highlight this difference is to consider Bacon's famous image of scientists as spiders, ants, or bees. (An illustrative paragraph to extend the discussion of the previous point.)

TS 6: As it turned out, the new science quickly adopted a method that drew on the contributions of both men, so that in a sense each of them can be considered a major contributor to the development of modern scientific thinking.

CONCLUSION

Comparative Essay B

GENERAL SUBJECT: Early Christianity

FOCUS 1: Gospel of Matthew and Paul's Epistle to the Romans

THESIS: The Gospel of Matthew and Paul's Epistle to the Romans are both laying the groundwork for a new religion based upon the life and teachings of Jesus Christ, but the visions of this new religion in the two texts are significantly different. The major differences stem from the fact that Matthew presents Christianity as the next step in Jewish history, while Paul distances Christianity from its Jewish roots.

TS 1: One of the most remarkable features of Matthew's Gospel is the way it repeatedly stresses the national identity of Jesus Christ in relation to the history of the Jewish people.

TS 2: Paul's Epistle to the Romans, by contrast, downplays the ethnic and national origins of Jesus in order to emphasize his international identity.

TS 3: Not surprisingly, Matthew's Gospel often links Jesus' message closely to traditional Jewish religious law and history.

TS 4: Paul's Epistle, on the other hand, places much more emphasis on faith in Jesus than it does on any notion of law or history.

TS 5: The Gospel of Matthew envisions the new religious community as having a distinctly Jewish identity— perhaps in the form of a radically reformed Judaism or a new version of Judaism living alongside more traditional communities.

TS 6: The Epistle to the Romans, by contrast, clearly sees the new religion as an international movement, with no distinctly Jewish roots or even any direct link to Judaism.

TS 7: One way to appreciate the different aspirations of these two Christian writers is to consider the two most famous acronyms associated with the development of early Christianity: INRI and IXTHUS. (An illustrative paragraph to highlight the main point in the comparison.)

CONCLUSION

Notice that in both these sample outlines, the argument starts by insisting that the two things being compared are sufficiently similar to bear the comparison.

7.6 | Writing Reviews of Fine and Performing Arts Events

A review of an arts event is, like the normal college essay, an interpretative argument. You are presenting your opinion of what you have seen and are seeking to persuade the reader to share that opinion. Like any argument, a review must have a clear logic (based on a firm opinion, or thesis), with an introduction and a sequence of paragraphs presenting well-organized evidence.

A review, however, has a few special requirements. To begin with, bear in mind that you are writing it for three different groups: those who have not seen the production and are wondering whether or not they should attend, those who have seen it and are interested in an informed opinion to compare with their own, and those who are putting on the production (the performers). Those in the first group will want to know a little about what the event consists of (what type of play or musical recital or dance or art show is involved), but they do not want to know too much (i.e., no "spoilers" that give away important information that may ruin their enjoyment if they decide to go). The second group will not want to read a mere description of the event; they will be seeking an interpretative opinion, an argument based on the evaluation of particular aspects of what the production offers (i.e., what they saw). The last group (the performers) will want to read very specific details of what you liked or did not like, so that they can understand what they are doing well and what they need to improve.

The following notes may help you produce a better review. There is a sample short review at the end of these notes.

1. It is customary to open a review by indicating the name, place, and time of the event you are reviewing. Identify those responsible for putting on the event, indicating (usually) the general content of the show. You should do this briefly, with no digressions. The introduction normally closes with the

writer's overall opinion of the event (the coordinating opinion), which is, in effect, the thesis of the review.

2. Your coordinating opinion at the end of the introduction must present your considered evaluation of the whole experience. Normally this opinion will fall into one of three categories: (a) unequivocal praise (everything is splendidly successful), (b) unequivocal criticism (everything is a mess), and, most commonly, (c) a mixed opinion (some things work well, but there are also some problems).

3. Once you have introduced the event and your opinion, in the sequence of paragraphs which follows (the argument), you will discuss one element of the event at a time, seeking to indicate to the reader why the production is worthwhile or not. You will not be able to cover all aspects of the event, so select the three or four most important features which helped to shape your reaction most decisively.

4. Remember that the purpose of the review is not (repeat not) simply to describe the event or the background to it (e.g., to retell the story of the play, to provide details about the paintings, to give a history of the author or the organization sponsoring the event): your task is to assess the quality of the experience. A very common mistake with review assignments is for the writer to digress into all sorts of other matters. So if you find yourself retelling the story of the play or talking at length about the writer or painter or anything not directly relevant to the argument, the review is going astray.

5. Be particularly careful with plays. The review is not a literary interpretation of the text (although that may enter into it briefly, especially if you are reviewing a new work). The review is an evaluation of the production, which is an interpretation of the play. Note that the terms *play* and *production*

mean significantly different things: the production is what you are concerned with, so in your review refer to the event as the *production*, not the *play*—unless you wish to say something about the script. The same is true with a musical or operatic production. In most cases, you are assessing the performance, not the musical score or the libretto.

6. Discuss only one aspect of the event in each paragraph. Begin the paragraph by announcing how this aspect affected your response (e.g., "One really successful part of this play is the set design, which brings out well the complex mood of the piece" or "Many of the paintings, however, are not very interesting, with banal subjects very conventionally presented"). Then in the paragraph discuss only that announced subject. Do not change the subject in mid-paragraph. If you want to change the subject to discuss another aspect of the event, then start a new paragraph.

7. Once you have introduced the subject of the paragraph, then you must introduce evidence from the show and argue how that evidence shaped your reaction. The quality of the review stems in large part from the way in which you do this. If, for example, you start the paragraph by saying that the supporting actors are not very good, then you must provide evidence (facts) from the production. And that evidence must be detailed.

   The question of detail is all important. For example, if you say something like "The main actress is very good, but the male lead is not up to her standard," you have expressed an opinion, but we need more detail. What does the main actress actually do on stage that makes you think this way about her performance? What does the male lead do or not do that makes you think this way about his performance? Note the difference between the above statements and the following:

The main actress is very good, especially in the way she controls her gestures and her voice at the key moments of the production. This is especially apparent in the final scene, where she sits down throughout, yet manages with her body movements and the controlled anger in her voice to convey fully just what the character is experiencing. However, the male lead is not up to her standard. He moves much too woodenly and speaks as if he is having trouble remembering his lines. He needs to inject some real feeling into many passages, particularly in his declaration of love in Act II.

Notice that in the example above there is enough detail for the actors whom you are praising and criticizing to understand why you think about their performance the way you do, so that, if they wanted, they could do something about it (whereas if all you say is "good" or "not so good" they have very little to go on). Your review will not be successful if you do not get into this sort of detail.

8. This level of detail applies also when you are reviewing works of art. Don't just sum up a painter or a work of art with a word or two of general praise or censure. Provide the supplementary details (taken directly from the works you are looking at), so that the reader understands the particulars out of which your opinion arises.

9. What the two above points mean, in practice, is that the review should consist of relatively few but substantial paragraphs rather than of many short paragraphs (in a 1000 word review, for example, you might have room for perhaps three paragraphs of argument after the introduction).

10. In organizing the review, you can choose to discuss what you want to. And remember that many things help to shape the

event apart from the most immediately obvious: the setting (the arrangement of the space), the price, the treatment of the audience or viewing public, the audience, the incidental music, the hanging of the paintings, the acoustics, and so on. At times some of these might be worth mentioning (if you think they had a significant impact). However, some issues are central to the event, and you can hardly choose to ignore them. For instance, in a review of a play, you must make some detailed mention of the acting. In an art show, you must spend considerable space discussing specific paintings (even if you cannot deal with them all). In a review of a musical performance, you need to discuss the quality of the playing or singing or both.

11. As you write the review, identify the people involved as you discuss them. "Mona Chisolm, who plays the heroine Janice, is well matched with Brad Ashley, in the role of Fred ..."; "The direction, by Alice McTavish, is crisp and effective ..."; "The first violin, Michael Tisdale, has difficulty in some places...." You do not need to identify everyone in the production, but identify those artists you do discuss.

12. It is customary in many reviews to keep to the present tense when you are discussing what is going on in the production (even though you saw it in the past). So, for example, when you discuss what the actors did, keep to the present tense: "In the opening scene the actors seem quite nervous, but they gather confidence as the play progresses. The director needs to pay some attention to improving this part of the production." Similarly, in discussing works of art, stay in the present tense when you are discussing particular works: "The colours in this work clash unexpectedly, but this makes the picture, in a curious way, effective, because it highlights the central focus." Use the past tense to discuss when you saw the play (i.e., in the opening paragraph), but stay in

the present tense throughout the discussion of the work or works.

13. It is customary to offer a short conclusion in which you restate your overall opinion, together with some facts about the continuing run of the production.

14. One final piece of advice: A review is much easier to write if you attend the event with some others and discuss what you have seen together immediately after the experience. If you take the time to discuss your reactions with others, your confidence in your opinions and your command of the particular details needed to back up your own views will be that much stronger.

7.6.1 | Sample Short Review of a Dramatic Production

Here is a sample review of an imaginary production. Pay particular attention to the way in which the writer introduces the review, establishes a central coordinating opinion, deals with one aspect of the production in each paragraph, and provides particular details to support the opinions that appear in the opening of each paragraph. Notice also the use of the present tense in discussions of the production.

> This week at the Malaspina University-College Theatre, Mountain Valley Theatre Company is offering its latest production, *No Time Like the Present* by Earl Courtenay, an engagingly written, funny, and, for the most part, successfully delivered bitter-sweet comedy about middle-age romance in a small Texas town in the 1980s. The play is something of a gamble for this young company, because the production style is mildly experimental in places, but, in spite of some unevenness in the playing and a few difficulties here and there, the production is well worth seeing.

The main asset in this production is the acting of the leading players. As Montague Jack, a middle-aged drifter down on his luck, Jim Beam provides an entertaining charm and a level of assured skill, both of which establish the character convincingly. His slow drawl and lazy, graceful movements, which explode into an extraordinary athletic energy in the brawl in Act II, keep our attention and provide an important dramatic intensity to the production. His performance is matched by Nora Roberts, who plays Alice, the owner of the local saloon. She establishes, above all with her wonderful facial expressions and her gravelly voice, an authentic sense of someone who has seen it all but is ready for more. Their skill and chemistry are particularly evident in the opening conversation between them in Act I, where they both convincingly come across as two experienced road warriors testing each other out in full knowledge of what they are doing. The easy pace and significant but subtle physical interactions between them evoke the characters and the mood perfectly.

The quality of these two leading players carries the main weight of the experimental dream sequences, when for a moment the action is suspended and we are taken directly into the buried fantasies of people who have almost forgotten how to dream. Roberts is especially effective at conveying the lyrical quality of her monologue: the intense longing in her voice and body movements generates a powerful sexual tension which suddenly illuminates the complexity of a character we may be tempted to take too lightly. Beam's acting in this scene is remarkably good, too, although the script offers him less to work with. The quality of his expressions as he deals with his memories and hopes is very impressive.

The supporting cast is not up to the quality of the principal players. Too often the acting is rather wooden (particularly in the case of Alan Blake, as the Sheriff, who moves as if he is reluctant to be there and who speaks in a monotone).

The lesser players seem to have some trouble establishing convincing accents (which move from the Southern States to Ireland and back to New England). However, Jennifer Braxton gives a wonderful but all-too-short cameo appearance as Wilma the inebriated singer. The quality of her voice really does suggest that she could deliver the goods if her neurons were all firing correctly, and she refuses to ham up the drunkenness, so that the comedy is always surgically precise (and all the funnier for that).

The direction (by Terry Stapleton) is, for the most part, deft. There are places, however, where the pace needs picking up (for example, in the long scene at the opening of Act II). And the blocking does get occasionally repetitive. Why, one wonders, are the chairs always arranged in the same position? There is room for considerably more visual variety than we get. In addition, the slowness of the scene changes is irritating. However, the comic scenes are well managed, and there is a good deal of very interesting business in the use of various props (e.g., the fake six gun and the old guitar). And I particularly like the way in which the director has controlled the tone of the piece, allowing the ironic resonance to manifest itself without overwhelming the comedy (he has wisely kept in check any desires of the cast members to play strictly for laughs).

The major technical aspects of the production are good, as well. The set (by Ryle Cannon) is splendidly evocative of a seedy old saloon. The colour of the wood and, above all, the floor provide just the right sense of a place which has seen its best days long ago. I do wonder a bit about the decoration on the walls; the picture of the baseball team seems a bit out of place and the antlers don't look as if they come from South Texas. Maybe I'm being too picky here. Lighting (by Patricia Foudy) is functional but unexciting (except in the dream sequences where the backlighting is spectacularly effective).

Other aspects of the production, in general, work very well. The costumes (by Christine Thompson) are really splendid, especially the shoes. The incidental music (composed by Claudia Smith and played by Wes Matchoff and Gloria Steiner) provides just the right introduction to the play and adds interest to the excessively lengthy scene changes. Like the production itself, the bluesy-funk style establishes some entertaining ambiguities, and Gloria Steiner's voice is very easy to listen to. I do, however, have some reservations about the make-up on the older townspeople (Mabel Courtenay, in particular), which seems to highlight the fact that these are young actors pretending to be older folks (the same goes for the hair).

No Time Like the Present, for all the criticisms one might like to make about this or that aspect of the production, is well worth the price of admission. It will make you laugh and yet leave you wondering about the way in which underneath the laughter there may be, as in much of life, a significant sadness lurking. The production continues its run at Malaspina University-College Theatre for the next two weeks (until April 17).

Essays about Literature

One of the commonest assignments in college requires the student to provide an argumentative essay on a work of literature—a novel, short story, philosophical work, political science treatise, epic poem, and so on. How a student is supposed to carry out this task can sometimes be rather confusing at first, and mistakes about what is expected may lead him to produce an unsatisfactory essay. This section seeks to clarify a few of the more important issues involved in such assignments.

8.1 | Preliminary Considerations

When you set out to write an interpretative essay on a literary work there are three important things to avoid: first, do not impose a quick snap judgement on the work or part of it; second, remember the difference between a summary and an interpretation; and third, do not think you are offering a useful interpretation of something when, in fact, you are merely explaining it away.

8.1.1 | *Imposing Snap Judgements*

A snap judgement is, as the name suggests, a response that has not given the text a fair hearing. The writer has simply imposed on the work a quick (and usually hostile) interpretation based on her own beliefs, her adherence to a rival set of principles, her own preferences, or her immediate response to a particular recommendation, theme, feature of the style, and so on.

You should, at the beginning of any attempt to interpret a work, treat the author with considerable respect. Assume he is an intelligent person who has something important to reveal in his argument or his fiction. If there is something bizarre or apparently offensive in the work, explore why that might be there, what it contributes to the work, what might be absent if it were removed or changed. That does not mean you have to approve of or endorse the text. What it does mean is that you have to take the trouble to understand it on its own terms, before arriving at a judgement.

For instance, many readers are quickly offended by Homer's *Iliad*, because it offers a vision of the world in which people kill each other in battle all the time and most of the deaths are horrific. That prompted the seventeenth-century poet and critic John Dryden to announce that Homer's heroes are "ungodly man killers ... a race of men who can never enjoy quiet in themselves till they have taken it from all the world." Before arriving at a similar conclusion, however, we have to explore *why* the men behave this way. How does their vision of the world prompt them to see value in this activity? Is there anything remarkable about this vision? How do people in that society feel about warfare? Why do they feel that way? And so on. To criticize the work without doing that makes as much sense as dismissing out of hand a work of science fiction or fantasy because it does not conform to our daily experience of the world around us or rejecting a philosophical argument because its initial assumptions about human nature are different from our own.

8.1.2 | Summarizing and Interpreting

The single most common mistake students make in writing argumentative essays about literary works is that they confuse a *summary* with an *interpretation*. A summary is simply a description of a work's contents; it translates the text into the essay writer's own words. An interpretation, on the other hand, seeks to provide the reader insight into how he might read a text (or part of it) so that he can understand it better.

When you are preparing to write an essay on a particular work, assume that the reader of your essay is thoroughly familiar with the text you are interpreting. She has read it many times and has it open in front of her. Because she has an excellent memory and has understood every word in the work, she has a thorough command of all the facts of the text. However, she is not sure why they matter, and she is hoping your essay will assist her with her problem. She is, if you wish, like a juror at a trial who has carefully inspected all the evidence many times and is waiting for you, the lawyer, to interpret that evidence (or some of it)—to tell her what is significant and why—so that she can deliver an informed verdict. Given that need, simply re-describing the evidence is no help to her at all. It is telling her what she already knows.

The surest and commonest way to write an unsuccessful interpretative essay on a work of literature is to offer what is little more than a summary of the argument or the story you are supposed to be assessing.

8.1.3 | Interpreting and Explaining Away

Interpreting a text is essentially an *exploration*. An interpretative argument is saying, in effect, "If we follow this possibility raised by the text itself we may be able to grasp the significance of certain details that we did not notice before and that make the text more intelligible to us." Explaining something away is essentially pasting a label on it, so that you do not have to think about it any further. Notice the following examples:

Macbeth kills King Duncan because he is ambitious.

Rousseau makes those recommendations because he is a sexist.

Mill talks that way about education because he's a liberal propagandist.

The scene with the porter in *Macbeth* is for comic relief.

King Lear gives away his kingdom because he is old and demented.

Achilles goes on a killing spree because he is a psychopath.

These statements, in themselves, explain virtually nothing. To claim that King Lear does what he does because he is old and demented or that Achilles kills because he's a psychopath removes any significance from their actions, because the argument is saying, in effect, that there is no logic to what they do. What forms of strange conduct would those words not "explain"? To sum up the reasons for Macbeth's actions with the word "ambitious" overlooks the fact that not all ambitious people kill. The word provides no insight into the particular details of his motivation. What does calling the Porter scene in *Macbeth* "comic relief" mean? If there is humour in the scene, how does that help us understand the play better? And what does the word "relief" contribute to an understanding of the text? And so on. To dismiss writers as intelligent as John Stuart Mill and Jean Jacques Rousseau with a handy label is to evade your responsibility to explore their arguments in detail. How do these arguments logically arise from basic principles they have announced? What is valuable about them? Where do problems emerge? Such facile one-word labels inform the reader of your essay, not just that you have not understood these texts, but that you have not even tried to understand them.

In general you should avoid attempting to interpret something simply by using a cheap and usually dismissive tag (*sexist*, *feminist*, *apologist*, *revisionist*, and so on), unless you are prepared to explore in detail the logic of the actions or the arguments those labels are meant to explain. Otherwise, all these terms are communicating to the reader of your essay is something like the following: "My explanation is that I cannot explain it, so I'm dismissing it using a relatively empty term that sounds meaningful."

Take particular care not to offer a summary snap judgement of a work based upon some perceived character flaw or bias in the author (e.g., "Nietzsche's whole argument here is a manifestation of his anti-Semitism. Also we need to remember that he was declared insane a few years after writing this book").

8.2 | Interpreting from the Outside and from the Inside

At this point, by way of clarifying a few matters, I need to venture briefly into the contested waters of how one ought to analyze a written text. It is beyond the scope of this book to navigate a clear and safe passage through such choppy seas, but, at the risk of oversimplifying complex issues, I would like to make a distinction that may help to illuminate whatever practical assistance I have to offer.

Let me begin, then, by proposing that there are two general approaches to interpreting a text: *from the outside* or *from the inside*. We approach a text from the outside when our interpretation is guided by information that is not contained within the text itself, and we approach it from the inside when we confine our attention exclusively to what the text contains, without reference to anything else. For instance, if we bring to the work a knowledge of the author's life or times and let details of his biography or of the social context of the age in which he lived shape the argument, then we are interpreting from the outside; if we ignore his life and times and focus only on the words on the page, we are interpreting from the inside, letting our argument grow out of the internal features of the work. I realize that there are some objections one might raise to this distinction, but please bear with me.

These two approaches, as we shall see, are not mutually exclusive; many of the most useful interpretations of particular texts combine them.

8.2.1 | *Clarifying the Assignment*

The first task a writer preparing to write an argument on a work of literature has to carry out is to make sure she understands what the assignment requires. Is she expected to read the work and write an interpretative argument from the outside or from the inside or both? Does the assignment specify that she is to provide an argument involving the historical context of the work, or can she ignore all matters of context? Notice the following sample essay topics:

1. Discuss the significance of Edgar in Emily Brontë's *Wuthering Heights*.

2. Assess Hobbes's notion of sovereignty in *Leviathan*. How would he respond to the charge that his proposals are a recipe for tyranny in the commonwealth?

3. In what ways might we consider Charles Darwin's *Origin of Species* a very derivative work, heavily reliant on the ideas of his predecessors?

4. What, if anything, is revolutionary about William Wordsworth's poetic style in *Lyrical Ballads*? Are we justified in seeing this work as a decisive shift in the writing of English lyric poetry?

These four assignments, each requiring the interpretation of a text, are not all making the same demands. The first two are inviting you to respond to the text on your own terms. You can deal with the topic by focusing all your attention on the text itself. The third and fourth clearly demand an argument about the work in relation to its historical context; you cannot cope with these topics satisfactorily without bringing into your essay material from outside.

Generally speaking, interpreting a work from the inside is commonly expected in most assignments on literature in the early years of undergraduate work (e.g., in first-year English and philosophy courses), where one purpose of the assignment is to encourage the student to read a text on her own and produce an interpretative argument based solely on that reading. In upper-division courses, by contrast, where a good deal of research is often emphasized, students are more frequently expected to incorporate contextual matters (e.g., history and biography) into their arguments.

We might note that the distinction I am making here between whether or not the historical context of a work should be a part of one's interpretation of it stems, in part, from the fact that we have traditionally had two different ways of understanding things, that is, two sorts of answers the question, "What is it?" Sometimes we explain what things are by describing the *properties they possess* (i.e., the formal characteristics which define them, the characteristics we see in them); at other times we answer that question by explaining their *origin* or *how they came to be* (i.e., the processes by which they were produced). For example, if someone poses the question, "Who are you?" you can define yourself by the character and qualities you now possess or you can define yourself by your family origins, your lineage. Or you can do both.

I stress this point here because, although these two ways of addressing the question "What is it?" are closely related, they are not the same, and a tendency to confuse the two can lead to serious errors in an interpretative argument. For example, if the focus of your interpretative argument is the significance of certain patterns in the language of the argument or the fiction, then you need to concentrate on exploring how those patterns work within the text, not on describing how they came to be there. If you fail to do so, you may be committing the *genetic fallacy*, the mistake of evaluating an argument or a fiction on the basis of its origins rather than on its own merits.

Here a relevant question may be in order: Should a significant change in one's knowledge of the context of a work change our interpretation of that work? Suppose, for example, we discovered that S.T. Coleridge's famous poem "The Rime of the Ancient Mariner" had been written by someone else. Would that change our understanding of the work? From a common-sense point of view, since the text remains exactly the same and the meanings of the words have not changed, the answer would seem to be no—of course not. The changed historical context would obviously have a decisive effect on any argument linking the poem with the biography of the author, but why should it change any argument about what the language of the poem is doing?

What all this means in practice is this: when you are writing an essay on a work of literature, you need initially to answer the following question: "Is my primary purpose here to offer an argument about the inner workings of the language of the text (i.e., to help the reader of my essay understand that text better), or is it to construct an argument about the way that text came to be written, or is it to do both?" Your answer to that question will obviously have a decisive effect on the nature of the argument and the structure of the essay. If you are uncertain what the assignment requires in this regard, make sure you check with the instructor.

8.2.2 | *Appealing to Context*

Given the above observations, unless the essay topic requires the writer to take the historical context of a work into account, she should normally ignore it or subordinate it to an interpretation based solely on what she reads in the work itself. In other words, the main focus of an interpretative essay should always remain on the contents of the text under discussion, without any undue emphasis on contextual matters.

There are, however, at least three places where an essay writer may need to appeal to the context of the work.

1. The first requirement of any intelligent interpretation of a work of literature is an informed sense of what the words in the text mean. In most cases, if we have any difficulty with that, a modern dictionary can help us out. However, many of the texts studied in college are not contemporary with us, and the language in them reflects this fact: often the words are strange, and sometimes familiar words have changed their meanings. To understand them properly we must refer to what they meant at the time the work was written (i.e., to their context). Hence, the greatest companion of every interpreter of a work written in English is the *Oxford English Dictionary*, which, in its definitions of words, traces their historical meanings. Fortunately for us, most critical editions of the texts we study spare us the trouble of consulting this lexicon all the time, by providing us with the information we need in footnotes (as in most modern editions of Shakespeare's plays, for example).

   A changed historical context can sometimes create serious difficulties for the interpretation of a work, especially when the language of an older text is now considered unacceptably offensive. That is commonly the case with racial epithets (for example, calling aboriginal people "injuns," or "savages," or "redskins," or referring to Jews as "kikes" or Afro-Americans as "niggers," all common practices until fairly recently). An appeal to the original context of the work can sometimes help to alleviate difficulties modern readers have with such language, but often, in spite of such appeals, the power of these racial slurs still seriously interferes with a modern reader's ability to judge the text. *Huckleberry Finn*, for example, universally acknowledged as a major work of American literature, creates significant problems for many modern readers because the word "nigger" occurs in it more than two hundred times. Attempts have been made to deal with this issue by banning the book or revising the offensive language. Such measures, however, raise a number of obvious objections.

This issue of the meanings of words can sometimes arise when we are dealing with a text that is a translation from a foreign language and that contains an important word difficult to render precisely in colloquial modern English. One might legitimately wish, as part of one's argument, to challenge the translation where the English text is potentially misleading in its rendition of the term (e.g., the habit of translating Aristotle's Greek word *hamartia* as "tragic flaw," Kafka's German word *Ungeziefer* as *insect*, Machiavelli's *virtù* as *virtue*, Rousseau's *amour propre* as *pride*, and so on). Such a challenge from outside the text is, of course, appropriate only if it contributes to your interpretative argument.

2. The authority of the historical context is also necessary sometimes in order to rein in any excessively whimsical interpretations based on the Humpty Dumpty principle that words and images can mean whatever we want them to mean. If, for example, a student wishes to argue that the phrase "the deep damnation of his taking-off" in *Macbeth* is a reference to a modern warplane setting out to drop bombs on innocent civilians, the best response is probably a gentle reminder that history informs us such weapons were not available in Shakespeare's day.

3. A contextual criticism (from outside the work) may also be an important part of your interpretation if the text you are discussing makes an egregious mistake by misrepresenting the facts or by misquoting someone else, especially if pointing out the mistake has a decisive effect on the argument the text is presenting and is relevant to the case you are making about it. Similarly, if the text is, deliberately or not, seriously distorting someone else's position on an issue, it might be important to point that out (once again, only if doing so helps the argument you are making).

Of course, calling attention to such errors is justified as a criticism only if the author could or should have known better. For example, we cannot fault Darwin's theory of inheritance on the ground that it does not match what later discoveries have revealed about the process (involving genes, DNA, and so on), any more than we can fault Dante for not having a direct knowledge of Homer's poems (to which he did not have access in a language he could read). And pointing out a mistake is not all that helpful if the error is trivial or irrelevant to your argument (e.g., a mistranslation of a sentence from John Locke in one of Rousseau's footnotes).

Such contextual criticism of factual errors is usually out of place in essays on literary fictions. For instance, reminding us that Shakespeare had an imperfect knowledge of the geography of Bohemia is on its own hardly a significant interpretative criticism of *The Winter's Tale*, although that point might be something you would want to mention if you were writing an essay about Shakespeare's general knowledge—or if the ways in which his depiction of Bohemia differed from the reality were somehow important to your interpretation of the play. Similarly, condemning a fiction based on historical events or characters because certain details contradict well-established historical facts is usually irrelevant: the term *fiction*, after all, means *made up*, and a writer of fiction is fully entitled to treat historical details from her sources as she likes. (It may, however, occasionally be of interest to consider what thematic, structural, or other purpose such deviations from the facts might serve.)

Apart from the situations mentioned above, you should normally avoid letting contextual facts shape your argument, and you should *never* offer as an insight into a text an interpretation whose *only* justification is that it answers to certain contextual facts. Consider, for example, this observation: "The stanza describing these sinners is significant because the figures depicted are Florentines whom Dante would have known." As it stands, this statement is a *non sequitur* because it is not clear to the reader why the fact that Dante would have known these sinners is significant to an understanding of the poem.

The reasons one should not give any special authority to contextual matters in an essay interpreting a work of literature are obvious enough. First, a detailed examination of a rich historical context is capable of yielding information to support any number of rival interpretations. As the saying goes, "If you torture the facts sufficiently, they will confess to anything." Appeals to context, after all, have been used to demonstrate that Shakespeare's texts must have been written by a conservative, a revolutionary, a Catholic, a Protestant, a skeptic, a soldier, a sailor, a law student, and any number of other possibilities. For that reason, establishing an apparent link between one or more contextual facts and some details of the text is not a very persuasive way to argue for a particular interpretation of those details.

Second, generalizations about context (for example, about what people believed in a certain age in the past) are, at best, superficial and, at worst, misleading. Then as now, on any particular issue there would have been all sorts of different opinions at work—some people would have been faithful adherents to the prevailing religious orthodoxy, others would have been skeptics, or atheists, or agnostics; some would have been very superstitious, others would have considered superstition ridiculous; some would have been conservative, others radical, others politically apathetic, and still others revolutionaries; some would have had opposite-sex relationships, some would have had same-sex relationships, and others would have been celibate; and so on. To suggest that they all must have shared a common ideology, attitude, habit, or vision of life flies in the face of what we know about human nature in complex societies.

Third, an argument that seeks to interpret a work with constant reference to the author's context overlooks the possibility that great authors can transcend the prevailing conventions of their times. In many cases the work they produce is a challenge to those very conventions and prevailing ideas. An interpretation that confines itself to explaining everything in a text by referring to the general or prevailing beliefs and practices of the author's contemporaries may be missing what is most important, original, and valuable in the work he has created.

For all these reasons, you should avoid interpretative arguments that rely on contextual explanations like the following:

1. We are meant to be sympathetic towards the ghost of Hamlet's father, because that's how Shakespeare's audience would have responded.

2. Gregor's grotesque transformation into a bug is obviously a symbol of Kafka's feelings about his own debilitating illness.

3. This phase of Descartes' argument for the existence of God is simply a manifestation of the Catholic faith of his time.

4. In her *Vindication of the Rights of Woman* Wollstonecraft treats Rousseau so harshly because the English public was appalled by what was going on in revolutionary France—events largely inspired, in their eyes, by Rousseau's writings.

Statements like this may or may not be true, but they are not very helpful unless the writer is prepared to explain how they illuminate the story or the argument we are exploring. As they stand, without that close link to details of the text, such assertions are one more example of explaining something away rather than interpreting it.

Appeals to context are often useful (and perfectly acceptable) if they serve *to introduce* an interpretative possibility. They become problematic, however, when such an appeal is used to privilege a particular interpretation or to close off further discussion. Notice the difference between the two following sentences:

> If we recall that Author X was, as a child, very harshly
> treated by his father, we might wish to explore how in this
> story the main character's hostility to his family may stem
> from his childhood experiences. For example …
> (The writer goes on to explore what evidence
> there is in the text to support this possibility.)

> If we recall that Author X was, as a child, very harshly
> treated by his father, then we can obviously trace the main
> character's hostility to his family in this story back to his
> childhood experiences.

Both interpretations open with an appeal to a biographical fact. But they use that fact in different ways: the first invites us to consider it as an interpretative possibility, a potentially interesting line of enquiry; the second insists that the contextual fact determines what the text means and suggests in its very firm wording that we do not need to reflect about the matter any further: the context has ruled, and that is that.

Of course, the writer of the first sentence does not need to know anything about Author X in order to invite the reader to "explore how much the main character's hostility to his family may stem from his childhood experiences." She is perfectly entitled to make that suggestion on her own. Providing the biographical fact is an interesting way to raise the suggestion, but it does not make that suggestion any more persuasive, because whether that interpretative line of enquiry is useful or not will be determined by only one thing: how well details in the text support it or, alternatively put, how much it illuminates certain details in the text.

What these remarks about arguments from the context of a work add up to is this: the persuasiveness of an interpretative argument can often be enhanced with contextual information but it does not depend on such information. Thus, so long as you understand the words in the text, you need not be deterred by ignorance of the author's life and times. Investigations into historical matters can be fascinating and enjoyable and tell us a great deal about the author and the writing of the book. But they have no particular authority when it comes to assessing the book on its own merits. So anyone who claims, for example, that a student needs to know a lot about an author and his times in order to write intelligently about one of his works is making a false claim—equivalent to saying that one cannot offer an intelligent assessment of a game of hockey without having expert knowledge of the history of the game or the biographies of all the players.

That also means, of course, that, unless your essay topic specifically requires you to address the context of a work, filling the essay with historical or biographical information is not going to make your argument any more persuasive. For that reason, you should rein in any temptations to provide long digressions about historical or biographical matters.

We might note, in passing, that if the purpose of the essay is to provide a biography of the author, then the emphasis I have described above would be reversed. Since the centre of interest in such an essay would be a historical narrative (rather than an interpretation of a particular work), details from various texts could be used to provide clues about the author's life. However, such an essay would not be literary interpretation.

8.2.3 | Appealing to Sources

One important element that can sometimes provide very useful clues about potentially interesting interpretative possibilities in a text is the author's use of the materials his culture has made available to him. For instance, he may pluck an idea from a contemporary or a predecessor and use it in his own argument or he may plunder a history book for a rich narrative or an interesting character.

In such cases, what is usually of particular interest is not the mere fact of the borrowing but rather the use the author has made of it (particularly the ways he may have changed the source material). For instance, the alterations Shakespeare makes to the facts taken from his historical sources can prompt interesting suggestions about a significant element in the story he has created (e.g., making Hotspur younger in *Henry IV, Part 1* so that he and Prince Hal are the same age emphasizes further the comparison between them). One does not have to know about that change in the source material to call attention to the significance of the age similarities, of course, but if one had not noticed it, the source might alert one to the fact. Similarly, the way a great scientist or philosopher has synthesized the ideas she has appropriated from others may provide insights into what is particularly important about her work.

An essay interpreting a work in relation to its sources needs to strike the correct balance, so that it does not end up spending too much time describing contextual sources when it should be focusing on what the author has done with that material. Here, for example, is a sample outline for an essay written on Charles Darwin's sources and his *Origin of Species*:

> ESSAY TOPIC: Discuss the importance of the scientific influences that shaped Charles Darwin's *Origin of Species*. Is that book simply a rehash of other people's ideas? If so, why should we consider Darwin a great scientist?

THESIS: Darwin's *Origin of Species* must be one of the most derivative great works in the history of science, since all its major ideas come from others. However, that fact helps one to appreciate the true nature of Darwin's genius.

TS 1: What, in essence, is the famous theory presented in *Origin of Species*? (The paragraph offers a definition of Darwin's theory, in order to identify the key terms in it.)

TS 2: The concept of evolution, of course, goes back to classical times, and the idea had been in the forefront of scientific discussions for at least a hundred years before Darwin's book was published. (The paragraph argues that evolution was very well known to Darwin.)

TS 3: Similarly, the key idea of descent with variation had been extensively treated well before *Origin of Species* appeared.

TS 4: Even the idea Darwin is usually given most credit for, the concept of natural selection, had been proposed and published in English well before 1859.

TS 5: The fact that so much of *Origin of Species* is "borrowed" material, however, should not blind us to Darwin's brilliance as a scientist. First of all, he had the insight to recognize the significance of ideas that people were talking about without realizing how powerful they might be. (The interpretative argument about Darwin's book begins here.)

TS 6: Second, Darwin realized that these ideas, as they stood, had little scientific status. Someone needed to demonstrate their explanatory value. (The paragraph looks at how *Origin of Species* was a response to this need. This point could be expanded into several other paragraphs, since there are a great many things Darwin explains in his book using his borrowed ideas.)

TS 7: Third, in writing *Origin of Species* Darwin had the courage and perseverance to gamble his entire scientific career and many years of his life on a theory that he knew he could not prove. (The paragraph discusses this point.)

TS 8: Finally, Darwin, like many scientists whose theories survive and prevail, was supremely lucky. Evidence critical to the success of his theory did eventually turn up years after his death.

CONCLUSION

This essay reviews three vital ideas Darwin borrowed and brings out just how derivative his theory in *Origin of Species* is. But then it turns to what the book does with those ideas and makes the case for its extraordinary contribution to science. The essay thus links contextual matters (the sources) to an interpretative assessment of the text, but the central emphasis is clear: the argument is about Darwin's text.

8.2.4 | Appealing to Authorial Intentions

For the same reasons as those given above about context, appeals to the author's intentions are of limited use and are never prescriptive. This point is obvious enough when we have no firm evidence for what the author intended (e.g., with Homer or Shakespeare), but it is equally valid if we do have unambiguous documentary evidence of what she intended to write or wished the work to mean. To insist that an author's intention occupies some privileged position and plays a determining role in assessing interpretative possibilities is to commit the *intentional fallacy*, the mistake of claiming that what a person intends to produce must define our understanding of what he did produce.

The reason for this point is obvious enough. I may intend to write an interesting, useful, and popular book on how to write essays. I may inform my relatives of that intention and even announce it in the book itself. But whether the book is interesting, useful, and popular is for the readers to decide by reading the book and assessing its contents. My wishes and intentions are beside the point. To paraphrase Bob Dylan: writers are postmen who deliver the mail; it is up to those who read the letters to determine what is in them and whether or not they are worth reading.

So, for example, if I want to propose that Machiavelli's *Prince* is a satire ridiculing the very conduct he is apparently promoting in the text, I need not be deterred by the fact that there is a letter from Machiavelli stating that he did not intend the work to be a satire. That historical evidence is interesting but irrelevant. First, an authentic letter may be deliberately deceptive and, second, Machiavelli may not have realized the full implications of what he had written. Conversely, if I wish to argue that *The Prince* is definitely not a satire, my argument does not become any more persuasive if I point to the letter stating that the author did not intend it to be one. A convincing argument about whether the work is a satire or not must rest on a close reading of what is in the text.

We should also, in general, be very wary of an author's comments on how we should understand her argument or her fiction. Writers and artists are often very poor interpreters of their own work (there is ample evidence for this assertion), and they can at times get very irritated when people see things in their work that they did not intend or mean or even notice. That should not surprise us, since creating a literary work is a very different task from evaluating it, and even if one is brilliant at the first activity one may not be competent at the second (although some writers are very good at both). That is one reason many authors wisely refuse to comment on what they have written.

Of course, statements of authorial intention may, like facts from an author's biography, provide interesting interpretative suggestions that introduce a discussion of a potentially illuminating insight. But they should not be used as authoritative declarations of how we are to understand a text. Once again, it is a matter of striking the appropriate balance.

One place where it is appropriate to talk of the author's intentions or wishes occurs when we use such phrases to discuss the sense we get of what is emerging from the text itself. For example:

1. This scene suggests that Ibsen does not intend us to see Nora as a feminist heroine in the modern sense; for him she is a tragic figure.

2. Homer wants us to confront the explicit brutalities of battlefield deaths.

3. Rousseau's intention in mentioning the authority of the Biblical accounts of creation is clearly ironic.

In statements like this, the essay writer is not referring to any clearly stated authorial intention outside the text. The words "intend," "wants," and "intention" and the author's name here mean, in effect, "From my reading of the text, this is what I think it is saying."

8.2.5 | Appealing to Literary Conventions

A popular but often lazy way of interpreting something in a text is an appeal to conventions: some element of the text is there because that's what the literary conventions of the work demand. Once we realize that, we do not have to worry any further about what it means. For example, one major problem for interpreters of *Hamlet* is explaining why the prince delays for so long in avenging his father. Well, one well-known explanation is "No delay, no play." In other words, we should not question the delay, because once Hamlet kills Claudius the play will be over, and so the delay is simply a convention demanded by a revenge drama in five acts.

Such an explanation is a variety of the genetic fallacy: by appealing to how something came to be present in the work, it is simply explaining away what we need to understand in order to follow the logic of the fiction. The delay, in other words, is an integral part of the text, and we need to understand it in terms of the details of that text. If the words of the text keep reminding us of the issue, we cannot simply explain it away as a convention and forget about it.

Another well-known example of this fallacy is the attempt to account for the abrupt and unexplained disappearance of the Fool in *King Lear* in the middle of the play by pointing out that the actor playing the Fool also played Cordelia and that, since she is about to reappear, the Fool has to vanish from the stage. Even if there were incontrovertible evidence for that historical fact, the explanation is no help at all in an interpretative argument where we are trying to account for the significance of the Fool within the context of the play itself.

Conventions are often essential ingredients in literary works, but the key question is not so much what is convention and what is not but rather how the writer has worked with the conventions he has drawn upon. Any revenge story (like *Hamlet*) obviously requires an elapse of time between the original act and the final revenge. What matters in an interpretation of such a work is how the writer has accounted for that period of time: What does the delay contribute thematically; what if anything about Hamlet's character makes the delay seem plausible; how does the delay help to build tension in the work; and so on? Similarly, if the acting conventions of Shakespeare's day required the disappearance of the Fool in the middle of the action, the issue for the interpreter is how the play manages to deal with that requirement (it is often fascinating to see how modern productions of *King Lear*, which do not have to worry about the same actor playing two roles, have dealt with this issue: some keep the Fool alive and present at Lear's side for the rest of the action, others have him disappear, and at least one has Lear kill him in a fit of mad rage).

8.2.6 | *Arguing about What Is Missing in a Text*

Authors of arguments and fictions are obviously free to shape their work the way they see fit, and interpreters of their texts normally have an obligation to confine their attention to the words on the page. However, there are times when a reader may legitimately introduce into an interpretative argument about a work something the writer has failed to include, because any piece of writing creates certain expectations that the text needs to address—or needs to have a good reason for not addressing.

Suppose, to take an obvious example, an author has written a work arguing that American military interventions around the world since World War Two have been, on the whole, a great success and has, in her argument, failed to make any mention of the wars in Vietnam, in Iraq, or in Afghanistan, without offering a reason for the omission. In any interpretative assessment of that book, one could legitimately point to that omission as a serious deficiency in the argument. The topic she has chosen—American interventions around the world since World War Two—creates an obvious expectation in the reader that her text is reasonably obliged to meet. If she is not prepared to meet it, then she should provide an explanation, because the omission could be very damaging to her argument.

Similarly, in a work of fiction the author's freedom to create an imaginary story as he sees fit does not relieve him of the obligation to make that story intelligible to us, and if there are things missing in the work that frustrate our attempts to make sense of what is going on, we are entitled to point that out—though, in the context of a literary essay, such criticism should be included only if it makes a useful contribution to the argument.

Of course, we have to be very careful in making such criticisms. For it may be the case that ambiguity in the argument or the story is an important part of the author's purpose, and we have no right to demand that all arguments or stories fit our notions of what they should contain. Sometimes, considering what an omission or ambiguity might contribute to the text can lead to interesting interpretive possibilities.

Once we have come to the conclusion that the omission or ambiguity does *not* accomplish anything valuable, we still have to make sure our criticism is legitimate. For example, a play is written, first and foremost, to be performed, and many things we find puzzling when we read the script may not matter in an actual production of that script (e.g., Hamlet's age, implausible coin-cidences, sudden inexplicable quarrels which launch the action, and so on). We should not apply to a play script the same criteria we bring bear when we read a novel. On the other hand, where significant omissions impede our ability to assent to the argu-ment or the fiction, calling attention to them may well be in order.

8.2.7 | Using a Conceptual Framework as the Basis for an Interpretation

A very useful and popular method of constructing an argument about a literary work is to bring to it a conceptual framework and an analytical vocabulary derived from some theory outside the work: e.g., a psychoanalytic approach to Kafka's *Metamorphosis*, a feminist interpretation of Ibsen's *A Doll's House*, a postcolonial study of Shakespeare's *The Tempest*, a Marxist interpretation of *On Liberty*, and so on. Such arguments typically apply a partic-ular theoretical framework (or parts of it) to the text, in order to highlight features in the work and to assist us in recognizing patterns we may not have paid sufficient attention to. A Marxist approach to *Metamorphosis*, for example, can illuminate for us in a very interesting way the importance of possible links between Gregor's transformation and the nature of his work, just as a fem-inist reading of *A Doll's House* can alert us to significant patterns in Ibsen's depiction of Nora Helmer.

There are, however, certain things a writer adopting this approach to a work needs to think about.

1. First, you cannot normally assume that readers of your essay will be familiar with details of the conceptual framework you are using or with its vocabulary. Hence you will prob-ably need to provide, after the introduction to the essay, a paragraph describing those parts of the theory you intend to apply and defining the key terms you will be using (e.g., *alienation, patriarchy, alterity, Oedipus complex, colonizing the*

consciousness, and so on). Such a paragraph should restrict itself to a succinct explanation only of those parts of the theory you mean to apply. Do not turn it into a full-blown summary of the entire theory.

Here, as an example of what I mean, is the introduction to an essay discussing Shakespeare's *Richard II* and *Hamlet*:

> In William Shakespeare's *Richard II* and *Hamlet*, there is an important dramatic conflict between characters who use language in different ways, that is, who seek to understand and deal with the world (including their role in it) by a characteristic use of words, so that the antagonism between the members of each pair also expresses an important conflict in the way human beings use language to deal with the issues facing them. We can characterize this central conflict in a number of ways. Most obviously, in both *Richard II* and in *Hamlet*, we witness confrontations between two very distinct characters: Richard and Bolingbroke in the former play, and Hamlet and Claudius in the latter. In each pairing, the first character has what we might call a strong "poetical" streak (using the term very loosely), that is, his response to experience is characterized by a marked tendency to immediate verbalizing in highly imaginative language. The second is a hard-headed pragmatic political realist, whose speaking style reflects his desire to use his public language as one more way to achieve certain very specific political goals. The first, as often as not, uses language to forestall any need for immediate action; the second sees language as an essential part of a plan of action—that is, as a tool with which to manipulate people.
>
> In his famous book *Pedagogy of the Oppressed* the famous modern pedagogical philosopher Paulo Freire distinguishes between two inauthentic uses of language.

As we attempt to analyze dialogue as a human phenomenon, we discover something which is the essence of dialogue itself: the word. But the word is more than just an instrument which makes dialogue possible; accordingly, we must seek its constitutive elements. Within the word we find two dimensions, reflection and action, in such radical interaction that if one is sacrificed—even in part—the other immediately suffers….

An unauthentic word, one which is unable to transform reality, results when dichotomy is imposed upon its constitutive elements. When a word is deprived of its dimension of action, reflection automatically suffers as well; and the word is changed into idle chatter, into verbalism, into an alienated and alienating "blah." It becomes an empty word, one which cannot denounce the world, for denunciation is impossible without a commitment to transform, and there is no transformation without action.

On the other hand, if action is emphasized exclusively, to the detriment of reflection, the word is converted into activism. The latter—action for action's sake—negates the true praxis and makes dialogue impossible. (75)

Freire's point is that significant human interaction requires dialogue, some shared interchange which involves a commitment to shared action. Such dialogue becomes impossible if the participants use language for personal purposes which undercut a common bond of love and concern for the human community.

Now, Hamlet and Richard are, from the perspective of this initial analysis, both chatterers, compulsive talkers who use language to protect themselves from action. (Paragraph goes on to discuss this point.)

> Operating against these two are Bolingbroke and
> Claudius, both of whom are shrewd political operators—
> or, in Freire's language, "activists"—who listen very
> carefully to others and use their language for the most
> part not for reflection but for action. (The paragraph
> goes on to discuss this point.)

Here the writer is using an analytical vocabulary ("chatterers" and "activists") derived from outside the text. She takes the time in the second paragraph to clarify the vocabulary she will be using in the essay, so that the reader understands clearly what she means. Once she has done that, she then starts applying the borrowed terms to the texts under discussion.

2. You should take care that the terminology of the theory does not transform your style into the mind-numbing and often incomprehensible prose typical of a great deal of academic writing. Your argument does not become any more persuasive or impressive simply because the language is obtuse. Try not to let the fact that many of your sources may be riddled with jargon infect your own writing. Use the terms you need, but always strive to keep your own style clear, concise, and readable. New writers are often tempted to rely too much on jargon when they don't completely understand the theory they are using, so make sure you understand the theory well enough to make use of it in your own words.

3. Most important, you should strive to maintain an appropriate balance between the theoretical concepts you are applying and the details of the work you are interpreting. You are using the theory (or part of it) to help the reader understand some elements of the text better, but if you get the emphasis wrong then your essay can easily become reductive and turn the text you are exploring into little more than an example of the theory you are applying.

For instance, a feminist interpretation of *A Doll's House* can be very useful in helping us see more clearly certain aspects of Nora's oppressive situation. But if that interpretation is so heavy handed that it makes the play little more than a simple *illustration* of the theory, so that everything in the play can be accounted for by the feminist principles being applied, then the essay, rather than enriching our understanding of the text, may well be limiting it. Once again, the issue is the difference between an interpretative argument that opens our eyes and one that puts blinkers on us.

For that reason, if you are using this approach to a text, you should always remain alert to parts of it that might not fit the theoretical framework, something that reminds us that no work of literature worth reading can be neatly compartmentalized and placed in a clearly labelled conceptual box without being distorted. After all, those who want to insist that *A Doll's House* is a well-known example of orthodox feminist principles (and that's all there is to it) may be incapable of seeing that the play is also a great dramatic tragedy.

8.3 | Writing Essays about Arguments

An essay interpreting an argument (e.g., a philosophy or political science text) typically selects one part of the argument and focuses on that in order to explore and assess what the text is saying, how the thinker has reached this point, and what might be valuable or problematic about his reasoning. As before, the purpose of the essay is to illuminate the text, so that the reader can return to the work with an enriched understanding of what is going on in the language of the argument.

8.3.1 | Dealing with Arguments on Their Own Terms

A serious and very irritating inadequacy in many student essays about such works is that the evaluation takes place without any sensitive entry into the text under consideration (i.e., it is a snap judgement). The essay writer simply imposes his views on the text under scrutiny, as in the following short argument:

> Thinker X makes a number of initial assumptions in developing his theory of the state. The most important of these assumptions are A, B, and C.
>
> But Thinker X is wrong, because the true starting assumptions should not be A, B, and C, which are wrong (or inadequate), but M, N, and P, which are true.
>
> Let's look at some examples of how Thinker X is wrong. Example 1 shows that because Thinker X does not believe or consider M, N, and P, he is wrong. If he had thought clearly about M, N, and P, he would have said something different.

The problem with an interpretative argument like this is that it consists of little more than mere assertion and does not deal at all with the nature of Thinker X's case. It may indeed be true that Thinker X's initial assumptions are claims we no longer believe to be adequate or true (or do not wish to be true), but that does not necessarily make his argument worthless. You need to examine his case in the light of its own assumptions. In addition, if your only case against Thinker X is a rival set of assumptions (M, N, and P), and you simply state these baldly without further ado, then we have no way of assessing in any detail the validity of Thinker X's position. Besides, what gives you the authority to say that your initial unsupported assumptions are any better than Thinker X's? All this process tends to achieve is to indicate that you do not agree with Thinker X's initial assumptions, but it still leaves the business of evaluating the argument in any further detail up to the reader, without any assistance from you. It also leaves you unable to appreciate the value of arguments which are based on principles you find unacceptable.

The same tendency to reduce an interpretation to a snap

judgement can occur if you simply dismiss an argument out of hand because one of its recommendations is by modern standards unacceptable, incomplete, or even wrong. In such a case, instead of just baldly rejecting Thinker X's claims and insisting upon the importance of your own, evaluate why he is making them, how they arise from his initial assumptions, and raise objections, questions, and so forth at key places in the argument. This way, the problem you perceive can become the inspiration for a more fruitful consideration of the argument.

For example, suppose you are writing a paper evaluating Hobbes's views on sovereignty in *Leviathan*: that in the modern state the sovereign authority should have complete power and answer to no one (a view about which you have strong reservations). Rather than simply expressing your disagreement with this view of sovereignty, explore why Hobbes is making this claim. How does he reason his way to this position? Does that argument make sense? Where would you want to challenge it?

So, for example, you can trace the logic of Hobbes's claim that giving all power to the sovereign is a logical outcome of his views of human beings, the state of nature, and the formation of the commonwealth. Now you can raise an awkward question: "How does Hobbes propose to deal with the issue of the corrupting effects of power?" If human beings are as nasty as he says they are and if the sovereignty will be in the hands of one human being or a small group of them, then how will his state protect itself from tyranny?

The next step would be to explore what Hobbes has to say about the question you raise, because, like many first-rate thinkers, he has anticipated the objection. Then ask yourself how adequate his responses are. In your analysis of these responses call attention to where his argument is strong and where it may be inadequate.

Notice what is happening here. You are always operating in direct contact with the text, arguing from the inside, leading the reader to your basic objections to (or unease with) Hobbes through the details of what Hobbes himself actually writes, so that as the reader goes through your essay, she is learning a great deal about Hobbes and about where you sense particular aspects of his theory may be vulnerable. Notice, too, what you are not doing: you are not simply imposing from outside a preformed judgement about what is or is not the best way for human beings to behave. You are not raising issues which do not come directly from the text itself, and whatever problems you have with Hobbes are arising from *his* treatment of the subject, not from some ideological position you prefer.

This process can be very simply summarized as follows:

Thinker X says that Y (some issue) is to be understood in such and such a way.
Why does Thinker X make this claim? (An exploration of the basis of Thinker X's argument.)
What is valuable about this analysis?
However, Thinker X's treatment here does invite one to raise some questions, alternative scenarios, counterexamples.
How would Thinker X deal with such potentially awkward questions?
This seems like a (satisfactory, unsatisfactory, illogical, inadequate, strained, limited, and so on) explanation.
This point, in fact, suggests an overall problem with the entire theory (or indicates just how fertile and useful Thinker X's position really is).
We can appreciate this problem clearly by considering another point (repeat the process).

Note that in the above structure you are giving Thinker X a good hearing in at least three respects: You are linking his position on a particular (and perhaps controversial) issue to the grounded argument he makes from first principles; you are conceding the fact that there is something in his case (as there almost always will be if you are dealing with a thinker who is not thoroughly simpleminded); and when you raise an objection or an awkward question, you are giving Thinker X the first chance to respond. In other words, you are striving to understand the problem in the terms defined by Thinker X.

In the above structure, to a considerable extent your evaluation of Thinker X's argument will therefore stem from the application of his principles to a particular problem, rather than from a rival set of assumptions. Of course, you may introduce rival assumptions, perhaps as a reminder that there are alternative ways of dealing with the awkwardness in the argument, but do not make those unproven assumptions carry more weight than they can bear. If you do wish to point out the inadequacy of Thinker X's initial assumptions, your argument will be much more persuasive if, instead of dismissing his assumptions from the outset, you can link the inadequacy of those assumptions to a significant problem with the argument he builds on them.

All of this is very different from simply dismissing Thinker X's case because you claim you have better (truer) initial assumptions than Thinker X does or because you find one of his conclusions unacceptable or because Thinker X lived many years ago, long before the things we believe are true were known.

It might be useful to remember that many arguments are very valuable and influential, not because they are universally convincing or come up with persuasive solutions to important problems (although some arguments do), but because they approach familiar problems in new ways and thus redirect how we understand and talk about them. For example, whether you find Marx's economic arguments convincing or not, you need to grasp his concept of *class*, for that is now an essential ingredient in many modern discussions of social issues (i.e., it is a concept we use to analyze and understand society). Similarly, no matter how satisfactory or unsatisfactory you may find Descartes' argument in his *Discourse on Method* and *Meditations*, it is important to recognize how he defines for us the single most difficult issue in modern biology and psychology: the problem of consciousness. Great thinkers, in other words, do not necessarily provide answers to disputatious questions; instead they redefine those questions and, in so doing, change the conversations we conduct about them.

8.3.2 | *Focus on Something Specific in the Argument*

The evaluative structure outlined above depends entirely on your selecting a very specific, clear, and important focus for your essay. In a relatively short essay, you cannot hope to provide a useful evaluation of a long argument in its entirety. What you want is a key place in the text that will enable you, in a close but restricted look, to offer significant insight into the case Thinker X is making. In a sophisticated lengthy argument there are a great many potentially useful entry points, but some may be more fertile than others. So you need to give careful thought to what specific part of Thinker X's case is going to provide the best focus for your evaluation.

Often a good focus for such an essay is a particular recommendation in the text, especially one which is, by modern standards rather strange: Plato's argument for censorship, Rousseau's program for educating women, Mill's plea for no government interference in education, Wollstonecraft's recommendations about passion in marriage, and so on. You should begin to generate all sorts of ideas for an essay, once you start asking yourself, "Why is the author making this recommendation? How did she reach this point? What are the strengths of this position? What is problematic about it?"

Alternatively, if you locate in Thinker X's text a striking and, in some ways, puzzling phrase, you can often organize your entire argument as an exploration of its significance. What does Thinker X mean by this assertion? How does she come to this conclusion? Is this a valuable insight? And so on. This, in fact, is a favourite way some instructors come up with essay topics and examination questions, as in the following examples:

Discuss what Nietzsche means in *Genealogy of Morals* when he claims "Only that which has no history can be defined."

How are we to understand Socrates' observation "No evil can happen to a good man"?

In *Social Contract*, Rousseau proposes the paradoxical idea that people must be "forced to be free." Is this a coherent idea or simply an example of his striking and sometimes paradoxical rhetorical style?

Any attempt to explore these short quotations in detail will quickly lead you to the heart of the argument in the text you are writing about.

Of particular interest in any argument (and an excellent source of useful essay topics) are those places where the writer disagrees with or dismisses another thinker. An attempt to answer the question, "Why is she disagreeing with her predecessor here, and what is significant about this disagreement?" will often lead to really significant aspects of the argument (e.g., Why does Nietzsche dismiss Descartes? Why does Aristotle reject Plato's Theory of Forms? Why does Wollstonecraft treat Rousseau so harshly? Why does Freud brush communism aside?).

8.3.3 | *Using Examples and Counterexamples*

Often an important part of evaluating an argument is the use of examples and counterexamples—that is, specific illustrations that illuminate or challenge part of the text you are looking at. For instance, if you want to drive home or sum up the implications of an argument you are examining, often an illustration is very helpful to a reader:

To appreciate just how fully Descartes is committed to an understanding of nature based on mechanical principles, we might consider how he viewed the pain of non-human animals. Believing that non-human animals do not have souls, he saw non-human animal behaviour as simply a matter of mechanical reaction, rather than as the expression of a conscious feeling. A painful yelp of a dog, in other words, was to him like the grinding of gears in a malfunctioning machine.... (The paragraph continues the illustration.)

In Nietzsche's view, then, all the competing systems of belief (democracy, socialism, science, orthodox religion, nationalism, and so on) are like organized activities taking place in a recreational complex in the middle of nature. Many different games are going on, each with its players, coaches, referees, fans, commentators, spectators, rule book and so on, and each group is proudly proclaiming that its game is the one true game, that it is the only activity truly based on an understanding of the natural world surrounding the complex.... (The paragraph goes on to develop the illustration.)

The purpose of such illustrative paragraphs is to communicate to the reader a clear sense of the part of the argument you are exploring. They do not advance your argument, but they clarify an aspect of the text that you wish to explore as part of your assessment of it.

A counterexample, by contrast, is an illustration that challenges a part of the argument you are examining. For instance, if the argument is claiming that all religious believers are bigoted fanatics, one can challenge that claim by pointing to a number of religious believers who are or were tolerant and humane. Counterexamples can come from historical events or characters, or they can be hypothetical situations. Their purpose is to say, in effect, "All right, I see what the argument is claiming, but what about this example? How does it affect the argument? How can what the writer is saying account for this?"

Consider Machiavelli's argument in *The Prince* that success-ful political rulers need to act in immoral ways (if necessary, lying and killing) in order to maintain their rule, a claim he backs up with a number of historical examples. Well, one way to challenge his argument here would be to offer up a rival list of rulers who refused to act in immoral ways and who prospered. Alternatively, one could produce some counterexamples of rulers who followed Machiavelli's advice and quickly came to grief. Such counterex-amples do not "disprove" what Machiavelli is saying, but they do invite the reader of your essay to recognize a potential inade-quacy in his argument.

Some of the most interesting counterarguments are hypo-thetical, that is, scenarios made up to point out some problem in an argument. The paragraph below provides an example of one such made-up counterexample (borrowed from John Cottingham). The writer wishes to raise an important question about Descartes' first proof for the existence of God (in his *Meditations*). Descartes' proof, very briefly put, goes something like this: human beings are imperfect, limited creatures, but they have clear and distinct ideas of perfection. Where do these ideas come from? They must originate in some entity that possesses that quality—that is, from God. Therefore, God exists.

> How are we to assess Descartes' argument here? Well, consider the following case. I come home to discover that my normal nine-year-old child has produced a complex diagram of a brilliant new computer design. So I reasonably infer that some mind other than my child's produced that design (or else she copied it from a diagram produced by such a mind). In either case, I conclude that such a mind must have been the source of the idea and that, therefore, such a mind must exist. To that extent, Descartes' argument seems plausible. But what if I come home and find my child has drawn a big square box with the label "really big new computer."

> In that case, I am far less likely to conclude that any such external source is necessarily the source of the idea, since my child is perfectly capable of coming up with that drawing by herself. If we consider the second possibility a better analogy to Descartes' proof than the first, then his argument does not appear all that plausible.

Notice what the writer has done here. He has offered a fictional analogy (the situation with his nine-year-old child) as a counterexample to Descartes' argument. His purpose is to draw the reader's attention in a vivid way to what he perceives to be a problem with Descartes' first proof for the existence of God.

Using examples and counterexamples well is an excellent way to make your assessments of philosophical works more interesting and incisive. Thus, as you explore various things you might want to say about an argument, keep thinking of possible examples of and counterexamples to claims made in the text.

8.3.4 | Sample Outlines

By way of illustrating some of the above matters, let me offer here some sample outlines for essays offering interpretative arguments about works of philosophy. Notice how they all focus on one particular aspect of the text and try to assess that in terms of the author's own argument.

Essay A
GENERAL SUBJECT: Mary Wollstonecraft's *A Vindication of the Rights of Woman*
FOCUS: Sexual passion in marriage
THESIS: Examining Wollstonecraft's arguments about passion in marriage offers a revealing insight into the strengths and limitations of her argument and, beyond that, of the liberal feminist agenda derived from it. The ideals Wollstonecraft espouses—independence, equality

between genders, and the subordination of sexual passion to rational virtue—threaten the survival of the family as a basic unit of our society.

TS 1: Wollstonecraft's view that sexual passion should play a subordinate role in married life may strike us as rather odd, but it arises logically out of her argument about virtue, independence, and education. (The paragraph explores how Wollstonecraft's views on marriage are linked to her argument for equal treatment for women in educational matters.)

TS 2: We can appreciate how important this stance is to her by looking closely at the following passage. (This illustrative paragraph takes a close look at a single passage from Wollstonecraft's argument.)

TS 3: One can see the logic of her case here. But one still might want to raise an objection: how is the family unit to remain together if women and men are to be educated equally, without any attention to family matters, and if sexual passion is no longer a priority in marriage? (The paragraph raises a question about Wollstonecraft's argument.)

TS 4: Wollstonecraft has anticipated this objection and offers a clear answer: passion is no basis for marriage because passion does not last. (The paragraph discusses Wollstonecraft's answer to the criticism raised in TS 3.)

TS 5: Wollstonecraft may well be correct in her assertion that sexual passion is not a firm, lasting basis for marriage. But we are still entitled to wonder if friendship between two rationally virtuous people educated for independence is an adequate substitute. (The paragraph assesses Wollstonecraft's answer in TS 4.)

TS 6: This feature of Wollstonecraft's argument leaves us with a question still very much on the minds of people today: if the family is the most important basic unit in our society, how well is it served by any agenda which emphasizes equality, independence, and rational virtue?

(The paragraph explores some of the consequences of this part of Wollstonecraft's argument.)

CONCLUSION

Essay B

GENERAL SUBJECT: Thomas Hobbes's *Leviathan*

FOCUS 1: Hobbes's concept of sovereignty

FOCUS 2: Hobbes's concept of sovereignty: the dangers of a corrupt sovereign

THESIS: One of the major questions one wants to raise about Hobbes's vision of the modern state is his insistence that the total power belongs to the sovereign. This would seem a dangerous idea which would lead away from the very things Hobbes believes justify the establishment of the commonwealth in the first place. Hobbes attempts to address this problem, but he does not do so in a way that is wholly satisfactory.

TS 1: Before assessing Hobbes's view of sovereignty, we should quickly review how he comes to define it the way he does. (Paragraph describes why Hobbes sees the sovereign in this way—i.e., it is tracing his reasoning from first principles. This paragraph is defining the issue, not starting the argument.)

TS 2: This concept obviously has some merits within the context of Hobbes's argument. (Paragraph argues that this concept makes sense in some respects.)

TS 3: However, the first question one would want to raise about it is this: How is the commonwealth to be protected from the corruption of the sovereign? (Paragraph goes on to argue that this is a real danger, especially given Hobbes's view of human nature.)

TS 4: There are two reasonable ways in which Hobbes seeks to answer this charge. (Paragraph goes on to argue that Hobbes's case takes care of this objection to some extent.)

TS 5: However, these aspects of Hobbes's argument

are problematic. (Paragraph goes on to argue that Hobbes's defence of this charge would not be entirely satisfactory.)

TS 6: To appreciate these problems let us consider the case of a corrupt sovereign. (Paragraph uses a historical counter-example to consolidate the points made above.)

CONCLUSION: The dangers of a corrupt sovereign are clearly something Hobbes takes into account. However, we have good reason to wonder about how satisfactory his treatment of this potential objection might be. (Paragraph sums up the argument.)

Essay C

GENERAL SUBJECT: Plato's *Republic*
FOCUS 1: The views on art expressed in Book X
FOCUS 2: Views on art in *Republic*: censorship by the state
THESIS: Many modern readers for understandable reasons find it difficult to accept the views on censorship expressed by Socrates in Plato's *Republic*. What's interesting, however, is how often many of those same readers invoke arguments identical to those Socrates makes in their discussions of modern aesthetic issues. That phenomenon is a testament to the continuing strength of the case Plato makes about artistic creativity and the need to control it.

TS 1: In order to understand why Socrates raises the issue of censorship, we need to recall what he says about the nature of the human soul and about knowledge. (The paragraph provides necessary background to the argument, which has not yet started.)

TS 2: Given this understanding of the human soul, we can readily understand one of Socrates' key objections to certain forms of art: they encourage those aspects of the human psyche detrimental to the harmony necessary to proper living. (Paragraph argues that this point about art has a certain justification for the reasons Socrates brings up.)

TS 3: A second reason for censorship is the particularly interesting point that debased art corrupts the understanding. Again, this point has considerable merit. (Paragraph argues that this defence of censorship is also persuasive.)

TS 4: It is important to remember, of course, that in the state Socrates is proposing, the rulers are perfectly virtuous, and thus their decisions in political matters, including censorship, would be wise and just. Hence, censorship would not only be logically justifiable but welcome.

TS 5: Most of us would still have some trouble agreeing with such state censorship, for we (or most of us) are unwilling to accept that our rulers are perfectly virtuous; moreover, we are all too familiar with historical examples of heavy-handed censorship in the name of a particular ideology. (The paragraph discusses the evils of censorship.)

TS 6: And yet, for all our dislike of censorship, arguments very similar to Plato's are common in certain modern discussions about the need for controls on artistic creativity. Consider, for example, how we respond to pornography or excessive violence in fiction (particularly on television). (Paragraph argues that Socrates' case for censorship is quite common in modern debates about TV programming.)

TS 7: Similar arguments are common in debates about what children should or should not be allowed to read or watch. In such discussions, many people (especially parents) come across as confirmed Platonists. (Paragraph provides examples of demands from different groups for a censoring of educational material and entertainment for children.)

CONCLUSION: What seems clear is that even in a country with a constitutional commitment to freedom of speech and artistic expression, Plato's arguments about censoring art still resonate.

Essay D

John Stuart Mill's *On Liberty*

FOCUS 1: Mill's concept of open free discussion

FOCUS 2: Mill's concept of open free discussion: some problems

THESIS: While justly famous as an eloquent statement of liberal principles, Mill's key concept of free and open discussion raises some important questions which Mill does not sufficiently address.

TS 1: Mill's essay is a stirring argument for a society in which individual liberties, especially freedom of speech, are promoted as actively as possible. (The paragraph reviews Mill's argument for the benefits of free speech.)

TS 2: Mill makes a persuasive case, but his argument prompts a few questions. The first and most obvious is this: Where are such free discussions to take place? (Paragraph argues that Mill's society does not have enough open places for discussion.)

TS 3: A related criticism calls attention to those who are excluded from such forums. Mill's argument does not seem to have much place for them. (Paragraph argues that many people will lack the qualifications to take part.)

TS 4: In defence of Mill, one might argue that these two objections are not insurmountable: there are ways of dealing with them in the context of his presentation. (Paragraph acknowledges the opposition and tries to answer the objections using Mill's theory.)

TS 5: This sounds all very well in theory, but in practice many people are going to be excluded. That is clear from the way Mill insists the debates should take place. (Paragraph argues that the defence of Mill in the previous paragraph is not adequate.)

TS 6: It doesn't take much imagination to visualize some of the more deleterious consequences of what might happen if we implemented Mill's recommendations as fully as he proposes. (The paragraph offers a counterexample.) CONCLUSION: The strength of Mill's case is the appeal of a rational liberal democracy, but its weaknesses stem from the same source. (Paragraph goes on to sum up the argument.)

8.3.5 | Evaluating the Style in Assessing Arguments

When you are writing an essay assessing a philosophical argument, most of the time you will be focusing on the logic of the case the text is presenting (as in the above examples). However, from time to time you should pause to reflect on another question: "What is the writer's style or tone contributing to the argument? Is there any ambiguity or irony I need to take into account? Are there any metaphorical elements shaping the case the author is making?" The reason for remaining alert to such queries is obvious enough: the way a writer expresses herself is an inextricable part of what she is saying. One cannot arbitrarily separate style and substance.

This is clear enough in extreme cases, like a satire, where the author's meaning is, in fact, the reverse of what she is apparently claiming. But the issue may be important, too, as soon as the writer introduces any ambiguities into her style, however slight, or seeks to advance the case she is making with poetic metaphors or narrative examples.

Of course, a great deal of philosophical writing, particularly in modern times, deliberately adopts a relatively unambiguous style marked by a very clear language, an absence of irony or poetic metaphor, and often a fairly technical vocabulary. Such a style is saying to the reader something like "What you really need to attend to here is the logic of my argument, which has no rhetorical frills." And, as long as that style is present, you can safely assess the argument by concentrating on the logic of the case the writer is making.

However, many writers on philosophical subjects deliberately adopt a much more elusive style, one marked by ambiguity, shifting tones, sarcasm, irony, metaphor, and so on. Plato's arguments are presented as dramatic dialogues (an inherently ambiguous form) and feature Socrates, the most slyly ironic philosopher of all (for that reason one needs to be careful about assuming that Socrates is always an unambiguous spokesperson for Plato's ideas). What people tend to like best and remember longest from these dialogues is not the arguments but the images and narratives Plato inserts into them (like the Ring of Gyges, the Allegory of the Cave, the Myth of Er, the death of Socrates, and so on). The precise meaning of these is not always clear cut.

In any assessment of an argument, therefore, attending to the writer's style is sometimes as important as tracing the author's reasoning. In the early Socratic dialogues, Plato's dramatic depiction of Socrates as a new kind of hero is every bit as integral to the work as any of the rational arguments Socrates advances to justify his activities. Descartes deliberately writes his *Discourse on Method* in colloquial French (rather than in Latin) and adopts a friendly, self-deprecating tone as part of his argument that the new science is a democratic activity everyone can understand, practice, and support. When Nietzsche urges his readers to see that truths are not discovered but created, that poetry trumps traditional philosophy, his own style is an eloquent part of that argument, and when Montaigne presents his plea for a pervasive skepticism, the elusive and urbane ironies throughout are an essential component of his message. Rousseau's influence stems not merely from the ideas he presents but from his passionate advocacy of those ideas. In Martin Luther King's "I Have a Dream" speech the compelling poetic intensity of the style carries the argument far more effectively than does the logical consistency or originality of the argument (especially when one listens to a recording of the speech).

What this adds up to is that in your essay about a philosophical argument you should remain alert to what the author's style may be contributing. Just because you are writing about what we call a work of philosophy, do not think you have to concentrate exclusively on the process of reasoning divorced from anything else. Often some attention to what looks like a minor rhetorical aspect of the style (a pattern in the imagery or references) may provide revealing insights into something important and worth incorporating into your argument, as in the following sample paragraph from an essay on Plato's portrayal of Socrates in the early dialogues:

> A fascinating detail in these depictions of Socrates' last days are the casual references to Achilles, the greatest hero in the Greek traditions (a direct reference in the *Apology* and a more veiled one in the *Crito*). What are they doing there? One possibility is that Plato wants to emphasize the heroic qualities of Socrates, because he knows that if his dialogues are to be successful in persuading people to pay attention to the philosophical way of life, he has to give them a dramatic hero, one every bit as compelling as Homer's great warrior leader. This small detail of the references to Achilles, in fact, suggests that the real aim of these dialogues may not be to set us debating about this or that argumentative point, but rather to help us recognize the value of a new way of life, one based not on old traditions but on the practices and beliefs of a new and worthy hero. Briefly put, Plato may well want his readers to set Socrates alongside Achilles or even to replace Achilles with Socrates as a role model for the good life. Whether that is, indeed, his goal or not, the strategy succeeded beyond anything Plato could have hoped: ever since these dialogues, and largely because of them, Socrates has been widely acknowledged as a figure worthy of the highest admiration, and many people have been first drawn to a philosophical way of life not by any argument promoting it but rather by Plato's picture of heroic Socrates in the days of his trial and its immediate aftermath.

This paragraph is not addressing any particular argument in the early dialogues. It has seized on an element in the style (the casual references to Achilles) and explored what these might contribute to our understanding of the text. Notice that the language is tentative; the essay writer is not insisting that these details are all important. However, paying attention to them enables him to make an intriguing suggestion that has a bearing on what may be a central purpose of the text.

In a similar way, one might call attention to (or even organize an entire essay around) Nietzsche's use of non-human animal imagery in *Genealogy of Morals* (birds of prey, lambs, herd animals, and so on). For these images are not there simply to illustrate his argument. They are an inherent part of his case that human beings are an animal species and that when we forget this fact we create all sorts of problems for ourselves. An attention to such matters is not always possible or even desirable. But when a philosophical text displays a pattern in its use of metaphor and imagery, it is almost always worth asking how that might contribute to the argument.

One stylistic feature that is often difficult to evaluate precisely is a writer's use of *irony*—those moments when you sense the language of a text is becoming ambiguous and bringing into play meanings other than (and perhaps even contradictory to) the literal meanings of the words. Obviously the presence of irony can significantly affect your interpretation of an argument, because you may not be sure if the writer means what he is apparently saying. For instance, deciding whether Machiavelli's *Prince* is a handbook for hard-headed politics or a satire depends upon a reader's response to the language: many sense irony there and are led to the idea that the work is clearly a satire; others argue that the language is unironic and that we are meant to take Machiavelli's advice literally (the uncertainty about this issue in discussions of Machiavelli stems, in my view, from his very inconsistent use of irony).

The failure to detect irony in the prose can lead to a serious misreading of a text. For example, the most famous satire in

English prose, Jonathan Swift's "A Modest Proposal" (in which the proposer argues that in order to solve Ireland's economic problems poor people should kill their babies at one year old and sell them to more prosperous citizens as a food delicacy) could be taken literally by some people who fail to recognize the irony: they either applaud the scheme as a fine idea or dismiss the author as inhumanly savage. Either response would indicate, obviously, that they have missed the entire point.

Detecting irony is one challenge facing an interpreter. Another is assessing how deep the irony runs: Is it simply a light ambiguity in the text, or is it deeper, something that points to a potentially serious criticism of an existing institution or habit or belief, or is it so strong that the tone is obviously sarcastic or satiric? As a result, if your interpretation of a text is going to call attention to irony in the writing, you will usually need to suggest how deep you think the irony runs and whether or not there is a critical edge to it (i.e., give the reader of your essay some guidance as to how she should read the irony present in the argument you are discussing). There is little point in suggesting ironic possibilities in the prose without indicating what they might add up to.

Here, for example, is a paragraph discussing a marked feature of Montaigne's style—the way he is always reminding us of prominent figures and works from the classical Greek and Roman past.

> Montaigne's frequent references to and quotations from classical Greek and Roman authors inevitably suggest a certain ironical attitude towards the present. The critical potential of this attitude should be obvious enough, since it involves setting up pagan thinkers and writers as a standard for living well in a modern Christian country. Thus, by implication at least, it calls into question the adequacy of prevailing Christian traditions (the absence of references to scripture and to the Christian present or past reinforces this point). Moreover, a number of the doctrines Montaigne

endorses have specifically pagan roots (as he reminds us) and lead to conclusions quite removed from the traditional values of Roman Catholic Christianity. Hence, beneath the urbane love of ancient learning and many of the witty quotations, there is a pervasive irony at work. But this critical attitude remains latent throughout. That is, Montaigne does not, for the most part, exploit his use of the past to develop any overtly searching criticism of those values and institutions most important in his own time. He is being very cautious here, for direct criticism of official secular and religious institutions could quickly get him into serious trouble. Since Montaigne is careful not to engage us directly in any potentially difficult questions about Christian faith or political allegiance or to turn the full force of classical examples against the major institutionalized powers of church and state in his own age, that critical attitude remains, as I say, latent. Nevertheless, it is there, and one does not have to read very much of Montaigne's prose to begin sensing that for him the pagan classical past is a much richer source of wise advice and fine examples of truly moral human beings (to say nothing of great literature) than is the Christian present.

Notice how this paragraph focuses on a pattern in Montaigne's prose (his constant references to the pagan past) and suggests that these have an ironic effect—rather than being mere decoration or wit, they are implicit criticisms of Christian Europe. The paragraph also attempts to weigh that irony, to assess how obvious and cutting it might be. His conclusion is that it is present but muted. Another interpreter of Montaigne might see it as rather more pointed than that.

Another way of raising the same issue is to ask yourself the following questions: Does the author have a hidden agenda? Is there a more revolutionary or confrontational message lurking beneath the ambiguities in the style? If so, what is it? Answers to

such questions are frequently elusive, and there can be considerable disagreement among interpreters about them. But obviously
if you sense such possibilities are present in a text, it is important
to trace how they shape your understanding of the argument.

Here, for example, is a paragraph from an essay interpreting Wollstonecraft's argument (in *A Vindication of the Rights of
Woman*) for reforming the treatment of women:

> A reader can see readily enough that Wollstonecraft is
> staking out an explicitly liberal position, but one may also
> wonder whether there is a much more radical purpose at
> work here. That is, to what extent is Wollstonecraft's agenda
> a reasonable-sounding Trojan Horse containing within it
> something much more potentially revolutionary than ques-
> tions of access, education, and minor political reforms? The
> radical potential of what Wollstonecraft is proposing comes
> from the frequent indications she gives that her real con-
> cern might not be simply providing more opportunities for
> middle-class women but rather something much bigger—
> extending her concepts of liberty and virtue much further
> than orthodox reform sentiment of the time would normally
> permit. For example, what exactly are we to make of com-
> ments like the following?
>
>> ... as sound politics diffuse liberty, mankind, including
>> woman, will become more wise and virtuous. (38)
>> ... but the nature of reason must be the same in all, if it
>> be an emanation of divinity, the tie that connects the
>> creature with the Creator. (53)
>
> Remarks like these create in this work a subdued theme that
> the progress of society requires the virtue of *all* the citizens.
> Since liberty is the essential precondition of such virtue, this
> work puts a certain pressure on the reader to recognize
> that there is a lot more a stake in this position than the

middle-class women whom Wollstonecraft repeatedly identifies as her sole concern. As for the liberty of the poor, now
that is something with much more radical implications.

> ... the very constitution of civil governments has put
> almost insuperable obstacles in the way to prevent the
> cultivation of the female understanding—yet virtue can
> be built on no other foundation! (54)

> If the progress of society depends upon virtue in the citizens,
> and if the present constitution of civil society is an almost
> insuperable obstacle, then the implication here appears
> obvious enough: if we are to progress, the present state of
> civil society must be changed. The logic of her argument
> invites us to ask the politically explosive question: Well, if
> we start granting middle-class women some measures of
> equality with middle-class men, then why stop there? What
> about poor women, poor men? Such questions may well get
> us thinking about changes considerably more radical than
> Wollstonecraft is, in other places, prepared openly to admit.

The writer here is raising questions about the ironical implications of certain parts of Wollstonecraft's argument. Since firm
answers to these questions are elusive, he has adopted a more
speculative tone, inviting the reader to see certain interpretative
possibilities in the text.

8.4 | Writing Essays about Fiction

8.4.1 | Selecting a Focus

As mentioned before, the best way to begin organizing an argumentative essay about a narrative fiction is to select something
very particular in the story and focus your attention exclusively
on that. If you are dealing with a well-written narrative, almost

anything you select to look at closely will enable you to offer an interpretative argument about important elements in the story. Here, for instance, is a partial list of possible choices:

1. What is the significance of a particular character or a particular moment in the career of a single character? Why is that moment important? What human possibility does that part of the fiction hold up to us? What does that moment reveal about something significant in the story? What would be missing if that moment or that character were not in the story? Often you can organize a useful interpretative essay around the contribution of an apparently minor character or event.

2. Does a particular character learn or fail to learn something important in the story? If the resolution of a narrative depends upon the education of a main character, then an important interpretative point in the story will undoubtedly be what that character has learned (or failed to learn). This question is often very fruitful if a major part of the narrative is a journey of some kind, as in *Huckleberry Finn* or *Gulliver's Travels* or *Heart of Darkness* or the *Odyssey*. Is the main character the same person at the end of the journey as at the start? If not, what has happened? Why is that significant? How does the character behave when he returns? Why?

3. What is the importance of the setting (the physical environment) or some aspect of it? How does this help to define for the readers the sense of nature presented in the text—or the sense of how the world operates, of the values of human life?

4. Is there an interesting recurring pattern in the fiction (e.g., in the treatment of women, the significance of food, the nature of work, the depiction of the gods, the images of nature, the attitude to money, the style of the clothes, and so on)? Is there one object in the story that is particularly significant?

5. Why does the story end the way it does? How does the conclusion affect our understanding of what has gone on? Is there any irony in the ending (i.e., any unresolved ambiguities)? Does that raise any questions and invite us to think about them?

6. Does the story call attention to any important ideas or themes? In what sense is there a conflict of ideas or attitudes being explored in the fiction?

7. What role does the narrator play in our response to the story? Is that voice reliable, playful, ironic? Does the narrator understand the significance of the story? How does that affect the interpretation?

8. Often a particular remark in a fiction (or the title itself) can make a useful focus for an essay (once again, a popular form of exam question or essay topic), as in, for example, one of the following:

    > What does Catherine in Brontë's *Wuthering Heights* mean by her famous remark, "Nelly, I am Heathcliff"? How does that help us to understand anything significant in the novel?

    > Discuss the significance of Conrad's title "Heart of Darkness."

    > What is significant, if anything, about Lily Briscoe's comment to herself in Woolf's *To the Lighthouse*: "Yes, she thought, laying down her brush in extreme fatigue, I have had my vision"?

And so on. Remember that in a relatively short essay you can deal only with one very particular aspect of the fiction, so select carefully, and confine the argument to the significance of that one feature you have selected. And make sure that you do not just describe what you have selected. Instead create an argumentative opinion about its significance. That will be your thesis, a statement or series of statements which says, in effect, "If we look closely at this single aspect of the fiction we can see ways in which it contributes something important to our understanding of the total story."

Structuring the rest of the essay, once you have a workable thesis, should follow the various principles outlined previously in this handbook. The result should be an outline something like the following:

Essay A

GENERAL SUBJECT: John Steinbeck's Short Story "The Chrysanthemums"

FOCUS 1: Elisa's character

FOCUS 2: Elisa's character: her weak sense of her own femininity

THESIS: Elisa is a strong but very vulnerable woman, vital enough to have strong ambitions but so insecure about her own femininity that she is finally unable to cope with the strain of transforming her life.

TS 1: When we first see Elisa, we get an immediate sense that she is hiding her sexuality from the rest of the world. (Paragraph examines the opening descriptions of Elisa and interprets key phrases to point out how she appears to be concealing her real self.)

TS 2: The speed and the energy with which Elisa later seeks to change herself reveal the extent of her dissatisfaction with the role she has been playing. (Paragraph discusses what happens as Elisa starts to respond to the crisis, arguing that she is seeking to move beyond her frustration.)

TS 3: But Elisa's new sense of herself does not last. She does not have the inner strength to develop into the mature, independent woman she would like to be.

CONCLUSION: This story narrates a series of everyday events, but the emotional drama Elisa goes through is really tense. (Paragraph goes on to summarize the main argument and reaffirm the thesis.)

Essay B
GENERAL SUBJECT: Homer's *Odyssey*
FOCUS: Home and hospitality in the *Odyssey*:
the significance of banquets
THESIS: In the *Odyssey*, the frequent and detailed attention to food and the rituals surrounding it serve constantly to reinforce a central concern of the poem, the vital civilizing importance of the home.
TS 1: Throughout the *Odyssey*, we witness the way in which food taken communally can act as a way of re-energizing human beings, enabling them to cope with their distress. This, in fact, emerges as one of the most important human values in the poem. (Paragraph argues for the restorative values of food brought out repeatedly in the poem.)
TS 2: The rituals surrounding food, especially the importance of welcoming guests to the feast and making sure everyone has enough, stress the importance of warm and open human interaction, even with strangers. (The paragraph argues the importance of hospitality as it is brought out by the references to food and feasting.)
TS 3: The occasions in which food is consumed are also moments in which the participants celebrate the artistic richness of their culture. Nowhere else in the poem is there so much attention paid to the significance of beauty in various forms. (Paragraph argues that all the things associated with the food—the serving dishes, the entertainment, and so on—reflect important values in the culture.)
TS 4: Given the cultural importance of food and feasting, we can more easily recognize why what the suitors are doing is so heinous: by invading Odysseus' home and forcefully

helping themselves to his resources, they are violating one of the most important principles of that society.

CONCLUSION: There is, of course, much more to the poem than the description of feasting, but we need to recognize these moments as especially important insights into the cultural life of the society depicted in the poem. (Paragraph restates and summarizes the central point of the argument.)

Essay C

GENERAL SUBJECT: Shakespeare's *Richard III*

FOCUS 1: The importance of Anne in the play

FOCUS 2: The first scene between Anne and Richard (I.3)

THESIS: Anne's role in I.3 is particularly important to the opening of the play because it reveals clearly to us not only the devilish cleverness of Richard but also the way in which his success depends upon the weaknesses of others.

TS 1: Richard's treatment of Anne in I.3 provides a very important look at the complex motivation and style of the play's hero. (Paragraph goes on to argue how the Richard-Anne confrontation reveals important things about Richard.)

TS 2: More importantly, perhaps, the scene reveals just how Anne's understandable weaknesses enable Richard to succeed. (Paragraph looks at how Anne's response to Richard's advances reveal important things about her character.)

TS 3: We can best appreciate these points by considering a key moment in the scene, the moment when Richard invites Anne to kill him. (In an illustrative paragraph, the writer takes a detailed look at five lines from the scene, to emphasize the points mentioned in the previous two paragraphs.)

CONCLUSION: This early success provides Richard with a sense of his own power and thus confirms for him that he really can achieve what he most wants. (Paragraph sums up the argument in the context of the entire play.)

The points to notice particularly here are, first, the argumentative nature of the thesis, which sets up an interpretative claim and, second, the opinionated topic sentences, which continue the argumentative style. They do not degenerate simply into sections of summary (retelling what goes on in the story). And notice how each argument depends upon an initial narrowing of the focus, so that the argument is concerned with only one aspect of the narrative.

8.4.2 | Avoiding a Structure that Is a List of Examples

One point to notice from the above sample outlines is this: when you are focusing on a pattern in the fiction (as in Essay B above, on banquets in the *Odyssey*), it is better to structure the essay as a series of argumentative points about the pattern you are looking at rather than as a series of examples. You notice, for example, that in Essay B each argumentative paragraph starts with a new assertion about the significance of banquets in the poem.

Consider the difference between the two outlines below, both arguing for the importance of a certain pattern in the imagery of a story:

Essay A
THESIS: The images of nature in the story evoke the main characters' paradoxical feelings about the landscape surrounding them.
TS 1: One example of the images of nature is ...
TS 2: A second example of natural imagery is ...
TS 3: A third example of natural imagery is ...
CONCLUSION

Essay B
THESIS: The images of nature in the story evoke the main characters' paradoxical feelings about the landscape surrounding them.

TS 1: We notice repeatedly that the descriptions of nature emphasize the harsh and threatening features of the landscape....
TS 2: However, the imagery also insists upon the beauty of the land surrounding the small, isolated community....
TS 3: In many features of the landscape there is also an almost hypnotic spiritual quality....
CONCLUSION

Notice the different structures. Both essays have the same thesis. In the first, the argument is structured as a series of examples of the thesis; in the second, the essay is structured as a series of arguments advancing the thesis (not just examples of more images from nature but a series of arguments about the entire pattern itself). The second organization will usually work much better than the first, because the first one will probably encourage you to summarize parts of the story and to repeat yourself from one example to the next.

8.4.3 | Dealing with Themes in Fictions

Fictions almost inevitably involve ideas (or themes): that is, as the story unfolds and we encounter characters, settings, turns of phrase in the narrative, and so on, we can understand them not only in terms of what role they play within the world of the story but also what larger meaning they might have. When we follow characters in action, what they do invites us to consider at least two things about them: first, who the characters are (their motivation, feelings, relationships to others, and so on—as if they were real and unique people) and, second, what those characters and their actions stand for (i.e., what they symbolize). So when one character quarrels with another, for example, we are witnessing, not just a conflict between two particular individuals, but also a conflict between the things they represent.

For example the story of Nora Helmer and her husband Torvald (in Ibsen's *A Doll's House*), as well as being about the particular details of these two individual characters, is also about the relationships of men and women in a middle-class marriage, about a woman's interactions with her children, her husband, and herself, about the realities of living in a modern conforming society, and so on, particularly for a young, intelligent wife. King Lear is not just an old person; he is also a man, a king, a leader of people, and a father. So when he speaks and acts he is doing so as a particular individual and as a representative of a certain type or group. And when the play ends with the dead bodies of Lear's three daughters on the stage, it is hard to resist the idea that in some important sense this play is about more than just the characters.

Another way of drawing attention to this issue is to ask an apparently simple question. What is *King Lear* about? Well, on one level the work is the dramatic depiction of one old man who undergoes horrific suffering and dies in misery. On another level, it is an exploration of certain themes or ideas: for example, conflicting views of nature, the importance of human bonding, the tragic effects of an inability to love, fathers and daughters, men and women, and so on. An exclusive focus on the character of Lear may tend to lose sight of the wider issues; an exclusive focus on some of the ideas may tend to lose sight of the particularities of the story.

Almost any object or location in a story can also acquire a symbolic significance (depending upon how it is described) and thus bring into play a range of associated ideas. The description of the interior of a house, for example, can give rise to ideas about the life people live there; clothing can often symbolize important things about an individual or a group. Colours are often significant, as well. In fact, some of the most famous symbols of American literature have distinctive colours: the red badge of courage, Hester's scarlet letter, Ahab's great white whale, and the green light at the end of Daisy Buchanan's dock. Those particular colours play an important part in any thematic discussion of the novels (one perceptive critic has suggested that, according to coast guard regulations, the light at the end of Daisy's dock should have been red, but obviously having Daisy, the object of Gatsby's intense yearning, associated with the symbolic suggestiveness of *red* and *a red light*, rather than with the colour *green*, would have significantly affected the thematic impact of the novel).

Sometimes, of course, the fiction will repeatedly call attention to a theme in a very explicit way. Slavery, for example, is a prominent and obvious theme in *Huckleberry Finn*; in Shakespeare's *Henry IV, Part I*, several people raise the issue of honour; Atwood's *Oryx and Crake* returns again and again to conversations about survival and the environment; Milton's *Paradise Lost* and Dante's *Inferno* explicitly invoke as a major concern the justice of God.

The ways in which a fiction calls attention to and explores ideas is thus a natural and useful subject for an interpretative essay. Such an approach is, as it were, answering the question "What is this story about?" by calling attention, not to the specific details of the fiction as elements in a unique and particular story, but rather to the more general ideas these details give rise to. Thus, a thematic interpretation often provides helpful insights into the wider ramifications of a fiction.

However, someone preparing such an interpretation should keep in mind a few cautionary principles:

1. A thematic approach to a fiction needs to remain sensitive to the relationship between the theme or idea and the specific details of the story, because, while some fictions are clearly created in the service of some idea or doctrine and almost every element in the story can be interpreted as a reference to that idea, other fictions invoke ideas only to subvert them, that is, to demonstrate their inadequacy as an explanation for a complex human experience; still other stories will introduce apparently clear themes and then complicate our understanding of them and often leave the issue hanging for the reader to ponder.

2. No worthwhile work of fiction can be satisfactorily interpreted *merely* by extracting from it the ideas or themes one discovers. Even in allegories that are obviously written to illustrate an idea, if the story is any good that quality will be due to the ways in which the style of the work brings the theme alive and conveys a sense of the emotional attractiveness of the ideas or the system of belief. If, for example, your entire essay on Dante's *Inferno* is an explanation of how various things in the poem refer to details of late medieval Catholic doctrine, and you end up discussing the logic of that doctrine, rather than the details of the poem, then you have rather missed the important interpretative point, which is this: "How has Dante's style made that belief emotionally intelligible and imaginatively stimulating, even to those of us who know nothing about and are not interested in the details of medieval Roman Catholicism?" Spare your readers a mere summary of the doctrine and talk about the way the poetry presents those ideas.

You should try to avoid the habit of isolating a theme from its context in the story and treating the work as if it is a rational argument. If that were the key to understanding a story, one wonders why the author would not spare himself the trouble of writing a fiction and just offer us the argument instead. That way of reading a story will probably lead you to miss something important. For instance, Milton's *Paradise Lost* is, as the narrator informs us, an attempt to "justify the ways of God to man," and there are a number of arguments put forward in the poem. If you take those arguments from their context and treat them as elements in a philosophical discourse, you may be able (perhaps) to show that Milton's justification is in line with certain Protestant doctrines. However, you will miss many of the most intriguing and disputatious elements of the poem: Why are the arguments and the characters of the "sinners" (Satan, Adam, and Eve) so much more emotionally convincing than God's arguments or God's character? How does our response to their arguments shape our understanding of God's ways? Could it be, as some have argued, that Milton's portrayal of these sinners undercuts any claims that God's actions are justified in any fully human meaning of that term?

If you find that your essay is discussing ideas without anchoring that discussion on an interpretation of particular details of the style, then your thematic analysis is probably turning into a relatively superficial summary of ideas rather than an interpretation of the fiction.

3. You should be very careful about taking what any one character (including the narrator) says in a fiction as the "moral" or "message" of the work. It may be, but before deciding that it is, ask yourself whether the details of the story (the character of that speaker, the context of his remarks, and the events in the narrative) endorse that "message" or not. In many cases, that utterance may be in the fiction in order to show that it is not an adequate summary statement explaining what is going on. Many interpreters of Greek tragic drama, for example, take the Chorus as the voice of the author informing us of the principal "moral" of the work; in so doing, they often misrepresent an essential feature of the play. A number of passages of Shakespeare taken out of context and offered up to us as isolated examples of Shakespearean "wisdom" are, if we examine them within the context of the works in which they appear, exposed as facile and inadequate statements (e.g., Polonius' advice to his son in *Hamlet*, Jaques' "Seven Ages of Man" speech in *As You Like It*, various moral comments on the action in *King Lear*, and so on). You should always bear in mind that many stories deliberately introduce ideas in order to show that the human experiences depicted in the fiction cannot be neatly summed up in some apparently significant generalization.

4. Try not to leap to an instantly thematic interpretation of something in the story. Let the importance of a particular detail emerge from the way the story presents it. A tree standing by itself in the yard is not always (or even usually) a symbol of the tree in the Garden of Eden, a white object is not necessarily a symbol of purity or death, a big unshaven man with black hair is not necessarily a symbol of evil, nor is every raven a sinister omen, and so on. It might be, and one should remain alert for that possibility, but whether it is or not depends upon how the story develops, what use the text makes of that detail. Arbitrarily imposing instantly symbolic and thematic meanings is an easy way to arrive at rather bizarre interpretations of a fiction.

5. A particularly useful form of thematic criticism (and a helpful style of literary interpretation generally) is to explore the ways in which the details of the fiction (the characters, places, events, structure, style, and so on) develop and, above all, challenge or complicate our understanding of some explicit thematic concern. *Huckleberry Finn*, for example, raises the issue of slavery, but more importantly it explores people's attitudes towards slavery (which is not the same thing). We may well applaud Huck as his opinions begin to change once he gets to know Jim and to formulate naive reflections on social injustice. That may tempt us see one sort of message emerging from the story. But we may then reflect upon the fact that as Huck is learning these important things he is relaxing on a raft that is effortlessly carrying Jim to the very centre of slavery and that once Huck gets there his response to the newly learned complexities he is facing is that he should head out west where he will not have to trouble himself with civilization and its problems. From this angle the book's message becomes much more complicated; what the novel is finally saying about slavery is not as straightforward as it may have appeared earlier.

Similarly, Fitzgerald's *The Great Gatsby* focuses on a central idea, what has come to be called the American Dream—the notion that one can simply reject the past, reinvent oneself, and live an entirely self-created life answering to one's dearest wishes. The novel, however, is anything but simplistic in its exploration of this idea. The actions of the characters, the effects of those actions, our different responses to them, and the way the story works out enormously complicate our feelings about that dream, so that making a simple judgement about it at the end of the narrative is extremely difficult.

Hence the key emphasis in thematic criticism should fall on how the fiction shapes the way we are to understand the ideas it presents. Does it make us enthusiastic for these ideas? Does it complicate our understanding of these ideas? Does it reveal the inadequacies of a simple faith in these ideas? Does it resolve conflicts between different ideas? Or does it leave them hanging? Bear in mind that often one of the important effects of a fiction is to remind us that some issues are more complicated than we like to believe.

Here for example, is a sample outline for an essay on a thematic concern in Homer's *Iliad*, written in response to the following questions: What is Homer's attitude to warfare? Can we call the *Iliad* a pro-war or anti-war poem?

> THESIS: Homer's vision of war in the *Iliad* is complex and ambiguous: war is destructive of valuable human life and yet at the same time is an affirmation of many of the highest values in human experience.
> TS 1: The first obvious thing we notice about Homer's depiction of war is its horrifying brutality and destructiveness. (This paragraph makes the first argumentative point.)
> TS 2: To appreciate just how forcefully the poem compels the reader to confront this aspect of war, consider the following

description of death on the battlefield. (The paragraph offers an illustration of the previous point.)

TS 3: Homer also goes to great lengths to bring out the wastefulness of the destructive enterprise, not only by naming almost all victims, but also by informing us of their families back home who will soon be grieving their loss. (The paragraph goes on to argue this point.)

TS 4: On the other hand, the poem repeatedly stresses the beauty and excitement of hazardous combat, creating a sense that the life of the battlefield warrior is a manifestation of truly worthy human qualities.

TS 5: Notice, for example, in the following passage how Athena's presence on the battlefield just before the first encounter brings to the men a vitality and excitement that brushes aside all thoughts of home. (The paragraph offers an illustration of the previous point.)

TS 6: The creative beauty of war is also emphasized by the attention paid to the astonishing quality of the weapons, particularly the shields.

TS 7: Warfare, too, in this vision of life is inherently part of the world, part of a cosmic and natural order by which the universe operates.

TS 8: The ambiguity at the heart of this vision of warfare is left unresolved. Warfare is horrible and beautiful, destructive and affirming, a denial of life and an irreducible part of life. (The paragraph argues this point.)

CONCLUSION

This essay is refusing to provide a simple answer to the question posed by the essay topic. Instead it is offering an argument that Homer's depiction of warfare in the *Iliad* is complicated. The poem, in other words, is challenging any notions we might have that Homer's vision of warfare is something easy to sum up and, beyond that, may well be inviting readers to rethink any naive assumptions they have about warfare.

8.5 | Writing Essays on Lyric Poetry

One form of writing that students often find particularly difficult is an essay on a lyric poem. On the face of it, this difficulty is curious, because students nowadays, thanks to the instant availability of popular songs every minute of the day and night, are more familiar with lyric poetry (in the form of song lyrics) than with any other literary form, and they spend a great deal of time listening to and discussing their own preferences. However, the source of the problem is not far to seek: writing an interpretative essay on a lyric poem demands a very detailed and precise attention to features of a poetic style (imagery, rhythm, rhyme, sentence structure, sound, and so on), and dealing with these properly requires considerable practice.

8.5.1 | What Is a Lyric Poem?

In the most general sense, *lyric poems* (as the term *lyric* suggests) are verses written to be sung or to bring out certain musical qualities in the language (or both). The term covers a wide variety of poetic styles, but we usually distinguish lyric poems from other forms of poetry (epics, satires, and so on) by a few or all of the following characteristics:

1. Typically, a lyric poem will be a short work featuring a speaker (often identified by the personal pronouns "I" and "me") focusing on his or her feelings about a particular experience. In that sense, a lyric poem generally has a very personal quality (often, as John Stuart Mill observed, it is not so much heard as "overheard").

2. A lyric poem tends to be a short meditation or reflection on an experience, or, to use a key metaphor, it is a speaker's exploration of her feelings about an experience. These feelings may be very clear and explicit (desolation, despair, joy,

disgust, anger, wonder, excitement, and so on) or they may be very ambiguous (the poem may be exploring a conflict of feelings about an experience or a sense that the speaker has lost feelings she once had or that she is having trouble coming to grips with her response to an experience).

3. A lyric poem will usually emphasize this exploration of feelings and not attempt to tell a story. If the poem is focusing on an event, what happens in the event is typically less important than the speaker's emotional response to that event; if the poem invokes an idea, what matters is usually not the rational consistency or the originality of the idea but the speaker's feelings about it.

In order to write an interpretative essay about a lyric poem, one needs to grasp the essential point emphasized above: a lyric poem is the *exploration* of personal feelings about an experience; it is not a *re-creation* of that experience. A poem written about something very sad is not designed to make the reader sad; its purpose is to invite the reader to understand the nature of the speaker's sadness in response to a particular event, to provide an emotionally intelligible insight into it. Hence, poems written on distressing subjects (e.g., death, sickness, loss) can often give the reader great pleasure. That pleasure comes, not from the subject matter or from the speaker's sadness, but from the skill with which the poem has illuminated what this sadness means to him.

Many lyric poems (like a great many songs) focus on an emotion and, in effect, ask us to swim in the feeling, without seeking to illuminate it in any way. What matters is that we surrender to the emotion (happy or sad), leave our keener perceptions behind, and direct no incisive critical questions at the emotional intelligence or honesty of what the speaker is saying. "Crying in my beer" lyrics usually fall into this category, as do the lyrics of a great many popular love songs and most verses on Hallmark greeting cards. Such poems tend to contain more sloppy emotionality than sense, and for that reason are often dismissed as sentimental or escapist.

Sentimentality in poetry is, of course, immensely popular, and many poets, songwriters, and singers have become rich and famous as skilful merchants of mere emotionality, appealing to a knee-jerk reaction in a listener or reader who has willingly detached his intelligence from his response, in order to surrender to a warm feeling. There is nothing particularly wrong with this (we have all had the experience of responding favourably to a song lyric we know is rubbish), as long as we do not mistake the sentimentality for anything too serious or insightful.

Lyric poems become more complicated (and more interesting) when the speaker is intelligently and honestly exploring a more complex range of feelings, when, for example, she is wrestling with a sense of loss that she does not entirely understand or that she feels partly responsible for, or when she is meditating on the significance of a perception or an event or a memory. The poem is inviting us, not to share or re-live the experience or to swim in a bath of emotional treacle, but to follow and gain some insight into her often ambiguous understanding of what she is going through.

8.5.2 | Interpreting a Lyric Poem

Anyone setting out to write an essay on a lyric poem first needs to make sure he understands the literal details of the poem, that is, the most surface-level and unambiguous features of the text (without any attempt to trace symbolic possibilities). This task requires a careful reading and re-reading of the poem in order to clarify as many of the following questions as possible:

1. Who is the speaker of the poem? Where is the speaker (in the city, in the country, at home, in a garden)? What season of year is it? What is the speaker looking at? Is the speaker

talking to anyone else, either present or imaginary (to a lover, to God, to another part of himself)? Is anything going on during the speaker's reflections? In many cases, there may be no clear answer to most of these questions, but where there are specific details about the speaker's identity and location, one needs to pay attention to them. In seeking to answer these questions, you might want to take the title of the poem into account; it can often provide a helpful sense of something central to the poem (e.g., Adrienne Rich's "Diving into the Wreck," T.S. Eliot's "Love Song of J. Alfred Prufrock," and Wallace Stevens's "The Idea of Order at Key West").

2. In sorting out these questions, do not confuse the speaking voice of the lyric with the author. It is true that many lyric poems strongly suggest that they are autobiographical reflections, but that is often not the case. Some poets will deliberately invent a persona who speaks the lines (that is, an assumed character, who may be entirely different from the author). Hence, it is generally a good idea to refer to the speaking voice as "the speaker" rather than to use the author's name. That practice will also remind you that biographical details of the poet's life are, for reasons stated earlier in this book, generally irrelevant in an essay interpreting a lyric poem.

3. As you read the poem, do not get confused about any time shifts. Pay attention to the verbs; these indicate whether the speaker is talking about the past, the present, or the future. This is particularly important in some meditative lyrics where comparing the past and the present is the central issue. In fact, if there is a shift back and forth like this, then that is almost certainly an important key to understanding the poem: e.g., the speaker recalls with joy the excitement of being young, turns to the present with sadness because that excitement is gone, and looks ahead to the future with

despair: this temporal structure is common in lyric poems (and especially in rock and roll songs).

4. What experience is the speaker addressing: love, loss, growing old, beauty in nature, a particular event or perception, an old memory, or something else? What, in the most general terms, is the poem about? Keep your answer to this question as literal as possible; do not leap to instantly symbolic interpretations. Do not, for example, immediately assume that Bob Dylan's "Mr. Tambourine Man" is about drugs and that the Tambourine Man must be the speaker's dope dealer. Begin with the literal details: the Tambourine Man is a musician with a tambourine.

5. From reading the lyric several times, what sense do you get of the speaker's feelings about the experience (e.g., is he reflective, sad, angry, bitter, joyful, confused, hopeful, puzzled, defeated, confident, resigned, and so on)? Are there any conflicting feelings at work? In trying to sort out the speaker's feelings about the experience he is dealing with, pay particular attention to any changes in or combinations of feelings. Does the speaker's mood shift from despair to joy, from happiness at a past memory to resignation at future prospects? If this is a love poem, what is the full range of the speaker's response about the experience (joy, bitterness, frustration, guilt, anger, despair, melancholy or some combination)? Lyric poems are often ambiguous, expressing contradictory and shifting feelings, and often they do not lead to a clear resolution of those feelings. As often as not, the speaker may be questioning her own feelings, unsure of what they all mean exactly.

You cannot proceed to organize an interpretative argument until you are as clear as you can be about all these literal details. If you find a poem's literal details confusing or unclear (and that is not uncommon), then discuss it with someone else, so that you arrive together at some understanding of the poem on a literal level.

As you sort out these questions, you should begin to shape an answer to the question crucial to any interpretation of a lyric poem: How do one or more particular features of the poem's style—that is, the way language is used in the poem—contribute to the exploration of feeling that is going on in it? What details of the text are shaping your response? To answer this question you need to attend carefully to all elements of the style, including the following:

1. How would you characterize the tone of the lyric? Do the words suggest a tone that is quiet, resigned, contemplative, angry, sad, joyful, and so on? What words in particular create that effect?

2. Is there a pattern in the choice of words? Pay particular attention to the adjectives and verbs. Are they helping to create a particular tone or mood? Are there any phrases that are especially effective? Are any words or lines repeated? If so, what does that contribute?

3. What about the sentences? Are they short and tentative or full of energy? Are there any questions asked? If so, what is the effect of such questions? What does the punctuation contribute? Does it force you to go through the sentence very slowly, dwelling on particular words, or does it allow the sentences to flow quickly and build up a certain momentum? If so, what does that contribute to your understanding of the speaker's mood?

4. How do the images in the lyric shape your sense of the speaker's response? Is there a pattern or a contrast in the imagery? How does what the images suggest help to define anything remarkable in the text?

5. What about the rhythm, the rhyme, and the other sound qualities of the language? How do these help to create a particular tone in the lyric?

6. How does the poem end? What tone does the language of the final lines establish?

You cannot begin to organize an essay until you have some sense of those elements in the poem (i.e., the stylistic features in the lyric) you intend to focus on and interpret in detail.

8.5.3 | *Structuring a Short Interpretative Essay on a Lyric Poem*

Once you have read and re-read the poem sufficiently to have a firm sense of the above issues, you can then move to organizing an essay which interprets the lyric or part of it. Remember that the function of this essay is to help the reader of your argument reach a better understanding of what is going on in the language of the lyric.

Generally speaking it is a good idea to start in the usual way with a subject-focus-thesis paragraph. This will identify the poem you are dealing with, call attention to the speaker and the experience he is exploring, and establish a thesis that argues for a certain interpretative judgement about the poem. The main part of the argument will seek to persuade the reader of that thesis by taking a very close look at certain elements in the style, that is, at the way the language of the poem contributes to the effects you describe.

Here's a sample introduction that follows the standard opening for a short, argumentative essay, with some topic sentences for the argumentative paragraphs:

> In Sonnet 73 Shakespeare returns to one of his favourite poetic themes, the disappointments of love. Here the speaker, addressing a lover or a dear friend, is clearly filled

with a sense that something is nearing an end in their relationship. It may be that he is old and trying to come to terms
with his approaching death or that he is just feeling old and
tired, emotionally empty and dead. In either case, the pre-
dominant mood of the poem, from start to finish, is a quiet
resignation, a tired acceptance of the inevitability of what
is happening. The style of the poem brings out repeatedly
the speaker's sombre, unexcited, even passive acknowledge-
ment that he is, emotionally or physically, about to die.

TS 1: We get a clear sense of this prevailing mood largely
through the imagery. (The paragraph goes on to discuss
how the sequence of images reinforces this sense.)

TS 2: The language, too, evokes a sense of resigned acceptance which speaks eloquently of the prevailing mood.
(Paragraph goes on to interpret particular words and
phrases to establish this point.)

TS 3: What is most remarkable in this evocative and sad reflection is that the speaker does not blame anyone, not even
himself. The constant emphasis on natural processes and the
subdued language suggest that the end is inevitably fated.
(Paragraph discusses this point.)

Notice how the main emphasis in this argument is not the experience the speaker is describing (the death of the relationship)
but rather the speaker's response to that experience, the range of
moods he goes through, as these emerge from the language, imagery, and rhythms of the poem.

To write a successful argumentative interpretation of a lyric
poem, you must grasp this principle that the interpretation looks
at how the language of the poem reveals things about the quality of the speaker's response. This is not easy at first, but unless
you commit yourself to doing it, you will not be interpreting

the poem. And please note, as before, that none of the paragraphs above is summarizing the details of the poem (that is, just re-describing the content in the essay writer's own words).

Here is another sample. Notice once again the characteristic emphasis in the argument linking aspects of the style of the poem to the range of feelings of the speaker.

SUBJECT: Frost's "Mending Wall"

FOCUS: The ambiguity of the speaker's feelings about the process of mending the wall

THESIS: Frost's language and, in particular, his imagery create throughout the poem a sense of the speaker's divided feelings about what he and his neighbour do every spring. The result is an intriguingly complex lyric about how human relationships are often characterized by a sense that firm boundaries between people are in some way unnatural and foolish and yet also necessary.

TS 1: The images of spring and the speaker's interest in them strongly suggest that the speaker feels there is something unnatural about the wall he and his neighbour are building. He is, to some extent, dissatisfied with the procedure, which, in his eyes, is rather silly. (Paragraph discusses one or two examples of these images to bring out the point.)

TS 2: At the same time, however, the way he describes the wall and the process of rebuilding indicates clearly that he finds the ritual enjoyable, almost magical, and, in a curious way, necessary. (Paragraph takes a detailed look at another part of the poem to establish this point.)

TS 3: Particularly significant in the lyric is the speaker's description of his neighbour. This injects into the poem a sudden sense of how the speaker is both fascinated and afraid of (or at least reluctant to challenge) his co-worker. (Paragraph goes on to look at the description of the neighbour in detail.)

CONCLUSION

8.5.4 | *Interpreting the Evidence in a Lyric Poem*

Remember that an interpretative argument about a lyric poem is an argument based on the interpretation of evidence: the writer of the essay is making claims about the text, providing evidence from the text, and interpreting the evidence. The most difficult challenge of this exercise is interpreting the evidence, that is, commenting on the parts of the lyric you have called attention to and showing how they reveal what you are claiming about the poem.

You cannot properly interpret the evidence from the text unless you are prepared to have a *really* close look at particular features of the style (the structure of the sentences, including the punctuation, the imagery, the choice of words, the sound, the rhythm, and so on) and to explore how these suggest certain important features of speaker's feelings.

Here, for example, is a sample paragraph from an essay on Frost's poem "Mending Wall":

> The process of repairing the wall is something the speaker, for all his sense that the ritual is unnatural and unnecessary, welcomes, because his neighbor is, if not a threat, at least someone who makes him uneasy. This uneasiness is suggested in the speaker's description of his neighbor:
>
> > I see him there
> > Bringing a stone grasped firmly by the top
> > In each hand, like an old-stone savage armed.
> > He moves in darkness as it seems to me,
> > Not of woods only and the shade of trees.
>
> The speaker sees his neighbor, in part, as a throwback, who "moves in darkness," that is, a person who moves in some unenlightened, mysterious, unseen, and potentially sinister manner. That remarkable phrase "old-stone

savage armed" conjures up a range of associations: a prehistoric wild, natural man, not only carrying a stone in each hand but also, in some sense, made out of stone (i.e., impervious to civilized feelings, a "savage"), in any case a different order of being from the speaker himself. And the word "armed" adds an entirely new dimension to the response, the feeling that there is a latent danger lurking in the man. The way the line is written, with the word "armed" emphasized by the rhythm and placed at the end of the sentence, so that we have to pause there, stresses the notion that for the speaker the neighbor has an intimidating quality that makes the speaker reluctant to challenge him. With this in mind, we may understand better why it is the speaker who initiates the annual ritual, is happy enough to "keep the wall between us as we go," and never tells his neighbor what he truly thinks about what they are doing together.

Here is another example, this time an interpretative paragraph from an essay on Eliot's "Love Song of J. Alfred Prufrock":

What is truly moving about Prufrock is his awareness of his own insufficiency and emotional cowardice: he knows what he needs to do, but cannot bring himself to do it. Nowhere is this more evident and telling than in the closing lines of the poem:

I have heard the mermaids singing, each to each.

I do not think that they will sing to me.

I have seen them riding seaward on the waves
Combing the white hair of the waves blown back
When the wind blows the water white and black.

> We have lingered in the chambers of the sea
> By sea-girls wreathed with seaweed red and brown
> Till human voices wake us, and we drown.

The imagery here of mermaids "singing," "riding seaward," and "combing" is richly suggestive of natural energy, beauty, sexuality, and freedom. The present participles of the verbs emphasize the driving motion brought out by the repetitive use of "blown" and "blows" and by the alliterative sounds and rhymes of "blown back ... black" and of that wonderfully alliterative phrase "white hair of the waves." Unlike so much of the rest of the poem, the imagery here brings out a sense of healthy, spontaneous, and joyful movement. But all these associations are invoked only to be instantly cancelled out ("I do not think that they will sing to me" and "Till human voices wake us, and we drown"). The flat, almost prosaic final line expresses a particularly bitter regret: as soon as Prufrock returns to a waking life, the beauty immediately vanishes and "we drown." What is apparent here, yet again, is that Prufrock is not a stupid or insensitive man. He understands what his life lacks, and he has visions of what he desires, but only in his dreams. Returning to a waking human life defeats his urgent wish for all the qualities evoked by that image of the sea girls. Prufrock is not ignorant of what he needs to do, but he lacks the emotional courage or energy to seek what will transform his life, and so he would sooner settle for what he knows he does not want. The shift in pronouns from "I" to "we" may be significant here, as well. It is as if he is inviting the reader to identify with him, to recognize that this exploration of a sensitive modern urban soul defeated by its own emotional inadequacies is a portrait, not just of Prufrock, but of ourselves.

Normally, you would not have to quote the passages as the above examples do (referring to the line numbers would be sufficient). I have done so here to make the interpretative comments easier to follow.

Notice how these paragraphs really look closely at the evidence they introduce. The speculations about the wider ramifications of the symbolism arise out of comments about particular details and direct the eye of the reader of the essay back to the text itself. The emphasis throughout is on assessing what we learn about the speaker's response to experience from particular patterns in the language of the text. This is very different from merely summing up the passage in your own words:

> In the final lines of the poem Prufrock talks about visions he has had of mermaids singing by the sea and riding the waves. He says they will not sing to him. These visions come to him at night, but they disappear when he wakes up....

If you remember that the reader of your essay is already very familiar with the poem, a summary like this is not telling her anything she does not already know.

Nor do the above interpretative paragraphs offer comments without a close attention to the evidence from the text. If you get into the habit of holding back on a discussion of particular details, you may offer potentially useful interpretation but without evidence. This will make the argument less persuasive and more difficult to follow, as in the following example.

> The poem closes with an image suggesting the freedom, beauty, and vital energy that Prufrock feels is missing in his life. This is in marked contrast to the details we have learned earlier about Prufrock's life. But in the end they are not enough to transform his emotional attitudes and responses....

These comments are more useful than a mere summary, but in order to work as convincing interpretative claims, they need to arise from a detailed look at text. Left by themselves like this, they are, in effect, the conclusions of an argument without any premises.

Generally speaking, any interpretation of a lyric poem that is not repeatedly calling attention to the significance of particular words and phrases in the text will not be providing enough interpretation, and simply providing more evidence (i.e., quotations) will not mitigate that lack.

8.5.5 | *Interpreting Symbolic Meanings in a Lyric Poem*

Lyric poems are inherently ambiguous, largely because the language and, above all, the images bring into play a series of symbolic associations, related meanings, and emotional connotations. In the above passage from "The Love Song of J. Alfred Prufrock," for example, the image of the mermaids is obviously not to be taken merely on a literal level. Yes, they are mermaids, but they are also clearly symbolic, as well, introducing a sense of beauty, freedom, naturalness, sexuality, and so on. The wall in Frost's poem, is, first and foremost, a stone wall separating two properties, but it is obviously also a symbol of the relationship between the speaker and his neighbour and, beyond that, of human relationships generally. A nuanced interpretation of the poem has to take these symbolic meanings into account.

However, a writer needs to be careful about symbolic meanings. It is important to let these grow out of the language of the poem and to avoid instantly imposing something arbitrary on the lyric (i.e., leap to an overstated conclusion). So it is wise to restrain any sudden tendency to translate the subject matter into something else that is not immediately prompted by words in the text, that is, to check any desire to make too great an imaginative leap (for example, by seeing the mermaids in Eliot's poem as symbols of death or depravity or something else with no obvious link to how the poem presents them). After all, if the reader of a lyric lets his hyperactive symbolic imagination run riot, then "Mary had a little lamb" can mean almost anything from a penetrating insight into Catholic religious spirituality to an exploration of strange relationships between human beings and woolly quadrupeds.

Often the persuasiveness of an argument introducing symbolic meanings will depend upon the tone the essay writer adopts. Using an overly firm, even aggressive language may make the interpretation sound unnecessarily reductive and ham-fisted; whereas, a more moderate tone, one which presents the idea as a suggestion for the reader of the essay to consider will often make the interpretation more effective.

8.5.6 | Dealing with Ideas in Lyric Poems

Because lyrics poems address a particular experience and are "about" something, they invariably deal with an idea (or theme). However, as I have repeatedly stressed, the central issue in the poem is not usually the idea or theme in itself, but rather the speaker's presentation of that idea. For instance, a lyric poem about love may well celebrate the idea "Love is a joyful experience," but what matters in any interpretation of the poem is not that idea (which is, after all, a very trite observation) but the way in which the language of the text presents the speaker's sense of her joy in love.

Most lyric poems are of very little philosophical interest (i.e., there are no complex logical arguments to follow, no startlingly original rational insights). As often as not, the philosophical content is very thin. For that reason, an interpretative essay on a lyric poem that spends its time discussing the "ideas" of the poem as if they were the chief concern of the work risks missing the point. These remarks apply especially to those lyric poems that explicitly set out an idea, as in the following lines from William Wordsworth's "Tintern Abbey":

> And I have felt
> A presence that disturbs me with the joy
> Of elevated thoughts; a sense sublime
> Of something far more deeply interfused,
> Whose dwelling is the light of setting suns,
> And the round ocean and the living air,
> And the blue sky, and in the mind of man:
> A motion and a spirit, that impels
> All thinking things, all objects of all thought,
> And rolls through all things.

Here the speaker is declaring his faith in an idea, and an interpretation of the poem should, of course, call attention to this point. But the idea itself is a very simple and common one (that nature inspires in one a sense of meaningful spiritual joy). So much so that no one would ever think of using these lines to prompt a philosophical discussion of pantheism. What is truly astonishing here, however, and what helps to make this one of the greatest poems ever written in English is the way the speaker brings out his absolute confidence in the idea, his unshakable sense of the spiritually unifying power and beauty of nature. And how does he do that? Well, in order to explore an answer to that question one has to look at the language: the sentence structure, the punctuation, the choice of words, the repetitions, the rhythm, the sound patterns, and so on.

At the risk of repeating myself unnecessarily, I urge the writer of an essay on lyric poetry to remember that if his argument is not exploring particular details of the language of the poem and showing how these illuminate the nature the speaker's feelings about an idea or an event or a perception or a memory (or whatever the subject matter of the poem is) then the essay is almost certainly a poor one. An interpretative argument that merely summarizes the literal details of the poem or describes the ideas detached from the way in which they are presented will provide the reader of the essay little insight into how he might better understand the lyric. I stress this point because many students find writing about poetic language difficult and, in order to say something about the text, prefer to write about anything other than significant features of the poetic style.

Answers to Exercises

2.6 | Recognizing the Form of Simple Arguments

1. Things equal to the same thing are equal to each other. Therefore if A equals B and if B equals C, *then A must equal C*. [This is a deductive argument based on a self-evident mathematical truth.]

2. The principle of free speech is one of the most important elements of our liberal democracy. Therefore *this student newspaper must be free to print opinions offensive to many people*. [This is a deductive argument based on an appeal to a shared principle.]

3. Last year six per cent of the machines manufactured in that plant had defective motors. *We may well*

have a serious problem that we need to investigate *further.* [This is an inductive argument based on a statistical measurement.]

4. All human beings suffering from a painful, fatal illness have the right to assisted suicide. *Therefore this terminally ill, suffering patient has the right to an assisted suicide.* [This is a deductive argument based on an appeal to a general principle.]

5. In this essay the writer frequently uses words like "perhaps," "maybe," and "alternatively." *This feature of the style suggests that the writer lacks confidence in her analysis.* [This is an inductive argument, based upon evidence taken from the text of the essay.]

6. Model X gets better mileage, costs less to purchase and to maintain, and has a better all-round rating in *Consumer Reports* than does Model Y. *Therefore, it probably makes more sense for me to purchase Model X rather than Model Y.* [This is an inductive argument based upon an examination of factual evidence.]

7. We all agree that the murder must have been committed by one of the three in the house—the husband, the wife, or the cook—and we've determined that neither the cook nor the wife could have done it. *Therefore, the husband must have done it.* [This is a deductive argument based on an appeal to shared assumptions.]

2.7 | Exercises in Deduction and Induction

Problem A

You begin with the assumption that one of the two drivers must have done it (since there are no other options). Then you measure (by observation) the heat of the engine in each car (by placing your hand on the hood or opening up each hood and sensing the heat). If one engine is significantly cooler than the other, then the car with the cooler engine has probably been there longer, and the driver at fault must be the one in the car with the warmer engine. The overall structure of the argument concerning the driver's guilt is deductive (either A or B must be at fault, and so if A is at fault then B is innocent, and vice versa) but the key test is inductive (it's very likely that the warmer engine is in the car that was more recently running, though it's not guaranteed—perhaps the resting driver left his engine running, for example).

Problem B

One deductive solution would be as follows: in the world there are more people with hair on their heads than there are hairs on any one person's head—that truth is surely self-evident. If that is the case, then there must be at least two people with the same number of hairs on their heads.

Problem C

The method here would be deductive. The man starts knowing that there is no point asking a simple direct question to whoever answers the door because he has no way of telling whether the answer is truthful or not. So he realizes some more complex question involving both brothers is required, because a lie and a truth combined might be more informative. So he finally comes up with the question "What would your brother tell me is the right road to Ipswich?" Whatever answer he gets will be a lie. The truthful brother would accurately report what his brother would say (which would be a lie), and the other brother would lie about his honest brother's response. So the traveller does not take the road indicated in the answer to his question and selects the other one. He could also ask, "If I had come here yesterday and asked you which is the correct road to Ipswich, what would you have said?" The answer would give him the correct road to take (the dishonest brother would falsely report what he would have said the day before, which would have been a lie, and a lie about a lie in this case would the truth; the truthful brother would honestly report what he would have said the day before, which would have been the truth).

Problem D
The woman facing the wall thinks deductively as follows: There are only five hats to choose from, three black hats and two white hats. Now, the person at the end of the line can see the two hats in front of him. If he saw two white hats, he would know he must have a black hat on and would have already said something. But he hasn't said anything. Therefore, I and the person immediately behind me must have either two black hats or one black and one white hat. Now, the person immediately behind me has also thought this through and come to the same conclusion. So if he sees I have a white hat, he would know that he must have a black hat and would have spoken out. But he hasn't said anything. So he's still not sure. Therefore, I must have a black hat on.

Problem E
The key idea here is that you have to bribe some other pirates to get their vote. In order to know which ones to bribe, you have to figure out what would happen if the vote failed and you were thrown overboard. You also know that all the pirates are thinking along the same lines as you are (since they are all perfectly rational).

You start by considering what happens if there are only 2 pirates: you and one other. In such a case, you propose that you get all the gold, and you vote in favour. The motion carries, and you get 100 coins and the other pirate gets 0. With 3 pirates (you, Pirate B, and Pirate C), you need to purchase 1 vote. You know that if you are thrown overboard,

Pirate C would get nothing (since the two remaining pirates would be in the two-pirate scenario). In this case, then, you propose that you get 99 coins, Pirate B gets 0, and Pirate C gets 1. With 4 pirates (you, Pirates B, C, and D), you still need to purchase only 1 vote. You know that if you are tossed overboard, the others will be back to the three-pirate scenario; Pirate C will become Pirate B and get 0. So you propose that you get 99 coins, Pirate B gets 0, Pirate C gets 1, and Pirate D gets 0. With 5 pirates, you need 3 votes and will need to bribe two of the others, those who would get 0 coins if you were tossed overboard. So you propose that you get 98 coins, Pirate B gets 0, Pirate C gets 1, Pirate D gets 0, and Pirate E gets 1. With 6 pirates, you still need 3 votes and need to bribe 2 of the others, those who would get 0 coins if you were thrown overboard. So you propose that you get 98 coins, Pirate B gets 0, Pirate C gets 1, Pirate D gets 0, Pirate E gets 1, and Pirate F gets 0. With 7 pirates, you must get 4 votes and thus bribe 3 pirates, those who will get 0 coins if you are thrown overboard. Hence, you propose that you get 97 coins, Pirate B gets 0, Pirate C gets 1, Pirate D gets 0, Pirate E gets 1, Pirate F gets 0, and Pirate G gets 1.

2.8.8 | Exercise in Simple Inductive Arguments

1. The ghost in *Hamlet* spends more time complaining about his ex-wife's remarriage than the fact that his brother murdered him. Clearly this demonstrates he is obsessed with his inadequate sexuality. [Here the conclusion is overstated. The fact is interesting, but the argument requires a more tentative conclusion.]

2. The ghost in *Hamlet* comes into Gertrude's bedroom to confront Hamlet, but his ex-wife cannot see him. This suggests something interesting: that Hamlet Senior, renowned as a warrior king, may not feel quite so

commanding and competent in the bedroom. [This conclusion is acceptable, since the language does not insist upon it but raises it as an interesting possibility.]

3. The driver's blood alcohol level was three times the legal limit. Three separate witnesses indicate that he was driving on the wrong side of the road without lights on, and the preliminary analysis shows that he was driving well above the speed limit. And the brakes on the car were defective. He might be to blame in the accident. [Given the evidence listed, the conclusion here seems understated. It should be much firmer than it is.]

4. We have conducted an experiment ten times under standard conditions in which we added a small piece of zinc to hydrochloric acid. Every time hydrogen gas was produced. Thus, the interaction of zinc and hydrochloric acid under similar conditions will always produce hydrogen gas. [The conclusion here may be slightly overstated, since there have only been ten trials. A successful experiment corroborates the hypothesis, enabling the experimenter to be more confident that it is not false; however, it does not conclusively prove the hypothesis.]

5. In this poem, nature is described as "green," "verdant," "ripe," "blooming," and "fertile." The writer is here suggesting that nature is a rich source of life. [The conclusion here seems acceptable, a reasonable interpretation of the facts.]

6. Odysseus obviously has a very cruel streak. We see this when he grinds out the eye of Polyphemos, the Cyclops, with a sharpened and burning pole and at the end when he slaughters the suitors and punishes the servants, some of them very brutally. [This conclusion seems appropriate given the evidence.]

7. The Liberal candidates promised that they would repeal the sales tax. Once in office, they refused to carry out that legislation. They are all liars. [The conclusion here is

obviously overstated. The party caucus may have gone against the wishes of many of its members in failing to honour its election promise.]

8. Some released sex offenders have committed new offences. We should never release any sex offenders, since they will always reoffend. [The conclusion here is overstated. The fact that *some* have reoffended does not entitle one to conclude that *all* will reoffend.]

9. My astrologer and the Ouija board have told me repeatedly me that it will rain on Friday. I think we should call off the picnic. [The conclusion here is entirely unwarranted, since it is based on unreliable evidence.]

2.10 | Exercise in Evaluating Short Arguments

1. The survey questionnaire on student plagiarism was completed by 85 per cent of the faculty. Three-quarters of the respondents said they definitely felt that plagiarism in first-year papers was on the increase. I think we may have a problem here that we should investigate further. [This is an inductive argument. The conclusion here is acceptable, since it expresses a possibility which seems warranted by the evidence, but is not a certainty.]

2. In the opening of the *Odyssey* the gods repeatedly state that anyone who violates someone else's home must be punished. This strongly suggests that there is some divine moral order in the world of this book. [This is an inductive argument. The conclusion is acceptable, once again because it is framed as a suggestion arising from evidence.]

3. The economy started to go downhill right after the present government was elected. Clearly, they do not know how to run a national economy. [This poor

inductive argument is making the mistake of assuming that because A happened after B, then A must be the cause of B.]

4. Of course, his argument is hopelessly wrong. After all, he's a Roman Catholic priest. What do you expect? [This is an unpersuasive inductive argument based on an *ad hominem* attack appealing to the hidden assumption that all Roman Catholic priests are hopeless at arguing.]

5. That film is pornographic; two or three scenes feature full male and female nudity. [This argument is unpersuasive since it rests on the false hidden assumption that all films featuring full male and female nudity are pornographic. Of course, the proper evaluation of the argument depends upon one's definition of *pornography*.]

6. This is a really good poem because it has a sonnet structure, with a basic blank verse rhythm, and a strong repetitive rhyme scheme. [This inductive argument is unpersuasive because it is based on a *non sequitur*. The general technical features of a poem are not the characteristics that define the quality of the work.]

7. Look, for the entire season this player led the team in scoring, in rebounding, in assists, and in blocked shots, and he played in every game during the season. He is clearly a strong candidate for the most valuable player on the team. [This inductive argument is acceptable. The evidence supporting the conclusion is strong.]

8. Students should all have to study first-year English at college because they all need at least two semesters of English. And my mother is in favour of the regulation, too. [This inductive argument is unpersuasive. The first part of it is begging the question, and the second reason is a *non sequitur*.]

4.3.2 | Exercise: Recognizing Potentially Useful Thesis Statements

1. Beth Henley's wonderful play *Crimes of the Heart* was turned into a commercially successful film. [This is a poor thesis, since it is a statement of fact.]

2. *The Duchess of Malfi* is a vastly overrated play, contradictory in its presentation of characters, ambiguous in its literal details, and excessively melodramatic in many crucial scenes. [This is a good thesis, perhaps somewhat overstated.]

3. Modern North Americans spend a great deal of money on supplies, veterinary medicine, and food for their pets. [This is a poor thesis, since it is a statement of fact.]

4. Modern North Americans spend far too much money on supplies, veterinary medicine, and food for their pets. [This is a workable thesis, since it expresses an argumentative opinion.]

5. McIntyre and Robinson, two medical researchers at McGill University, conducted five separate studies of fetal alcohol syndrome. They concluded that it is a serious problem in modern society. [This is a poor thesis, since it is a statement of fact.]

6. The study by McIntyre and Robinson, two medical researchers at McGill University, which concluded that fetal alcohol syndrome is a serious problem, is a badly flawed study that produced very misleading conclusions. [This is a useful thesis, since it states a clear and energetic opinion.]

7. Frost's poem "Mending Wall" is constructed around a central image of two men repairing a wall between their two properties. [This is a poor thesis, since it is a statement of fact.]

8. In Frost's poem "Mending Wall" the central image of the two men repairing a wall brings out the

paradoxical feelings of the speaker regarding figurative boundaries in human relationships. In doing so, the poem captures the ways in which fear of otherness interferes with the development of mutual understanding on both personal and political levels. [This is a useful thesis, since it expresses an interpretative opinion.]

9. In *A Vindication of the Rights of Woman*, Wollstonecraft devotes considerable time to discussing the education of women. [This is a poor thesis, since it is a statement of fact.]

10. I quite enjoyed the film *Titanic*. [This is a poor thesis, since it states a weak and vague personal opinion.]

11. *Titanic* is such a sentimental and poorly scripted and acted work that one wonders what on earth our public standards had come to in 1997, such that the film won so many awards and so many people all over the world flocked to see it several times. Whatever the sociological explanation, the film is undeserving of the accolades it received. [This is a very strong and workable thesis, since it expresses an opinion.]

12. We should be paying more attention to dealing with spousal abuse in our society. [This statement expresses an opinion, but the opinion could (and should) be stronger and clearer. As it stands, the thesis is very weak.]

13. Violence against women is a common problem in modern society. [This is a poor thesis, since it is a statement of fact.]

14. Violence against women is, quite simply, the most serious crime in our society. [This is a useful thesis, since it expresses a clear and strong opinion. However, the claim is extreme (*most serious crime in our society*). Whether or not this thesis is too strong (i.e., exaggerated) will depend upon the argument that follows. The writer has to establish not only that

violence against women is a serious crime but that it is more serious than any other crime (rape, murder, and so on). Once the argument is finished, the writer will have to decide whether he has made that case or whether he should moderate the thesis (e.g., by saying "one of the most serious crimes in our society").]

15. New Cadillacs are more expensive than new Honda Civics. [This is a poor thesis, since it is a statement of fact.]

16. A new Cadillac is, in the long run, a much better investment than a new Honda Civic. [This is a useful thesis, since it states an opinion we might dispute.]

4.5.1 | Exercises in Opening Paragraphs

Example A
The film *To Rangoon on a Trading Ship* tells the story of Martin, a teenage runaway on a cargo boat which sails from London to the Far East. On board the ship are two other stowaways, Gumby and Sian, two friends, who know nothing about Martin's presence. The ship is called the *Narnia*. The captain is called Fred Jones. He hates stowaways and is keen to punish them whenever he finds them. Rangoon is in the Far East. The story is set in the early 1900s. Pirates chase the ship at one point. At another time, the ship joins a group of navy ships sailing off to a war in the Pacific. Martin is nineteen years old. He is played by Adam Blimph.

[This opening paragraph is much too scattered, with one random factual detail following another. It does not define a focus or offer a thesis.]

Example B
The film *To Rangoon on a Trading Ship* came out in 2014. It is the best film I have ever seen. Everything about it was splendid. Everybody should see it.

[This opening paragraph expresses an opinion (a thesis) but is much too short. We need a more extensive introduction and a clearly defined focus.]

Example C
To Rangoon on a Trading Ship, a recent adventure film, tells the story of some young stowaways on a cargo vessel going to the Far East in the early years of this century. Martin, a young London boy, and two other teenagers, Gumby and Sian, escape from oppressive situations at home by stowing away on the *Narnia*, a vessel bound for exotic places. The ship and the young stowaways encounter all sorts of adventures, but ultimately the story resolves itself happily. The work contains many predictable elements, including a wicked captain, some pirates, brave teenagers who help each other, a storm at sea, a mutiny, and so on. These scenes are quite familiar to anyone who has ever seen or read many sea yarns aimed at a young audience. However, for a number of reasons, particularly the script, the direction, and the acting of the lead characters, this is not just another conventional romantic adventure aimed at the younger set. It is in many ways a mature, amusing, and inventive reworking of a traditional genre, well worth the price of admission, even for skeptical adults.

[This opening paragraph is useful. It identifies the work, defines a focus, and establishes a clear thesis at the end.]

Example D
To Rangoon on a Trading Ship is a recent film directed by Sue McPherson. I really like her films because they usually combine a good script with some excellent camera work. Her first film, Manhattan by Night, won several prizes at film festivals, and in 2010 another work won her an award for best screenplay. McPherson is a filmmaker from Canada.

She attended film school in New York and was in the graduating class that produced a number of excellent Canadian filmmakers, including Alice Jackson and Terry Bright. I really like all their films. I think it's a shame that more Canadians don't support Canadian filmmakers by paying more attention to their work. That's why so many good directors go south to the United States. Anyway, McPherson's film is another excellent example of the high quality work that can be done by Canadians.

[This is a poor thesis, largely because it is stuffed with all sorts of irrelevant biographical details and observations about Canadian films. We need a more clearly defined focus and a sharper thesis.]

Exercise 2

Paragraph A
Homer's *Odyssey* recounts the adventures of the Greek hero Odysseus, in his return home from the Trojan War. In fact, much of the book is taken up with various tests of this epic hero, encounters in which he has to demonstrate his ability to overcome obstacles of various kinds. In the process of following Odysseus through these adventures, we, as readers, come to recognize many important qualities of the central character. We also learn a great a deal about what he values and about the nature of the world he lives in. There are many episodes in this exciting story which might serve to introduce us to these issues, for in virtually every adventure we learn something important about the hero and his values. One obvious and famous example is the story of his encounter with Polyphemos, the Cyclops. A close inspection of this incident tells us a great deal about what is most important in the poem. In fact, if we attend carefully to what is going on here, we come to understand some central

features of Odysseus' character: his insatiable curiosity, his daring, his cunning, his ruthlessness, and his very strong, even egotistical, sense of himself.

[This is a useful opening paragraph. It defines a clear focus (one incident in the poem) and establishes a workable thesis.]

Paragraph B
Homer's *Odyssey* recounts the adventures of the Greek hero Odysseus, in his return home from the Trojan War. This is a very old story, composed by the poet Homer at some point in the eighth century BCE and passed on for many generations before it was written down. At first the poem existed only as an oral composition; it was recited by bards. Only later was it put into the form in which we have it today. No one really knows whether or not a poet named Homer actually existed or not. Homer also composed the *Iliad*, the story of Achilles. Both of these books played a central role in Greek religion and education, and they have been important parts of the tradition in Western literature ever since. The *Odyssey* was probably written after the *Iliad*. The *Odyssey* is a much easier poem to read than the *Iliad*. The story moves much more quickly, and there are a lot more adventures. One adventure that is particularly well known and important is the encounter with Polyphemos. This essay will discuss this episode, focusing on its importance.

[This introduction is not very helpful. It spends too much time talking about the historical details of Homer's poems. It does indicate a focus, but establishes no clear thesis about that focus. The last sentence is merely a promissory note.]

Paragraph C
The Bible is one of the most important texts in Western society. Christianity has helped lay many of our moral

foundations, and these are still an important part of modern society. For instance, many people still follow the Ten Commandments. However, not all of Christian beliefs still fit into our modern world. So the Bible is a source of oppression. There are many examples of this. For example the creation story clearly is oppressive to women. The dominion of people over nature also endorses oppression of non-human animals. And there is lots of killing of people by the Israelites in the name of the Lord. This also is oppressive. And the story of Abraham and Isaac is oppressive as well.

[This introduction is quite poor. The general observations about Christianity and oppression are irrelevant. There is no clear indication of a focus, and we are left in some doubt about the precise nature of the thesis.]

Paragraph D

One of the central issues of the book of Genesis is the relationship between particular characters and the Lord. Repeatedly in the narrative, God selects an individual for special attention, and that individual becomes, in effect, an example of the appropriate relationship between God and humanity, a role model for the faithful. An obvious example of this point is Abraham, one of the most important of the patriarchs. He displays complete faith in God, and God rewards him with the Covenant. But Abraham's faith makes large demands on him, and we are forced to recognize in him just what a truly meaningful relationship to the Lord demands. Many places in the Abraham story bring out this point, but we can best appreciate it by exploring in detail the famous account of Abraham's sacrifice of Isaac. This section of Genesis explicitly and compellingly offers us an insight into the religious life defined and illustrated in the Old Testament, an apparently harsh but passionate and compelling belief. Abraham's sacrifice of Isaac illustrates a paradoxical conception of relationship to God in which total sacrifice is required—even the sacrifice of moral principles—but in which everything an individual sacrifices is returned to him.

[This is a useful introduction. By the end of it the reader understands clearly what the essay will be looking at and what the writer is claiming about it.]

Exercise 3

Paragraph E
There's a lot of talk these days about how we just have to do something about guns. Guns have always been a part of civilization. Human beings have used guns for hunting and for sport for centuries. A gun is also an expression of human creativity. Many guns are fine objects of art. And anyway if we don't have guns the government will control us even more than they do now. Besides, the right to protect ourselves is obviously important. And guns don't kill people; people kill people. If we cannot have guns then how are we going to fend off the police when they start attacking our homes? Are we supposed to use kitchen utensils? So I say we should forget about any further gun control legislation. That's what this essay will argue.

[This introduction is too scattered. It does offer a focus and a thesis, but these are presented quite awkwardly. Moreover, the rather flippant tone does not inspire confidence in the reader.]

Paragraph F
The question of increased governmental control over guns raises a number of important issues that the public seems eager to discuss. In fact, few subjects stir more passionate

and widespread national debates than the issue of gun ownership and gun legislation. Every story about someone running amok with a gun—and these, we know, are frequent enough—has a lot of people calling for more regulations and restrictions on the sale of guns. In some quarters to oppose such legislation is seen at once as a sign of one's right-wing, red-neck credentials. So anyone who wishes to argue reasonably that those opposing more gun legislation may have a good case, or at least a case worth paying attention to, is unlikely to get a proper hearing in many forums. However, the attempt to present such a case must be made, because bringing down more restrictive legislation on guns will not merely do nothing to deal with our concerns about lethal weapons in the wrong hands, but will also threaten a number of other important personal rights which we take for granted.

[This is a useful introduction, much better than the previous one.]

6.4.2 | Exercise in Argumentative Topic Sentences

1. The language the judge used in his ruling illustrates that he did not take the plaintiffs' concerns seriously because they were teenagers. [This is a useful topic sentence that clearly establishes the subject matter of the paragraph—the language the judge used in his ruling—and the argumentative point that the judge did not take the plaintiffs seriously.]

2. Later in the novel Huck meets up with two confidence men. Together they plan a number of tricks on the citizens of small towns along the river. [These sentences are statements of fact. They do not put anything argumentative on the table.]

3. Some of the salaries paid to average professional

athletes are very high. It is not uncommon to read about a journeyman player receiving a salary of several millions of dollars a year. [These two sentences are not useful topic sentences. They are statements of fact.]

4. The poem repeatedly describes the narrator's anger with visceral, gory language that links her past trauma to the violence she witnesses in the slaughterhouse. [These sentences work well in declaring the topic of the paragraph. They express an interpretative opinion.]

5. A second major erroneous claim made by the proponents of the Keystone pipeline in order to "sell" the project to the general public is that it will create a number of well-paying, long-term jobs. Such a claim is dubious at best. [These sentences establish a firm and opinionated topic for the paragraph.]

6. Robert de Niro has appeared in many different films. He has been a leading actor for many years. He has received a number of prestigious awards for acting. [These three sentences are all statements of fact and thus not very helpful in establishing the topic of the paragraph.]

Index

from the publisher

A name never says it all, but the word "broadview" expresses a good deal of the philosophy behind our company. We are open to a broad range of academic approaches and political viewpoints. We pay attention to the broad impact book publishing and book printing has in the wider world; we began using recycled stock more than a decade ago, and for some years now we have used 100% recycled paper for most titles. As a Canadian-based company we naturally publish a number of titles with a Canadian emphasis, but our publishing program overall is internationally oriented and broad-ranging. Our individual titles often appeal to a broad readership too; many are of interest as much to general readers as to academics and students.

Founded in 1985, Broadview remains a fully independent company owned by its shareholders—not an imprint or subsidiary of a larger multinational.

If you would like to find out more about Broadview and about the books we publish, please visit us at **www.broadviewpress.com**. And if you'd like to place an order through the site, we'd like to show our appreciation by extending a special discount to you: by entering the code below you will receive a 20% discount on purchases made through the Broadview website.

Discount code: **broadview20%**

Thank you for choosing Broadview.

Please note: this offer applies only to sales of
bound books within the United States or Canada.

The interior of this book is printed on 100% recycled paper.